LEISURE IN BRITAIN 1780-1939

Leisure

JOHN K. WALTON
JAMES WALVIN *editors*

n Britain

1780-1939

MANCHESTER
UNIVERSITY PRESS

Published by MANCHESTER UNIVERSITY PRESS
Oxford Road, Manchester M13 9PL
and 51 Washington Street, Dover, N.H. 03820, USA

British Library cataloguing in publication data
Leisure in Britain 1780-1939.
    1. Recreation – Great Britain – History – 18th century
    2. Recreation – Great Britain – History – 19th century
    3. Recreation – Great Britain – History – 20th century
    I. Walton, John K.   II. Walvin, James
    306'.48'0941   GV75
    ISBN 0-7190-0912-X

Library of Congress cataloging in publication data
Main entry under title:
Leisure in England, 1790-1939.
    Includes bibliographical references.
    Contents: 'The oddest combination of town and country':
popular culture and the London fairs, 1800-1860 / Mark
Judd – The cinema and cinema-going in Birmingham in the
1930s / Jeffrey Richards – The performing arts in Newcastle
upon Tyne, 1840-1870 / Kathleen Barker – [etc.]
    1. England – Popular culture – Addresses, essays,
lectures. 2. Leisure – England – Addresses, essays, lectures.
I. Walton, John K. II. Walvin, James.
NX543.L45 1983   790'.0942   82-62251
ISBN 0-7190-0912-X

Photoset in Monophoto Ehrhardt *with* Bauer Bodoni *display*
Printed in Great Britain
by Butler & Tanner Ltd, Frome and London

CONTENTS

I JOHN K. WALTON
JAMES WALVIN

Introduction

The history of leisure in industrial England has attracted growing interest among a wide range of scholars. But the proliferation of published work over the last ten years has only scratched the surface of this important theme in modern English history. Many aspects of the subject remain completely unexplored. This is particularly the case when we consider leisure in its regional and local context.[1]

Social historians of industrial England have long been aware of the value of a local and regional dimension to their work. Regional surveys of economic history have a long and distinguished pedigree, but it was Asa Briggs's *Chartist Studies* in 1959 which really pioneered the comparative use of local case-studies to illuminate a chosen theme. That hardy perennial, the standard of living debate, was nourished from an early stage by careful detailed investigations of particular localities. These revealed the complexity of regional and local differences, and exposed the perils of facile generalisations about developments at the national level.[2] The last twenty years have seen a spate of books, articles and theses dealing with important themes at the level of the locality and to a lesser extent the region. Recent collections of essays, for instance, have brought together work of this kind on topics as varied as landownership and industrial development, working-class and middle-class housing, and popular education.[3] Studies of early modern England have moved even more rapidly in this direction over the last decade, a trend given added impetus by the growing interest in urban history.[4]

Local studies have both a negative and a positive value. They undermine superficial, over-generalised interpretations by illustrating the diversity of local experiences. The result of this enhanced complexity need not be chaotic and unmanageable, however, though it may become very difficult to master if, to paraphrase David Cannadine, every Camberwell acquires its Dyos.[5] Even so, the multiplication of well-chosen examples should eventually enable us to ask more satisfying questions about the reasons for regional and local variations, and about the extent to which general trends can be identified among the inevitable welter of crosscurrents. A localised field of enquiry allows deeper analysis, and in the process neglected themes can acquire an unsuspected importance as new sources are exploited, often in highly labour-intensive ways. The extra dimension to historical understanding which can be provided by the study of chosen themes in their local settings ought eventually to lead to the writing of a new kind of national history, which will incorporate and explain the rich variety of regional and local experiences.

The social history of leisure is a relatively recent preoccupation of

historians, and early attempts at wide-ranging synthesis and the identification of general trends have suffered from the lack of a common core
of comparative evidence, and the uncertain status of their examples,
which were drawn from a wide variety of geographical areas and social
contexts. Peter Bailey, in his *Leisure and Class in Victorian England*,
recognised the problem and tried to tackle it by incorporating a 'modest
running casestudy' of Bolton into his argument. This approach gave
additional weight to the particular experience of the Lancashire cotton
towns, without resolving the difficulty of arriving at a convincing national
interpretation.[6] The other general surveys of themes in the social history
of leisure have sought to take account of regional differences, but their
main task has been to generate introductory hypotheses. These now need
to be tested at the local level in various kinds of setting, and new themes
need to be investigated, before a more informed and contextually-aware
synthesis can be attempted.[7]

Historians of leisure have explored themes which have been strongly
influenced by the availability of sources and the preoccupations of existing historiography. Attempts at repression and control, and the promotion by those in authority of 'respectable', 'improving' or merely 'safe'
alternative activities, generate evidence in judicial and local government
records, and in the archives of voluntary organisations, all of which have
a high survival rate. Local newspaper coverage of such initiatives was
also good. Parliamentary papers provide further evidence on working-
class leisure activities, though viewed mainly from above and as social
pathology. The abundance of such documentation increases the attraction exerted on historians by the more obvious aspects of the relationship
between leisure and class. This is especially true of the treatment of
working-class leisure as an expression of class identity and culture under
attack from the repressive and manipulative forces of middle-class authority. Over-simplified presentations of a dichotomy between 'class expression' and 'social control' have come under fire from widely differing
angles, but the subject area remains attractive and rewarding, not least
because of its close relationship with other important themes in modern
social history.[8] There is a similar urge to study the commercialisation of
sports and recreations, another well-documented field in which company
records, licensing records and a specialist press become increasingly
available during the second half of the nineteenth century. Here, leisure
is drawn into close relationship with another well-established interest,
the study of living standards and economic development.[9] On the other
hand, the survival of pre-industrial and early industrial leisure forms is
poorly and patchily documented, and was often recorded by disapprov-
ing contemporaries. As a result, historians eager to identify major

changes in leisure activities have probably tended to underplay the strong elements of continuity.[10]

It is also clear that the absence of appropriate sources, and the silence of existing ones, makes certain important themes particularly difficult to pursue. For example, in the explosion of feminist historiography we are now learning a great deal about the sexual division of labour, but very little has yet surfaced on the sexual division of leisure. It has also proved difficult to reconstruct the composition of the audiences at spectator sports and large-scale entertainments, traditional or commercial (an admittedly debatable dichotomy), whether from a sexual or a social structural perspective.[11] Most taxing of all, perhaps, is the bias in the sources towards large-scale, organised leisure forms which generated their own literature and attracted outside commentary. It is difficult, on the other hand, to analyse or even describe the informal use of free time by the individual and the family outside a commercial or institutional context, especially within the home: the balance between what Cunningham calls 'public leisure and private leisure' has been heavily tilted in favour of the former.[12] The predilections of historians have also led to a concentration on the perceived problems of working–class leisure, with the result that the abundant evidence on the middle and upper classes, while not neglected, has been under-utilised.[13]

Even the most popular themes as yet have received very patchy coverage in terms of geographical range and types of economic and social environment. Attention has focused particularly on London and the textile towns, and several studies of resorts are available in book or thesis form. But rural areas, small towns, suburbs and, indeed, most kinds of urban and industrial environment have been neglected by historians of leisure-related themes.[14] Of course, leisure cannot and should not be abstracted from the total social history of which it forms a part, and some general urban histories and works on cognate topics contain interesting material on leisure, broadly interpreted; but many kinds of place still require sustained and specialised attention.

This book is intended as a contribution towards the collective enterprise of preparing for the next stage of national generalisation about the social history of leisure in modern England: a stage which will need to be informed by a fuller awareness of regional and social differences which only local and sectional empirical studies can provide. A more modest aim, but of immediate and practical value, is to enable students to test generalisations, to weigh the difficulties of the evidence, and to generate new ideas of their own, using a manageable range of material which will take them beyond the introductory generalisations of the textbooks which are now available. Apart from the contribution to research and teaching, however, we hope that the essays which follow have been written in such a way that they will be accessible to interested readers outside the academic community. As will be apparent, however, we have no pretensions to developing a grand theory of the social history of leisure, and nor do we intend to spend time agonising over the definition of this polymorphous but distinctive area of enquiry. Our own grand theories and precise definitions would probably not have been shared by our contributors, and we have no desire to impose a doctrinaire strait-jacket on them. We are also aware that our coverage of neglected themes and places is less than total. The content of this book reflects, for example, a continuing bias towards urban settings, and a persisting lack of research on women and leisure; and we have confined our attention to England, ignoring other parts of the British Isles. Many other omissions are only too apparent. The same would have been true, however, if the book had been three times as long.

All but two of the following essays are based on particular localities, and explore in a local setting themes which have been underworked or which have been previously explored in a different context. The last two essays, on reading in the working-class home and on children's leisure pursuits, explore informal and largely unorganised activities which are difficult to piece together from conventional sources. The use of oral history is beginning to make an impact, however, for a period later than those covered by these essays. Each of the essays covers new ground in terms of approach, location or subject matter, and each should provide further essential pieces in the recovery of the complex geographical and social mosaic which makes up the social history of English leisure.

We begin, appropriately, in London, for despite the impressive work of Stedman Jones, Altick, Cunningham and Vicinus (among others),[15] there remain many gaps in our knowledge of the social history of London leisure. This is especially true of the period covered by Mark Judd's analysis of the London fairs, which brings out at once the importance and adaptability of custom and tradition in a uniquely cosmopolitan urban setting.[16] In the case of Birmingham, with its equally distinctive economy and social structure, there has been some interesting work on eighteenth-century artisan culture, the subsequent impact of labour discipline with the coming of the steam engine, and the restrictions on popular recreations imposed by a local authority which was influenced to an unusual extent by organised Nonconformity.[17] These analyses, however, stop short in the later nineteenth century, and Jeffrey Richards shows for the first time how the mid-Victorian arguments about fairs, music-halls and Sunday observance were perpetuated into the inter-war years as the focus of dissension shifted to the conduct and influence of the cinema. Richards's essay covers an under-researched field and points to the need for further work on twentieth-century themes.

Kathleen Barker's survey of the performing arts in early- and mid-Victorian Newcastle upon Tyne draws our attention to another gap. We know surprisingly little about the provision (and enjoyment) of commercial theatrical, musical and variety entertainment in the provinces, despite the valuable work of Martha Vicinus, Peter Bailey and Douglas Reid.[18] Newcastle seems to have been surprisingly rich in polite entertainment, and unusually tardy and limited in its music-hall provision. But we need to know more about other places before we can begin to assess the range of experiences; and any attempted explanation of Newcastle's peculiarities could only be tentative at this stage.

Robert Poole and David Russell cover much better-documented geographical areas, but the very density of existing material on Oldham and the West Riding textile district imposes additional obligations on these authors. The controversy over the social and political structure of Oldham, set in train by Foster and Musson, shows no sign of abating, and Poole's rich analysis of the persistence of customary attitudes and practices in the observance of popular festivities makes an interesting, if largely implicit, contribution to this debate.[19] Poole's main concern, however, is with the Wakes themselves, and his wide range of evidence reinforces the growing tendency to emphasise the continuities in those popular recreations which spanned the first half of the nineteenth century and beyond, even (perhaps especially) in this area of spectacularly rapid urban growth and factory industrialisation. Russell, on the other hand, tackles political questions head-on in his pioneering study of the popular musical societies of the West Riding of Yorkshire. He does not make extravagant claims, and his conclusions are tentative; but this reflects realism rather than faint-heartedness. He brings an interesting and worthwhile new perspective to the relationship between leisure and class, while shedding light on a hitherto-neglected cultural phenomenon which achieved a mass following and built strong and effective bridges between the classes in the region.

The relationship, both positive and negative, between employers' paternalism and working-class leisure has attracted some attention from historians, but the emphasis has usually been concentrated on related and contingent issues such as labour discipline, religion, education and (above all) politics and industrial relations.[20] Redfern's work on leisure in Crewe is particularly welcome because it offers a detailed examination of the extent and manner of employer involvement in a classic 'company town'. Although the London and North Western Railway's provision of leisure facilities seems to have been sufficient to stunt the growth of local commercialised leisure, much of the organisation, energy and initiative came independently, from the workers themselves, and the company rapidly retreated into a narrower interpretation of its social responsibilities by the turn of the century, leaving a vacuum which its obvious successor, the town council, was unwilling to fill. To set this case-study in context, however, we need further material on large Victorian firms, including some of less spectacular size. But the limits to the recreational role of even the giant and locally dominant L N W R seem instructive, even in isolation.[21]

As might be expected, the specialised leisure towns are rather better documented for our purposes than other kinds of place, at least in thesis form. Most of the studies of individual resorts, however, concentrate on landownership, architecture and high society rather than the amenities and recreational activities on which these towns depended.[22] Existing interpretations of seaside towns are particularly neglectful of the increasingly important and distinctive role played by local government in the provision of amusements and amenities, in sharp contrast to its reluctance at Crewe. The papers by Roberts and Walton should help to rectify this omission by giving local government the central place it deserves in explaining the remarkable rise of two of the most successful resorts in Victorian and Edwardian England, Blackpool and Bournemouth. The choice of these leading resorts does, however, reflect a general tendency to concentrate on the 'success stories' and to neglect the more modest achievements of the lesser resorts, whose experiences probably came closer to the national norm. The inclusion of May's paper on Ilfracombe should help to redress this balance, while conjuring up, along with Roberts's study of entertainment in Bournemouth, a picture of middle-class leisure styles which will redress our general preoccupation with the lower orders.

Finally, we move on from local studies to accommodate two other ways of providing detailed analysis of themes in leisure history. David Vincent's study of reading in the working-class home opens out a hitherto neglected theme on which evidence is hard to come by, and James Walvin pieces together evidence from a variety of sources to offer a study of children's leisure activities. These approaches through life-cycle stages and particular kinds of activity should remind us that many important aspects of the social history of leisure are too thinly documented to respond to locally-based research, and that other ways of making sense of this heterogeneous subject must be pursued alongside the local and regional approach. Even within this framework, however, we remain all too well aware of the amount of unexplored territory which remains; but we hope that this collection of essays will at least alert students to the complexity of the problems of generalisation in this fascinating field, while encouraging researchers to fill in some more of the gaps in our knowledge.

NOTES

1 See H. Cunningham, *Leisure in the Industrial Revolution* (1980), p. 200.

2 A. Briggs (ed.), *Chartist Studies* (1959); A. J. Taylor (ed.), *The Standard of Living in Britain in the Industrial Revolution* (1975), chapters 2, 7; T. R. Gourvish, 'The cost of living in Glasgow in the early nineteenth century', *Economic History Review* 2nd series 25 (1972), pp. 65–80; E. Hopkins, 'Small town aristocrats of labour and their standard of living 1840–1914', *ibid.* 28 (1975), pp. 222–42; and others.

3 J. T. Ward and R. G. Wilson (eds.), *Land and Industry* (1971); S. D. Chapman (ed.), *The History of Working-Class Housing* (Newton Abbot, 1971); M. A. Simpson and T. H. Lloyd (eds.), *Middle Class Housing in Britain* (Newton Abbot, 1977); P. McCann (ed.), *Popular education and socialization in the nineteenth century* (1977).

4 P. Clark and P. Slack (eds.), *Crisis and Order in English Towns* (1972), and *English Towns in Transition* (1976); *Urban History Yearbook*, 1974-, *passim*.

5 Cannadine drew attention to this problem at a S.S.R.C. seminar held in the Department of Geography, University of Lancaster, 1978.

6 P. Bailey, *Leisure and Class in Victorian England* (1978). These comments are not intended to detract from the value of this excellent book.

7 Apart from Bailey, the pioneers have been R. W. Malcolmson, *Popular Recreations in English Society 1700–1850* (Cambridge, 1973); J. Walvin, *Leisure and Society 1830–1950* (1978); and H. Cunningham, *Leisure in the Industrial Revolution* (1980), whose bibliography can be recommended to those in search of further reading.

8 G. Stedman Jones, 'Class expression *versus* social control', *History Workshop* 4 (1977), pp. 163–70; F. M. L. Thompson, 'Social control in Victorian Britain', *Economic History Review* N.S. 34 (1981), pp. 200–4.

9 Tony Mason, *Association Football and English Society 1863–1915* (1980) is a particularly stimulating book which fits loosely into this category.

10 Even the revisionist Cunningham may lean too far in this direction in *Leisure and the Industrial Revolution*, chapter 2.

11 For attempts to overcome this problem see Mason, *Association Football*, pp. 138–74, and D. Reid, 'Popular theatre in Victorian Birmingham', in D. Bradby, L. James and B. Sharratt (eds.), *Performance and Politics in Popular Drama* (Cambridge, 1980), pp. 65–89.

12 Cunningham, *Leisure in the Industrial Revolution*, chapter 3.

13 Exceptions include D. C. Itzkovitz, *Peculiar Privilege: a Social History of English Fox-Hunting* (1977); L. Davidoff, *The Best Circles* (1973); W. Weber, *Music amd the Middle Class* (1975). Others can be found in Cunningham's bibliography.

14 Studies focusing on aspects of leisure in particular economic and social settings include H. Meller, *Leisure and the Changing City* (1976), on Bristol; S. Yeo, *Religion and Voluntary Organisations in Crisis* (1976), on Reading; D. Reid, 'Popular theatre' (above, note 11); 'The decline of St Monday', *Past and Present* 71 (1976), pp. 76–101; and 'Popular culture and the march of progress', in R. D. Storch (ed.), *Popular Culture in Nineteenth-Century Britain: Persistence and Change* (1982), all on Birmingham; A. Howkins, *Whitsun in Nineteenth-Century Oxfordshire* (1973); J. D. Marshall and J. K. Walton, *The Lake Counties from*

1830 to the Mid-Twentieth Century (Manchester, 1981), chapters 7 and 8. Storch, in *Popular Culture*, rightly remarks on the general neglect of southern towns by modern historians.

15 G. Stedman Jones, 'Working-class culture and working-class politics in London, 1870–1900: some notes on the remaking of a working class', *Journal of Social History* 7 (1974), pp. 460–508; H. Cunningham, 'The metropolitan fairs: a case study in the social control of leisure', in A. P. Donajgrodzki (ed.), *Social Control in Nineteenth-Century Britain* (1978), pp. 163–84; R. Altick, *The Shows of London* (1978); M. Vicinus, *The Industrial Muse* (1974), chapter 6.

16 Cf. Cunningham, 'Fairs', Reid, 'Popular culture', J. K. Walton and R. Poole, 'The Lancashire wakes in the nineteenth century', in Storch (ed.), *Popular Culture*; and Poole, 'Oldham Wakes', this volume.

17 Reid, articles cited above; J. Money, *Experience and Identity* (Manchester, 1977); E. P. Hennock, *Fit amd Proper Persons* (1973).

18 Reid, articles cited; Vicinus, *Industrial Muse*; Bailey, *Leisure and Class*.

19 J. O. Foster, *Class Struggle and the Industrial Revolution* (1974); A. E. Musson, 'Class struggle and the labour aristocracy', *Social History* 1 (1976), pp. 335–56, and Foster's reply, *ibid.* pp. 357–66; G. Stedman Jones, 'Class struggle and the industrial revolution', *New Left Review* 90 (1975), pp. 35–69; D. S. Gadian, 'Class consciousness in Oldham and other north-west industrial towns', *Historical Journal* 21 (1978), pp. 161–72; R. Sykes, 'Some aspects of working-class consciousness in Oldham, 1830–42', *ibid.* 23 (1980), pp. 167–79.

20 See especially P. Joyce, *Work, Society and Politics* (Brighton, 1980); but there is an extensive literature on the policies of paternalistic employers, especially in cotton and mining, although their treatment of leisure is generally subordinated to other themes.

21 Cf. Yeo, *Religion and Voluntary Organisations in Crisis*, for Reading biscuit manufacturers, and Meller, *Leisure and the Changing City*, for the civic endeavours of Bristol's chocolate and tobacco magnates.

22 Exceptions include D. Cannadine, *Lords and Landlords: the Aristocracy and the Towns, 1774–1967* (1980) on Eastbourne, and F. B. May, 'The Development of Ilfracombe as a resort in the nineteenth century', M.A. thesis, Univ. of Wales, 1978.

2 MARK JUDD
'The oddest combination
popular culture and the

George Cruikshank

# of town and country':
London fairs, 1800-60

Fairs, wakes, animal baitings and other traditional entertainments provide some of the few insights into the activities and attitudes of a largely sub-literate section of early industrial English society. To the modern social historian they are as valuable a source as riots, festivals, chapbooks and ballads to an understanding of the beliefs and values that motivated plebeian behaviour. And yet until recent years such amusements had been given over to well-intentioned but uncritical amateur and antiquarian histories. The growing acceptance of leisure as a valid concern of the historian has done much to place popular recreations in a fuller social context. However, recreations such as fairs became near-obligatory social occasions and with their emphasis on communal activity and play were distinct from the simple freedom from work – 'leisure'. They may justly be considered an intrinsic part of English popular culture.

Popular culture is an amorphous term, but for the purposes of this chapter will be taken to mean 'a system of shared meanings, attitudes and values, and the symbolic forms (performances, artifacts) in which they are embodied'.[1] In pre-industrial England the culture of the inarticulate poorer classes had been expressed in the symbolic performances of the yearly festivals (both religious and secular), bread riots, songs, tales, parochial sports, charivaris and trade rituals. This 'low' or 'vulgar' culture was predominantly oral and its observation was mainly local and depended on face to face contact between the participants. In the first half of the nineteenth century this traditional culture was clearly on the wane. A wide variety of forces were reshaping the nature of popular culture. The increasing provision of education to all levels of society raised literacy rates and coupled with major technological advances in the printing industry served to undermine the primitive beliefs sustained by the oral tradition; the rise of Methodism and the reforming zeal of evangelicals (led by Wilberforce and Hannah More), promoted the principles of sobriety, respectability and self-discipline and laid the ideological foundation for the attack on the violent animal sports and other unruly forms of leisure by such groups as the Society for the Suppression of Vice and the RSPCA, founded in 1802 and 1824 respectively. The building of the railways bridged the gulf between town and country and by facilitating population mobility eroded that identification with the community which lay at the heart of local customary observances. The rise of industrial capitalism demanded new labouring habits: as the working day became increasingly regulated by the factory clock, so the fairs, wakes and religious holidays – adapted to the seasonal rhythms of agricultural work – came under pressure. Above all the process of urbanisation, fuelled by a population explosion and immigration from the countryside and Ireland, alienated the new generation of city dwellers from the pre-industrial village traditions without immediately providing an alternative urban culture other than that centred on the alehouse.

Such fundamental changes in the modes of working-class life and leisure in the first half of the nineteenth century constituted what William Howitt called a 'mighty revolution'.[2] The transition of popular culture was quite apparent in London. At the end of the eighteenth century many manifestations of the old culture were visible on the London streets. Trade rituals continued unabated, milk-maids and chimney-sweeps still paraded and danced on May Day and Bartholomew Fair remained the climax of the annual cycle of metropolitan fairs. Joseph Strutt's 1801 catalogue of popular pastimes demonstrated that very little had changed from John Stow's survey of Tudor London. The expression of local derision still took the form of 'rough music'. Puppet showmen, jugglers, tumblers and ballad singers continued to thrive on the streets; pedestrians in the Strand could witness the performances of dancing dogs, bears and learned pigs; and bulls were still hunted through the backstreets of Smithfield and Bethnal Green and baited on Westminster's Tothill Fields. In the courts and alleys of the rookeries of Westminster, cock-fighting, dog-fighting, ratting and badger-baiting appealed not only to costermongers but also to dissolute aristocrats. Only Southwark Fair (abolished by the Corporation of London in 1763), Shrove Tuesday throwing at cocks (prohibited in 1758), and may-poles had failed to survive the eighteenth century.[3]

The following century witnessed some profound changes. A transport revolution and the allied growth of extensive suburbs put a widening geographical as well as social distance between the capital's working and middle classes. Moral reforming bodies such as the London City Mission, The Ragged Schools Union, Model Dwelling Companies and the Christian Socialists had by 1860 made some headway in their efforts to 'civilise' the poor of the metropolis. Rowdy Bartholomew Fair was finally suppressed by the Corporation of London in 1854 and Greenwich Fair was to follow in 1857. The atavistic animal sports had all but died out by the end of the century, craft rituals (such as the observance of Saint Monday) had faded away, timetabled bank holidays had replaced the traditional holidays and the more fortunate street performers had moved indoors to the music halls.[4] 'The dominant cultural institutions' of late Victorian working-class London, Gareth Stedman Jones argues, were 'the pub, the sporting paper, the race-course and music hall'.[5]

Stedman Jones asserts that London working-class culture was unique: 'its focal points were not politics and education, but entertainment, sport and leisure time activity'.[6] It must be strongly reiterated that popular culture was a regional phenomenon and the case of London challenges received generalisations about much of nineteenth-century English urban culture. The factors shaping the nature of London popular culture were often quite different to those in the industrial north. The factory never became the dominant unit of production in the capital and skilled craftsmen remained very important in such small-scale industries as clock-making, shoe-making, furniture-making, coach-building and silk-weaving. Consequently the old artisan culture with its guilds, trade feasts, ritual drinking and holidays was perpetuated relatively longer into the nineteenth century. Before 1850 the concept of craft consciousness or 'vertical solidarity' was as important as the 'horizontal solidarity' of class in understanding how working Londoners viewed each other.[7] London life was further distinguished by the presence of a distinct adolescent or apprentice culture whose own traditions mirrored those of their elders. The immigrant communities, particularly those of the Jews, Irish and French Huguenots, contributed to the uniquely cosmopolitan London culture and in the slums of Whitechapel, Ratcliffe Highway, Wapping and St Giles a sub-culture existed among resident soldiers, sailors and professional thieves which had changed very little from that described in the picaresque literature of the Elizabethan period. High literacy rates and the wider availability of cheap printed matter together with the relative weakness of Methodist and temperance movements were further ingredients in a distinctive urban culture and tradition which contrasted sharply with the new cities further north.

In many ways an academic study of London popular culture remains a futile task because of the difficulty of seeing the festivals through the eyes of the participants: all the gestures and innuendoes and much of the humour are lost to the twentieth century. However, London fairs provide perhaps the clearest window into the recreations and transitional culture of the London poor in the first half of the nineteenth century.

There were many varieties of fair to be found in and around London. Some, notably the oldest and most famous – Bartholomew, Southwark and May Fairs – were devoted purely to pleasure and entertainment. Originally, however, fairs had been markets for local products and many of the long-established fairs on the periphery of the city (for example, Barnet 'Welsh' Fair and Croydon Fair) maintained this function well into the Victorian period. Statute fairs or 'mops' were ostensibly kept for the autumn hiring of agricultural labour and even in 1850 there was still a scattering of these fairs in metropolitan Essex. Such fairs usually had medieval origins and frequently had a royal charter in addition to the sanction of local custom. At the opposite extreme were the temporary and spontaneous fairs which appeared to celebrate royal jubilees, when the Thames froze over, or simply when a suitable plot of land became available (as happened at King's Cross and Chalk Farm in the 1840s). Just as transient were the Saturday night street fairs described by Mayhew.[8] Thus the term 'fair' is in itself a generalisation. Most English fairs combined the roles of market place, labour exchange, amusement park, and even museum. However in London, at least, the pleasure fair was beginning to predominate.

Between 1750 and 1850 over sixty different fairs have been traced within a fifteen-mile radius of Charing Cross.[9] Not all the London fairs survived the period in question; Southwark Fair and May Fair were both abolished in the 1760s. The Metropolitan Police Act of 1822 was wielded to abolish Bow, Brook Green (Hammersmith), Stepney, Tothill and Edmonton Fairs in the 1820s.[10] Yet fairs were far from a declining form of popular recreation in London. The suppressions should not over-shadow the fact that several new fairs originated in the period 1800-60, including those at Deptford, Chalk Farm, King's Cross and Battersea Fields. Stepney Fair was very successfully revived in 1843 and old rural fairs at Mitcham, Barnet, Wanstead, Croydon and Fairlop developed into major cockney carnivals. There is little doubt about the enduring popularity of the metropolitan fairs. The advent of the steamships on the Thames brought annual crowds of over a hundred thousand people to Greenwich Fair in the 1820s, an attendance bolstered by the arrival of the London and Greenwich Railway in 1838. A crowd estimated in excess of two hundred thousand patronised the newly revived Stepney Fair in 1843 and in his autobiography the showman George Sanger recalled that in 1848 the Easter Fair at Stepney was 'then the biggest gathering of its kind in England'.[11]

Fairs were a prime element of the traditional culture in the sense that they were perennial climaxes of the recreational calendar. It has been argued that 'wakes and fairs were intimately involved in the seasonal rhythms of agricultural life' and certainly rural fairs tended to take place after the major tasks of the farming year: the spring sowing, the summer hay harvest and the main corn harvest.[12] The incidence of the London fairs offers some insight into the survival of a traditional holiday calendar based on the cycle of rural labour within an urban environment. In common with the rest of the country London had no winter fairs. This is significant because throughout England winter was a season of under-employment, and London was no different. Most building work ceased; the frozen Baltic reduced timber imports and halted work in the dependent trades; work opportunities in the docks dropped dramatically after December and the ancillary services and consumer industries geared to serving upper class tastes found little demand after the end of the autumn 'London Season.' In a local economy as diversified as that of the capital there were exceptions (for example, the coal-heavers, chimney-sweeps and porters); but nevertheless one can argue that London, like rural areas, experienced an annual cycle of summer prosperity and winter poverty.[13] The high incidence of spring/early summer metropolitan fairs (Barnet, Greenwich, Stepney, Bow, Kingston, Peckham, Wanstead and Wandsworth all held their fairs between Easter and Whitsun) conforms to the rural pattern.[14] Here, however, similarities with the traditional rural calendar end. Fair activity around London in late September and early October (Michaelmas) was decidedly muted. There was no metropolitan equivalent to the post-harvest climax of the rural festival calendar. However, this discrepancy is largely explained by the knowledge that Michaelmas was the traditional hiring time for agricultural labour – a function customarily filled by the statute fairs. In London the role of the hiring fair had been largely superseded by other well-developed labour agencies: the trade guild, the public house and the dockland 'houses of call'.

Easter and Whitsun were the most notable London plebeian holidays. Although Londoners did not enjoy old festivals such as Plough Monday, Shrove Tuesday or May Day to anything like the same extent as their country counterparts, there is little doubt that Easter and Whitsun more than adequately replaced them as the most widely observed of the yearly celebrations in the capital. Greenwich and Stepney, the most popular fairs of the 1840s, were held at Easter and Whitsuntide, as were the new fairs at Chalk Farm and Deptford which successfully became established, whereas the most notable casualties, Southwark and Bartholomew Fairs, were held outside the recognised holiday times. The most ambitious attempt to institute a new fair outside the season, the 'New Bartholomew Fair' at Hoxton, was a total failure. The annual timing of London fairs anticipated rather than followed the legislated bank holidays of the second half of the nineteenth century. Thus it is very probable that the traditional and long-established London holiday calendar more than the annual rhythms of urban work determined the pattern of fairs between 1800 and 1860. As one critic of Greenwich Fair angrily complained in 1856: 'The whole mischief seems to have no other sanction but that of custom, which pleads against the reason, the common sense, and the common humanity of all'.[15]

> There's dancing, kissing, courting too,
> And a great many more such things to do,
> Getting drunk I do declare,
> When they go to see Bow Fair.
>
> There's hallowing, singing, cracking nuts,
> Some cramming sausages down their guts,
> Gin and gingerbread, I do declare,
> Is what they get when they go Bow Fair.
>
> – 'The Humours of Bow Fair' (anon., *c.* 1800)

All moveables of wonder from all parts,
Are here, Albinoes, painted Indians, Dwarfs,
The Horse of Knowledge, and the Learned Pig,
The Stone-eater, the Man that swallows fire,
Giants, Ventriloquists, the Invisible Girl,
The Bust that speaks, and moves its goggling eyes,
The Wax-work, Clock-work, all the marvellous craft
Of modern Merlins, wild Beasts, Puppet Shows,
All out-o'-th'-way, far-fetch'd, perverted things,
All freaks of Nature, all Promeathean thoughts
Of Man; his dullness, madness, and their feats,
All jumbled up together to make up
This Parliament of Monsters ...

> – William Wordsworth, *The Prelude* (Book VII, 679-91), on
> Bartholomew Fair (1805)

The principal trends in a transitional urban culture may be discovered in the customs, shows and exhibitions of the fairground. Both pieces of verse, for example, offer insights into the culture of two of London's biggest fairs. 'The Humours of Bow Fair' describes a popular London fair from the inside, through the eyes of a participant in the current popular, 'low' or illiterate culture. Indeed the very form of the evidence, the broadside ballad, was in itself an intrinsic part of that culture. The ballad is written in a mood of celebration, the overall impression is of a carnival atmosphere. Wordsworth provides an accurate and comprehensive catalogue of exactly what Londoners could see at Bartholomew Fair in the early nineteenth century. His description was written out of a spirit of curiosity but also startled bewilderment at the more traditional entertainments of the London poor. However sympathetic the poet may have been towards English radicalism, his impression of the fair was still framed by the attitudes and values of 'learned' or 'high' culture. Despite his political sympathies Wordsworth could not cross the cultural divide separating him from the English poor he romanticised. The very line "All out-o'-th'-way, far-fetch'd, perverted things' shows his inability to enter the world of traditional culture. This step is even more difficult for the modern historian.

Fortunately, in London at least some remnants of this culture have survived. Bartholomew Fair, which was held every September in Smithfield, is particularly well documented. The very location of the fair was significant. Smithfield was part of an ancient London recreational tradition. Horse-racing had been staged there as early as the twelfth century; in late medieval times it had been noted for sword-fighting exhibitions (Ben Jonson referred to the 'sword and buckler age of Smithfield' in the introduction to his play, *Bartholomew Fair*); in Tudor times John Stow described Bartholomew Day wrestling matches between citizens of the City of London and 'inhabitants of the suburbs'; Smithfield had been used as a prize-fighting venue in the eighteenth century and even after the abolition of the fair itself in 1854, Mayhew described regular Friday afternoon donkey races in the market place among the London coster-monger community.[16]

Bartholomew Fair itself had originated in 1133 and as an ancient chartered fair held a Court of Pie Powder (a medieval summary court) for resolving petty disputes and offences and, more importantly, to license the stalls and booths. This last function of the court provides details of the names of the entertainers and offers a unique opportunity for a numerical analysis of which fairground amusements were most prevalent in London.[17] Sample studies have been made of the two five-year periods most fully and accurately documented in the court book. Table 2.1 lists the total number of licences issued for the different categories of stalls and exhibitions.[18]

Table 2.1   Bartholomew fair stall licences, number and (%)

	1790-4	1830-4
Gingerbread sellers	167 (35.5)	90 (33.7)
Toy sellers	109 (23)	60 (22.5)
Animals (Exhibits of freaks and menageries etc.)	37 (7.8)	25 (9.4)
Exhibitions/peep shows (mechanical objects, clock-work, glassblowing etc.)	31 (6.5)	39 (14.6)
Puppet shows	33 (7)	
Dramas (drolls, medleys, pantomimes, comedies)	23 (4.8)	19 (7.1)
Roundabouts & swings	21 (4.4)	–
Physical agility (tumbling, rope & wire dancing, conjuring, dexterity)	18 (3.8)	15 (5.6)
Human freaks (dwarfs, giants etc.)	18 (3.8)	15 (5.6)
Waxworks	8 (1.7)	4 (1.5)
Others	8 (1.7)	–
Total	473	267

The statistics plot accurately the decline in the scale of the fair. Indeed the doubling of stall rents in 1840 by the City of London's Markets Committee effectively banished the major shows and exhibitions, leaving behind only the itinerant pedlars and destroying the fair as a popular festival. Nevertheless what does emerge is the wide cross-section of entertainments and the durability of certain forms of amusement. The disappearance of the swings and roundabouts by 1830 is explained by a successful Lord Mayor's prohibition (on the grounds of safety) rather than by any radical change in popular tastes. Prints of the 1838 Coronation Fair in Hyde Park show that swings and roundabouts remained very popular fairground amusements. The absence of puppet shows is not so easily explained: Mayhew's accounts of the Punch and Judy and 'Fantoccini' men suggest that knockabout puppet shows still retained popular favour, particularly among children.[19]

A further examination of exactly what entertainments were on offer is most informative to an understanding of the nature and pace of change within plebeian London culture. Henry Morley, writing in 1859, compiled a catalogue of the entertainments at Bartholomew Fair in 1748.[20] In that year the fair featured theatrical representations of 'The Bloody Contest between Charles the Twelfth and Peter the Great, Czar of Muscovy', the ancient chapbook and folk-tale of 'The Blind Beggar of Bethnal Green' and 'The Adventures of Roderick Random and his friend Strap'. In addition there was a droll 'The Constant Quaker, or, The Humours of Wapping' and a pantomime (typical of this enduring genre) 'Harlequin's Frolics'. Other exhibitions included a waxwork gallery of the 'Court of the Queen of Hungary' and the inevitable range of freaks from the human and animal worlds, which that year included 'The Young Oronatu Savage', a twelve-foot-long and 120-stone hog attended by 'the amazing little dwarf' – 'the smallest man in the world', and 'Maria Theresa, the Amazing Corsican Fairy'. Elsewhere there were firework shows and displays of Italian sword dances, hornpipes and other traditional folk dances. The amusements were rounded off by puppet shows and a more orthodox menagerie which presented camels, hyenas and panthers to an inquisitive audience. The impression given by Morley is corroborated by a newspaper account of 1752. 'The Chronicle' reported that the attractions included 'the learned horse', 'the American Dwarf', 'the tall lady from Norfolk, and the short one from Durham', 'the surprising learned pig', ribbon and breeches sellers, 'the scrapers of cat-gut', Punch and Judy showmen and 'the usual group of fire-eaters, ribbon weavers, rope and wire dancers, conjurors and wild beastesses [sic] and not above five hundred pick-pockets . . .'.[21] Seventy years later William Hone assembled a detailed and revealing list of the twenty-two major shows at the 1825 Bartholomew Fair. No fewer than eight of the shows exhibited assorted human curiosities – dwarfs, giants, Indians; a further five shows featured jugglers, tumblers, rope-dancers, clowns and displays of equestrianism; two of the major commercial fairground menageries, the collections of Wombell and Atkins, were present alongside a less reputable assembly of animal freaks which in this year included three 'learned horses', 'The Mare with Seven Feet' and 'Toby the Swinish Philosopher' (a pig which according to Hone had a fine grasp of arithmetic and the alphabet and could draw up accounts and tell the time), hurdy-gurdy players, a peep-show and exhibitions of glass-blowing and waxworks. The remaining stalls were filled with itinerant vendors of gingerbread, toys, shell-fish and hot foods.[22]

The same showmen attended the other major London and provincial fairs. At the time of Hone's description, 1825, Bartholomew Fair was in relative decline, but further east down the River Thames Greenwich Fair was very much in the ascendant, and it maintained a very similar culture and atmosphere: 'It was a never to be forgotten orgy of noise, swings, dancing-booths, oil lamps, fried fish, fat women, giants, dwarfs, gingerbread nuts, unappreciated actors, jugglers and acrobats, mud, dirt, drink, gin, beer and skittles.'[23]

Analysis of the various displays is not made easier by the fact that their juxtaposition was not far short of anarchic. At the 1825 Bartholomew Fair a peep-show presented the celebrated murder of William Weare followed by a portrayal of the conversion of St Paul, while waxwork representations of the current royal family took their places alongside figures of Mother Shipton, an Irish giant and an inevitable murderer, Abraham Thornton. Eight years later there was no more order: there was an exhibition of views from the New Testament 'joined to the very similar association of Views of the details of the Red Barn Murder' and this particular collection was completed by a boa constrictor and a mis-shapen sheep.[24]

Nevertheless much can be learned about the leisure-time tastes of Londoners from this apparent chaos. Puppet shows, roundabouts and 'high' dramas came and went, but otherwise the entertainments were remarkably consistent over the hundred years between 1750 and 1850. Music, dancing, eating, drinking, gaping at physical monstrosities and curiosities, laughing at clowns, marvelling at the antics of apparently intelligent animals and at feats of human agility and dexterity: all these proved remarkably durable as the typical London fair-time amusements. Indeed displays of tumbling, dancing, balancing and the ritual feasts had descended virtually unaltered from the medieval fairs.

The London fairground exhibitions testify to the popular obsession with spectacular and sanguine crimes. Murders remained a perennial fascination of the fair audiences in much the same way as they dominated the contemporary popular literature. It was perhaps no accident that the old May Fair had been held on a plot of land adjacent to the Tyburn gallows and there in the mid eighteenth century gingerbread men had been shaped to resemble famous felons, while puppets carried out mock executions. The popular preoccupation with violent crime in London increased rather than diminished with the passage of time. In 1834, some seven years after the event, there were five separate 'panoramics' and 'phantasmagoricas' depicting the murder of Maria Marten at the Red

Barn. George Sanger, the showman, recalled that this murder was particularly popular in the London area and made a special point of including it in his peep-show when he visited Brentford Fair in 1833. The murders perpetrated by William Rush in 1849 were no less lucrative. A peep-show proprietor informed Mayhew: 'There was more [money] took with Rush's murder than there ever has been by the battle of Waterloo itself'.[25] The phenomenon of the Red Barn and Rush murders illustrates that the fairground showmen played no lesser part in perpetuating the bloody legends which haunted the popular psyche than the 'penny dreadfuls', ballads and chapbooks; indeed the peep-shows may have been more important as they made no demands on the literacy of the audience.

The fascination with strangely 'gifted' or unusual animals was a very prominent theme within pre-Victorian London popular culture. Many of these freak shows were clearly cheap frauds (for example, the afore-mentioned 'Mare with Seven Feet' did not have seven legs – as one handbill claimed – but three extra bones growing out of its fetlock joints), yet their appeal was enduring. A giant hog became something of an emblem for Bartholomew Fair and its ritual roasting was one of the fair's great climaxes. Interestingly the every-popular 'learned' animals also found an audience at more respectable fixed venues outside the fair-ground. In 1785 Southey observed that the learned pig resident in a Charing Cross exhibition was a 'far greater object of admiration to the English than ever was Sir Isaac Newton'. Public gullibility remained undiminished in the 1840s when an Italian, Signor Cappelli, earned a living by displaying his 'family of learned cats' in a shop in fashionable Regent Street, and nearby in Bond Street 'the Scientific Java Sparrows' – allegedly proficient in seven languages and all Oxford undergraduates – could fool an audience educated enough to know better.[26] Highly-trained animals (dancing bears, dogs and monkeys) were a long-estab-lished part of the old London street culture, but the popularity enjoyed by the 'learned' animals both in fairs and in more fashionable venues in the first half of the nineteenth century is a revealing insight into the co-existence and intermingling of very ancient popular beliefs with the quasi-scientific outlook of the 'age of improvement'.

The evolution of galleries of stereotyped or 'stock' characters formed an integral part of the old pre-industrial popular culture and the shows of the London fairs serve to reinforce this observation.[27] Stereotypes were most commonly drawn along national, racial or occupational lines. 'Inhuman' Turks and negro 'cannibals' appeared year after year at Bartholomew Fair. In 1833 a troop of Chinese sewing-needle swallowers were recommended as being of especial interest to the 'Knights of the Thimble' (i.e. tailors) and clockwork figures depicted mechanics 'fully

employed' with 'the costume of their various trades . . . well observed'.[28]
Perhaps the best example of the way in which the fairs helped to fasten
these stereotypes in the popular consciousness was a performance of *The
Shipwreck'd Lovers* at Bartholomew Fair in 1759. It was 'Interspersed
with the comical and diverting Humours and adventures of Lieutenant
Fireball, a true English Tar; Noddy Nestlecock, a distressed Beau; Snivel
Thimble, a Taylor; Split Farthing, an old usurer; and Glisterpipe, a
finical surgeon.'[29] Indeed the many descriptions of fair audiences emphasise the extent to which the London poor classified each other in the
language and imagery of their trades rather than class. This is very
apparent in the broadside ballads describing the London fairs:

> . . . The Watermen with Wapping whores
> Over the fields do come by scores
> From Billingsgate comes fish fag Nan
> Some Thames Street Carman is her flash man
> Soft-cinder Sue, scavenger Dick,
> Both arm in arm doth fondly trip . . .

('The Humours of Bow Fair')

Waxworks were another important part of the culture of London fairs.
They were first recorded at Bartholomew Fair in 1647 and their lasting
appeal to Londoners is still reflected by the continuing success of the
Madame Tussaud's collection. A bewildering array of contemporary,
historical and mythological characters were commemorated in wax at the
fairs and they provide further evidence of the extremely wide range of
popular tastes. Domestic and foreign monarchs and statesmen were
always popular, but literature, the Bible and folk-lore were constantly
but randomly raided for commercial effigies. The collection described
by Hone in 1825 was typically representative: it featured likenesses of
George IV, Princess Amelia, Elizabeth I, Mary Queen of Scots, Jane
Shore (mistress of Edward II), Othello, O'Bryen ('the famous Irish
Giant') and John and Margaret Scott (a Scottish centenarian couple).
Such collections did much to convey popular and folk history to a
semi-literate audience.[30]

The waxworks, panoramas and peep-shows demonstrate that spectacular murders, military feats, royalty, traditional folk-tales, dragons,
ghosts, witches and human and animal abnormalities remained firmly
embedded in the popular imagination in the fifty years before the Great
Exhibition of 1851, but the popular political consciousness of
seventeenth-century London, as described by Peter Burke, is notably
absent.[31] Plays and drolls at the fairs dealing with political subject matter
were few and far between. Occasional peep-show representations of the
Tolpuddle Martyrs and the demonstration of the Grand Consolidated

Trades Union appeared in the 1830s, yet these were isolated examples and were far outnumbered by peep-shows, transparencies, waxworks and panoramas detailing royal jubilees, coronations, marriages and deaths. The uneasy relationship between fairground culture and radical politics was illustrated by the experience of George Sanger at Newport's 1839 Whitsun Fair where Chartist rioters abused and assaulted the showmen, eventually driving the fair out of the town. Although clearly frightened at the time, with hindsight Sanger could later remark: 'All the same it made an excellent subject for my father's peep-show ... In addition to the Newport Riots we later added the trial of [the Chartist leaders] Frost, Williams and Jones ...'.[32] The attitude of the showmen towards the radical politics of the day had more to do with curiosity and commercial opportunism than commitment. Political indifference was a marked characteristic of the London street culture; Guy Fawkes's Day was traditionally used for the expression of political feeling, the Guy representing any public figure who had offended the popular mood. Towards mid-century the Pope and Cardinal Wiseman were regular 'Guys' until they were superseded by assorted Czars after the British entry into the Crimean War in 1854. As the interviews of Henry Mayhew reveal, such political feeling was superficial and fleeting among the street-folk; a seller of Guys confided: 'The year they was chalking "No Popery" all about the walls, I had one dressed up in a long black garment, with a red cross on his bosom. I'm sure I don't know what it meant, but they told me it would be popular.'[33]

Although the London fairs provide only the most oblique of insights into the relationship between radical politics and popular culture, they do cast some light on a neglected London phenomenon – the non-political street gangs. Accounts of fairs and other major recreational events such as prize-fights are enlivened by the activities of such groups as the 'Lady Holland Mob' at Bartholomew Fair and the 'Swell Mob' of Greenwich Fair. To the enemies of popular recreations these largely adolescent gangs were the necessary proof of the debauching nature of London fairs. Following an orgy of petty thieving and vandalism after Hampstead's West End Fair by the 'Bird Street Gang' in 1819 local magistrates felt vindicated in suppressing the fair the next year. 'The Swell Mob', who worked using gaudily-clad women as decoys at Greenwich and Bartholomew Fairs in the 1830s, were little more than flamboyant and well-organised pick-pockets who operated out of the fringes of the London underworld and were the latest in a long line which dates back to the picaresque characters of Elizabethan literature. However, the 'Lady Holland Mob' of Bartholomew Fair reveals rather more about the survival of seventeenth-century urban traditions well into the nineteenth century. Bartholomew Fair had customarily opened at midnight when a riotous mob assembled to carry an effigy of Lady Holland through the streets of Smithfield. The tradition had originated in the Commonwealth period when Lady Holland had given sanctuary at Holland House to the Fair's players from harassment by Puritan zealots, yet as late as 1822 an estimated crowd of five thousand gathered outside the Cloth and Shears public house to celebrate this ritual. The exploits of the Lady Holland Mob had steadily become a front for much criminal activity and they were never effectively controlled before the formation of the City Police in 1832.[34]

This midnight procession of the effigy to celebrate the Proclamation of Bartholomew Fair draws attention to the extent to which traditional London culture survived into the eighteenth and nineteenth centuries. In the eighteenth century the fair was ceremonially declared open by the Lord Mayor and this civic opening had strong affinities with the European spirit of carnival: 'The moment the coach is discovered to be approaching all the instruments of music, base drums, fiddles and crankee trumpets, broken bassoons and salt-boxes are in readiness to salute his lordship with a grand concert, while the emperors and Kings, Harlequins and Columbines, and even punch and the devil are arrayed in splendid attire.'[35]

Street processions were a long-established feature of London popular culture and had accompanied the May Day and Midsummer Eve festivities. Several of the London fairs served to maintain this old tradition. Charlton's Horn Fair started only after a procession from Cuckold's Point, Deptford, had reached the Kent village and the participants had passed three times around the local church. In the eighteenth century Fairlop Fair began with a procession of block-makers and watermen from Wapping to Hainault Forest in Essex; Deptford Fair (which started only in the 1820s) developed out of the annual Trinity Monday water procession on the Thames from Trinity House, London, to Trinity House, Deptford.

Charlton's Horn Fair provides probably the best example of the survival of very primitive traditions in the London area well into the modern period. The Fair was so named because (at least until 1800) all participants had worn horns to go to the Fair. There is little doubt that in the popular imagination Charlton Fair was associated with cuckolding. In legend and popular belief the fair had begun when King John had enjoyed the favours of the wife of the local miller during a hunting expedition. The King was said to have compensated the aggrieved husband by granting him the tract of land from Charlton to the aptly named Cuckold's Point, and a charter to hold a fair. To confirm the strong survival of this version of the fair's origins one only has to examine the broadside ballads of the late eighteenth century which frequently retell the story of King John and the miller's wife. One ballad actually ends with the lines. 'For this Fair is kept, that you may go, With your Friends t'Ride as Cuckolds all a'row.'[36] Charlton Horn Fair grew to resemble a mass annual charivari: the expression of local popular justice and community defamation and derision which had been widespread across Europe in the early modern period.[37] In the eighteenth century Londoners had proceeded to Charlton disguised as wolves, bears, lions, Frenchmen, Spaniards, Russians and Turks. In his autobiography, one William Fuller told how he travelled from London to Charlton: 'I was dressed in my land-ladie's best gown and other women's attire, and to Horn Fair we went.'[38] The procession was accompanied by 'rough music' – trumpets, bells, cymbals, salt boxes and drums – another of the symbolic forms of the European charivari. Although Charlton Fair was not a spontaneous expression of local derision and justice in cases of sexual irregularities, the fair was a conscious attempt at least to uphold the traditional symbols of the charivari. A broadside of 1768, 'A New Summons to Horn Fair', warned revellers that they must come with a 'horn new tipt with gold' and 'other accoutrements fit for a gentleman cuckold' or face the punishment of sexual mockery: '... Hereof fail not at your peril, for if you do, you will be fined by our court and ... be obliged to ride with the Fumblers, and undergo the ridicule of women.'[39] Although the processions had ceased by the nineteenth century, Charlton Fair retained important elements of the old traditions. In 1825 the pleasure-seekers still wore masks and assumed female clothing and William Hone wrote that the 'fair was still a kind of carnival or masquerade' even though it had been moved out of the local churchyard to a private field.[40] Charlton Fair was not a unique survival. Charivaris were still a feature of the streets of England's largest city during the 1820s. A dozen Bermondsey women were charged with riotous behaviour in 1825 after assembling outside the house of an elderly man who had allegedly raped a girl 'labouring under imbecility of mind', burning his effigy in a bonfire and having 'saluted his ears with music from marrowbones and cleavers and old tin pots'. Chimney-sweeps also maintained the charivari tradition, using a pair of carrots to denote the cuckold's horns in their street parades.[41] Charlton Fair and the charivaris are a fascinating glimpse into the old London popular culture and there were undoubtedly more similar survivals (for example, the chimney-sweeps continued their 'grotesque' and 'fantastic' May Day dances at Hammersmith's Brook Green Fair), but our knowledge of them is always likely to remain fragmented because of the unconscious puritanism of many of the old folklorists (on whom we must still rely) when faced with traditions which shocked their moral sensibilities and belied their ideas of social 'progress'.

The perpetuation of pre-industrial culture at the London fairs owed much to the presence of the pedlar class. Even in the 1850s they upheld the semi-literate culture of the chapbook and broadside ballad as street minstrels, patterers and song sellers. At the fairs this class was represented by the toy and gingerbread sellers who formed the majority of licensed stall holders at Bartholomew Fair and as that fair was run down by the City authorities, it was they, and not the professional showmen, who were the last to quit Smithfield. These migrant tinkers and chapmen normally wintered on the fringes of London before taking their shows and wares on the summer circuit of metropolitan and provincial fairs. Although enjoying little respectability, this tramping fraternity was an intrinsic part of the fairground culture and they actually developed their own distinct fairs at Stepney, and, late in the nineteenth century, the 'Gypsy Fair' on Wanstead Flats. Even now their descendants are still to be seen on Epsom Downs on Derby Day. Their summer perambulations helped produce the cultural interplay between London and its immediate countryside which shored up the traditional rural culture in the capital and prompted one observer to describe Bartholomew Fair as 'the oddest combination of town and country ever brought together'.[42]

London's commercial tea and pleasure gardens supply further evidence of the persistence of rural beliefs and customs within metropolitan society. Until the mid eighteenth century May Day festivities were observed at the London Spa in Clerkenwell, where chimney-sweeps and milk-maids performed their traditional dances to fiddle and tabor music. Highgate's Eel Pie House and Hornsey Wood House were used well into the nineteenth century by the London poor who went out 'palming' in Hornsey Wood. As late as the 1850s, the Surrey Zoological Gardens in Walworth still held 'country fairs' which included 'may-pole gaieties', juggling acts and gypsy displays, which, unlike the fairs, middle-class patrons could enjoy without risk to their respectability. When London's fairs came under increasing pressure from evangelicals, police and magistrates from the 1820s onwards, the later pleasure gardens preserved many of the traditional fairground entertainments. Small menageries, learned horses, pantomimes and displays of hornpipe dancing, tumbling, posturing and rope dancing were common features of the gardens at Sadlers Wells, Vauxhall and Cremorne in the first half of the nineteenth century. These city retreats ensured that traditional cultural conventions were never entirely swamped by the new demands of urban and industrial life.[43]

Even the enemies of London fairs appreciated that they perpetuated traditional modes of leisure, and indeed the antiquity of the fairs was cited as proof of their obsolescence. By the 1850s reformers claimed that working-class improvement had rendered the old fairground amusements redundant. In a tract of 1856, calling for the suppression of that 'focus of London iniquity', Greenwich Fair, the Reverend C. F. S. Money referred to the Fair as 'the toy of overgrown children' and a 'barbarous relic of a bygone age'. He concluded his tirade by warning that failure to abolish Greenwich Fair 'would be inconsistent with those efforts we are making to ameliorate the condition and elevate the tastes of our working class'.[44] Certainly the fair showmen were not immune to the rise of the ethos of rational recreation. After describing to Mayhew how he had to modify his act and perform 'werry steady and werry slow and leave out all comic words and business' a Punch and Judy showman bitterly complained: 'It's the march of hintellect wot's a doing all this.'[45] Nevertheless the sanction of antiquity and custom did preserve many London fairs. Chartered fairs were particularly resilient. In the 1760s the City of London's Lands Committee twice seriously discussed the abolition of Bartholomew Fair, but were thwarted because the owner of the charter, Lord Kensington, could not be persuaded to sell his rights to the Fair. It was not until 1829 when the Kensington estate finally agreed to part with the rights that the City Corporation could legally begin to extinguish the revelries of Bartholomew Fair. The notorious Charlton Fair possessed a charter and was not suppressed until 1871 whereas the more orderly and popular but unchartered fair at nearby Greenwich was abolished fifteen years earlier.

There is much to be learned from the entertainments and traditions of the London fairs in the first half of the nineteenth century. London society was uniquely cosmopolitan and this was reflected in the fairgrounds themselves. The fairs maintained a culture which preserved several rural ritual practices and beliefs in the heart of Europe's biggest city. Its survival owed much to the itinerant class of pedlars, tinkers and chapmen and to the adolescents and journeymen who carried Lady Holland's effigy through the Smithfield streets. Fairground culture was as non-political as the contemporary 'penny dreadfuls' or the traditional chapbooks. It was an escape from the awareness of economic and social ills.

The most striking feature of the popular culture was the resilience and immutability of the various forms of entertainment. Music, dancing, farces, menageries and displays of curiosities provide a constant thread throughout the period. What changes took place – the introduction of more peep-shows, transparencies and mechanical exhibits – simply reflected technological advances in the craft of the showmen. This process was to continue, throughout the century, to produce the automated and mechanised contraptions which dominate and characterise modern fairgrounds.[46]

In pre-Victorian England fairs had been part of a pre-industrial way of life which sanctioned such atavistic sports as bull-baiting, dog-fighting and ratting, and indeed they remained the most enduring manifestation of that most brutal and ill-disciplined culture. However, in nineteenth-century London, the fairs, unlike the animal sports, proved to be a far from moribund recreation. The old fair showmen made decisive contributions to the evolution of Victorian London leisure and also go some way to devalue assertions that the early nineteenth century saw something of a vacuum in the provision of popular recreations. Fairground jugglers, acrobats and tumblers produced the talent and an established audience for the nascent circus industry; zoological gardens developed out of the travelling menageries, and the music halls became secure venues and provided a livelihood for many of the street singers and patterers. The Great Exhibition of 1851, the invention of photography and the wider availability of cheap pictorial papers did undermine the old fairground exhibitions, but, despite the exertions of moral reformers, such shows were never successfully harnessed to the ideal of rational instruction and even the popular success of the later showplaces of the London exhibition industry, Crystal Palace, Olympia and Alexandra Palace, owed as much to an interest in mechanical and natural curiosities generated in the earlier fairgrounds as to the 'march of intellect'.

The fairs of the London area emphasise that in nineteenth-century England there were very marked differences in the patterns of leisure and recreations between the major urban centres. London's distinctive social, economic and cultural history had produced long-established and remarkably enduring urban recreational traditions. At Bartholomew and Charlton Fairs extremely old rituals and popular beliefs can be detected impinging on, and surviving in, an age of rational education, industrialisation and rapid urban growth. Yet, the fairs were at the same time a dynamic and regenerative influence in the evolution of modern popular leisure. Such developments are clear with the benefits of historical hindsight. But, above all else, through the eyes of the participants (perhaps the most important perspective in the study of popular culture) the fairs were ends in themselves – opportunities for a total release from the everyday pressures of work and economic survival. They remained recreations in the most basic and exact sense of that word.

NOTES

1 P. Burke, *Popular Culture in Early Modern Europe* (1978), Prologue.
2 W. Howitt, *The Rural Life of England* (1840 edn.), p. 515.
3 J. Strutt, *The Sports and Pastimes of the People of England* (1801); J. Stow, *A Survey of London*, (1603, 1838 edn.) (reprinted 1908).

4 G. Stedman Jones, 'Working-class culture and working-class politics in London, 1870–1900: Some notes on the remaking of a working class', *Journal of Social History* 7 (1974), pp. 460–508.

5 *Ibid.*, p. 479.

6 *Ibid.*

7 E. P. Thompson, 'Patrician society, plebeian culture', *Journal of Social History* 7 (1974).

8 H. Mayhew, *London Labour and the London Poor* 4 vols. (1861–2), vol. 1., pp. 11–12.

9 Anon. *An Exact List of all the Fairs in England and Wales* (1752); W. Owen, *Owen's Book of Fairs* (1820 edn.); Victoria County Histories of Middlesex, Kent, Surrey and Essex.

10 H. Cunningham, 'The metropolitan fairs: a case study in the social control of leisure', in A. P. Donajgrodzki (ed.), *Social Control in Nineteenth-Century Britain* (1978).

11 G. Sanger, *Seventy Years a Showman* (1938 edn.), p. 102.

12 R. W. Malcolmson, *Popular Recreations in English Society 1700–1850* (Cambridge, 1973), p. 24.

13 G. Stedman Jones, *Outcast London* (Oxford, 1971), chapter 2.

14 One problem of this approach is that the time span of 1800–60 invalidates many rural-urban distinctions. For example, in 1800 Croydon Fair specialised in the sale of horses, bullocks, sheep, toys and walnuts and was thus clearly a market for local rural products, however, by 1860 the railway had reached Croydon and the Fair was established as one of the major metropolitan fairs worked by the commercial fairground entertainers.

15 C. F. S. Money, *Greenwich Fair: a Nursery For Crime* (*c.* 1856), p. 14.

16 J. Strutt, *op. cit.* (1838 edn.), p. 81; W. Fitzstephen, *Description of the City of London* (1772 edn.), p. 36; H. Mayhew, *op. cit.*, vol. 1., p. 30.

17 Guildhall Library, MS. *Bartholomew Fair Pie Powder Court Book, 1790–1854.*

18 Unfortunately, this table is only a crude representation of the different categories of entertainment on offer at the Fair. It disguises some very sharp annual fluctuations (for example, in 1792 there were ten different licensed puppet shows, in 1795 there were only three). Surviving handbill advertisements suggest that many of these shows did include a wider variety of entertainments; however as the survival of such handbills is entirely random, in order to obtain some consistency only the classification registered with the licence fee has been used.

19 H. Mayhew, *op. cit.*, vol. 3, pp. 51–72.

20 H. Morley, *Memoirs of Bartholomew Fair* (1880 edn.), pp. 335–6.

21 *The Chronicle*, September 1752 (Guildhall Library Noble Collection).

22 W. Hone, *The Every-Day Book*, 2 vols. (1826–7), pp. 1169–1252.

23 J. Hollingshead, *My Lifetime*, 2 vols. (1895), vol. 1, p. 17.

24 Guildhall Library, Noble Collection: Catalogue of Bartholomew Fair 1833.

25 H. Mayhew, *op. cit.*, vol. 3, p. 97.

26 R. D. Altick, *The Shows of London* (1978), pp. 35, 40, 306.

27 P. Burke, *op. cit.*, chapter 6.

28 Guildhall Library, Noble Collection: Catalogue of Bartholomew Fair 1833.

29 S. Rosenfeld, *The Theatre of the London Fairs in the Eighteenth Century* (1960), p. 61.

30 W. Hone, *op. cit.*, and Guildhall Noble Collection.

31 P. Burke, 'Popular culture in seventeenth-century London', *London Journal* 3 (1977).

32 G. Sanger, *op. cit.*, p. 37.

33 H. Mayhew, *op. cit.*, vol. 3, p. 75.

34 H. Morley, *op. cit.*, chapter 23.

35 Anon., *The History and Origin of Bartholomew Fair* (1808), p. 13.

36 *The Counsellor's Speech For Horn Fair* (1770).

37 E. P. Thompson, 'Rough music', *Annales* (1972), pp. 288-312; P. Burke, *Popular Culture in Early Modern Europe*, pp. 198-9.

38 W. Hone, *op. cit.*, vol. 1, p. 1386.

39 *A New Summons to Horn Fair* (1768), Guildhall Library.

40 W. Hone, *op. cit.*, vol. 1, p. 1386.

41 *Bell's Life in London and Sporting Chronicle*, 18 September 1825; 10 February 1822; 5 May 1822.

42 J. Hollingshead, *op. cit.*, p. 19; R. Samuel, 'Comers and goers' in H. J. Dyos and M. Wolff (eds.), *The Victorian City*, vol. I, (1973), p. 133.

43 W. Wroth, *The London Pleasure Gardens of the Eighteenth Century* (1896); W. Wroth, *Cremorne and the Later London Gardens* (1907); British Museum, Royal Surrey Zoological Gardens Collection (th. Cts. 51-8).

44 C. F. S. Money, *op. cit.*, pp. 15-16.

45 H. Mayhew, *op. cit.*, vol. 3, pp. 51-2.

46 H. Cunningham, *op. cit.*; S. Alexander, *St Giles's Fair, 1830-1914*, History Workshop Pamphlets 2 (1970).

3 JEFFREY RICHARDS
The cinema and cinema-going in Birmingham in the 1930s

The cinema is primarily a sort of public lounge. It is a blend of an English club and a continental café; at once the most public and the most secluded of places. It has affinities with both church and alcove. One can go alone, à deux, *en famille* or in bands. One can take one's children there to keep them quiet; or one can take one's girl there to be quiet oneself. Punctuality and decorum are of little or no consequence. One can drop in and out at will ... One can proverbially filch ideas for a new dress, or 'get off' with one's neighbour. One can enjoy a little nap as easily as the luxury of a good laugh or a good cry. In wet weather it is an escape from the rain; in winter a means of keeping warm. Schoolboys, whose holidays are drawing to a close, know that prevalent epidemics can often be caught there. The cinema is a pastime and a distraction, an excuse for not doing something else or sitting listlessly at home.

Thus, in his memorable manifesto for modernist cinema buildings, published in 1930, did P. Morton Shand summarise the social function of the cinema.[1]

Cinemagoing was indisputably the most popular form of recreation in the 1930s. In 1934, the first year for which reliable statistics exist, there were an average 18.5 million admissions to cinemas every week and a total of 963 million admissions for the year. By 1939, the number had risen to 20–22 million a week.[2]

It is clear that the bulk of this mass audience was drawn from the working class. An analysis of the seat tickets sold in 1934 reveals that 'nearly 4 out of every 5 persons visiting the cinema paid not more than 1 shilling for admission', in other words took took the cheap seats.[3] The majority of cinemas were to be found in the working-class urban industrial areas. A succession of surveys confirmed the nature of audience composition. The National Council of Public Morals' enquiry into the cinema in 1917 concluded: 'The picture house is the cheapest, most accessible, and the most widely enjoyed form of public entertainment; it is most popular in the poorest districts, and is attended by a very large number of children and young people.'[4] *The Social Survey of Merseyside* (1934) concluded that 'the manual working class go more frequently than Class B [i.e. lower middle class] ... working class children, it appears, nearly all attend the cinema at least once weekly'.[5] The Wartime Social Survey into cinemagoing (1943) found that 'the lower economic groups and those with elementary education go to the cinema more than the higher economic groups and those with higher education. Factory workers, clerical and distributive workers go rather more than any other occupation groups'.[6]

Cinemagoing was as important to the unemployed as to the employed.[7] E. W. Bakke found this in his study of Woolwich and it was confirmed by the Carnegie Trust's study of unemployed youth in Glasgow, Cardiff and Liverpool between 1936 and 1939.[8] The trust concluded that 'attendance at cinemas was the most important single activity of the young men of the enquiry'. About eighty per cent attended at least once a week and twenty-five per cent more often. The trust saw the appeal of the cinemas as wish-fulfilment, escapism, topicality and the warmth of the buildings.

Cinemagoing was thus regular and habitual, assuming a dominant role both in working-class leisure and in the life of the young. It also tended to be local; so that the neighbourhood cinema assumed a place in community life not dissimilar to that of the local pub. But it was not only the working classes who went to the cinema. Throughout the 1920s and 1930s films became increasingly respectable and widened their audience appeal. As the Commission on Educational and Cultural Films disarmingly put it in 1932: 'A fellow of an Oxford College no longer feels an embarrassed explanation to be necessary when he is recognized leaving a cinema. A growing number of cultivated and unaffected people enjoy going to the pictures.'[9] By the end of the decade important sections of opinion had even been converted to the virtues of Hollywood films, which had traditionally been regarded with fear and distaste by both the political and critical establishments.[10]

The enormous influence and impact of cinema was widely accepted. When John Buchan said in the House of Commons: 'Whether we are interested in the film or not we cannot deny its enormous public importance. It is the most powerful engine of propaganda and advertisement on the globe today. It appeals to every class. It has an enormous influence on the education of youth. It is an amazing platform for the dissemination of ideas good or bad', he was merely echoing the stated views of many public figures from the Prime Minister and the Archbishop of Canterbury down.[11] It was indeed this belief which led the Conservative Party to make extensive use of film in its publicity and propaganda.[12]

Important social changes were wrought by the cinema. Its surface influence in matters of fashion, courtship, image-making and role-playing was obvious. *The New Survey of London Life and Labour* (1934) recorded:[13]

> The influence of films can be traced in the clothes and appearance of the women and in the furnishings of their houses. Girls copy the fashions of their favourite film star. At the time of writing, girls in all classes of society wear 'Garbo' coats and wave their hair *à la* Norma Shearer or Lillian Harvey. It is impossible to measure the effect the films must have on the outlook and habits of the people.

But the cinema's influence went deeper. Husbands and wives attended the cinema regularly together, breaking through the strict separation of the sexes that the predominance of the pub seems to have entailed.[14] In the view of many authoritative commentators, the cinema as the chief in a whole range of alternative leisure pursuits to the pub had played its part in the diminution of drunkenness. Many chief constables, testifying to the National Council of Public Morals' enquiry in 1917, said so, as did Seebohm Rowntree in his study of York in the 1930s.[15] This view was summed up by the Earl of Dudley, when opening the new Warley Cinema in 1934: 'Those who are old enough to remember the days before the war can recollect the appalling amount of drunkenness we used to see every day. The fact that in these days drunkenness has practically entirely disappeared I put down very largely to the good effect of the cinema industry.'[16]

The popularity of cinemagoing with the working classes and the strongly held belief in the potential of films to inflame them led to the content of films being strictly controlled. Although there were regular calls for State censorship, the British Board of Film Censors, set up in 1913, was an unofficial body, established by the cinema industry itself. The industry wanted to establish uniform regulation of films to prevent the seven hundred local licensing authorities giving different verdicts on the suitability of films and thus threatening the industry's viability. But they also wanted to gain respectability. They had secured the working-class audience and now wanted to add the middle class. Their solution was to disarm the criticism of film content that came from various middle–class pressure groups. The Censors exercised a total and systematic control, over film content. Working closely with government departments, they purged from the screen anything that might harm the perceived *status quo* morally, socially or politically, leaving the cinema to emphasise romance, adventure, vicarious excitement and wish fulfilment.[17] The cinema therefore came to function, according to critic Richard Winnington, as 'a narcotic, rivalling or even superseding the church in the valuable respect of providing the masses with an escape dream'.[18] The new opiate was so strong that in 1937 George Orwell was led to include it with a memorable list of placebos ('fish and chips, art silk stockings, tinned salmon, cutprice chocolate, the movies, the radio, strong tea and the football pools') which had, he believed, 'quite likely ... between them averted revolution'.[19]

The experience of Birmingham provides a useful case study of the development of the cinema in provincial cities during the 1930s and of the attempts by local pressure groups to limit and control its presumed influence. The first public exhibition of films in Britain was by the Lumière Brothers in February 1896 at the Regent Street Polytechnic in London. In May of the same year a programme of Lumière Films was featured as part of a variety bill at the Empire Theatre, Hurst Street, Birmingham, and was so popular that it was rebooked for August. Its success heralded an explosion of film-shows, initially at fairgrounds, variety theatres and public halls. Soon primitive cinemas were being created. Initially existing buildings were converted, often shops, which were blacked out, filled with seats and became known as 'penny gaffs', like the cheap theatres before them. But it is an index of the cinema's rapid eclipsing of its entertainment rivals that increasingly it was theatres, music halls and even churches that were converted. In Birmingham three of the earliest cinemas, Pringle's Picture Palace, Gooch Street, the King's Hall, Corporation Street, and the Queen's Hall, Edward Street, were church conversions. Of Birmingham's six music halls, four had become cinemas by 1920. Of the seven theatres, the three melodrama houses – the Metropole, Snow Hill, the Theatre Royal, Aston, and the Carlton, Saltley – all rapidly succumbed.[20]

Birmingham's first purpose-built cinema was the Electric Picture Palace, Station Street, opened in 1908. It was soon joined by more lavish and palatial city centre houses, such as the Picture House, New Street (1910), described as 'Birmingham's premier picture lounge' and the Scala, Smallbrook Street (1914), 'the last word in kinemas'. But the bulk of cinemas were in the central and inner suburban working-class areas. The war set the seal on the arrival of the new craze. The first issue of a new Birmingham-based trade journal, *Films*, launched in 1915, declared: 'Pictures are about the most popular things in the civilised world just now and pictures are probably more crowded than at any time since their successful inauguration.' There were at least fifty seven cinemas operating in Birmingham in 1915.[21]

With the great boom in cinema-building in the 1920s, the days of the 'penny gaffs' began to pass. There were about four thousand cinemas in operation nationally in 1921 and it was estimated that another two thousand were needed to meet the public demand. The old, plain, modest rectangular boxes began to be superseded by ever larger, more imposing, magnificent and lavishly decorated structures, designed in a wide variety of styles from Moorish to Ionic, from Tudor to Egyptian, from Gothic to Assyrian, providing as one brochure put it: 'acres of seats in a garden of dreams'.[22] By 1928, there were seventy-four cinemas in Birmingham; by 1935, a hundred; and by 1939, 109.[23] The comparatively small increase in cinema numbers between 1915 and 1928 conceals the fact that many old cinemas had been demolished and replaced, sometimes on the same sites, by new ones. So while the overall number did not increase greatly, the quality and capacity of the accommodation did. Many of the oldest silent cinemas went, either because it was deemed too expensive to wire them for sound when talkies arrived in 1929 or because they were declared unsafe. *The Birmingham Gazette* (30 August 1935) estimated that at least fourteen silent houses in the city did not make the changeover to sound. No fewer than nineteen cinemas, including the old Electric Palace in Station Street, were declared structurally deficient by the justices in 1931 and closed down.[24] So rapidly did the old houses disappear that in 1936 F. R. Buckley, film critic of the *Evening Despatch*, suggested half-humorously that the Globe, Newtown Row, should be preserved as a specimen of the pre-war super-cinema.[25]

Birmingham was in the forefront of cinema developments. The first 'atmospheric' cinema outside London, the Alhambra, Moseley Road (now demolished), was opened in 1928. The idea of the 'atmospheric' was to give the illusion of being outdoors in some exotic locale. The Alhambra had a ceiling painted Mediterranean blue, a great glass bowl in the centre filling the auditorium with artificial sunlight, and the decor and setting of a Moorish courtyard. It was the ultimate concept of the building as escapist fantasy.[26]

Birmingham also boasted the first News Theatre outside London. The very first News Theatre, providing a continuous programme of newsreel and documentary films, opened in New York in 1929; the first British one in London in 1930. In Birmingham, British Movietone News acquired the Oxford Cinema, High Street, and opened it as the News Theatre in 1932, with the slogan 'Round the World in 50 minutes'. It was in fact officially opened by the Chancellor of the Exchequer, Neville Chamberlain, a local M.P., on 18 January. He declared that it answered the need to entertain and inform: 'The talkie picture with its presentment of authentic actual events opens our mind and directs our attention to new interests. My experience is that the more interest one can acquire the easier it is to get away from the tedium and monotony of our everyday life.' A second News Theatre, the Tatler, was built on the site of the Electric Palace, Station Street, and opened in 1937.[27]

But both these developments were eclipsed by the Odeon chain, brainchild of the Birmingham-born scrap-metal merchant turned cinema owner, Oscar Deutsch. He began his ambitious programme of cinema-building in Birmingham with the Odeon, Perry Barr, built in Moorish style in 1930. But it was not long before the distinctive Odeon house style, a distillation of the Modern movement in architecture, was perfected by Birmingham architects Harry Weedon and Cecil Clavering. With its streamlined curves, clean lines, fin towers, cream faience tiling, art deco embellishments and night-time floodlighting, the Odeon became one of the most distinctive contributions to 1930s architecture. Deutsch's aim was to build Odeons in every town and city in the land, and at its height his empire embraced some three hundred cinemas. He opened thirty-seven new cinemas in 1937 alone. Birmingham remained his base of operations until 1939 when he finally moved to London.[28]

By the 1930s cinemas had become a matter of civic pride and were regarded as vital social amenities. When the Tudor Cinema, Haunch Lane, was opened in 1929 by Alderman A. H. James, Deputy Lord Mayor of Birmingham, *The Birmingham News* (6 April 1929) reported: 'Built in the heart of the new population that has sprung up in the Billesley and Yardley Wood areas, the Tudor Theatre is an attempt to provide a centre of amusement and recreation of high class character in a district previously unprovided for in this essential respect.' Indeed the main feature of cinema-building in the 1930s was the provision of cinemas for the outer suburbs, the inner city and inner suburban areas having been well provided for already. It signalled the decisive acceptance of the cinema as a respectable, indeed indispensable, form of entertainment by the middle class. In Birmingham, cinemas sprang up in Kingstanding (Odeon, 1935), Shirley (Odeon, 1935), Quinton (Danilo, 1933), Sheldon (Sheldon Cinema, 1937), Great Barr (Clifton, 1938; Beacon, 1938) and Kings Norton (Kings Norton Cinema, 1938).[29]

The great development in terms of film technology was the arrival of talkies. Councillor G. F. Macdonald, a former president of the Cinematograph Exhibitors Association, expressed the initial reaction of exhibitors when he said in 1929 that talkies were 'an interesting novelty but he doubted whether they would take the place permanently of the silent film'.[30] But when *The Singing Fool*, Birmingham's first talkie, was shown at the Futurist, John Bright Street, in 1929, *The Town Crier* (12 April 1929) reported under the headline 'Amazing Scenes at the Futurist': 'For four weeks the house has borne the appearance of a besieged citadel, great queues controlled by a special force of police encircling the building from morning to night and in spite of the fact that five performances have been given each day the public demand to see and hear this wonderful film has still not been satisfied.' One hundred thousand people had seen it and there was no sign of a diminution of demand. It broke all records, running from 18 March to 11 May 1929, a run not broken until *Gone With The Wind* arrived. Exhibitors, with the cost of converting their cinemas in mind, remained cautious but by 1930 *The Birmingham Gazette* concluded that talkies were here to stay.[31] Movie patronage was up by thirty per cent. Cinemas continued to prosper throughout the 1930s and although they closed for one week at the outbreak of World War II, they reopened to enjoy perhaps their greatest era of popularity.

The rise of the cinema led inevitably to a new round in the continuing debate about the nature and use of working-class leisure. It is entirely appropriate that this debate should be examined in the context of Birmingham since that city was the *fons et origo* of the 'Civic Gospel'. The civilising mission of the municipal authorities had been preached by influential Nonconformist ministers like George Dawson and practised by dynamic municipal leaders like Birmingham's Mayor, Joseph Chamberlain. Under Chamberlain, water and gas were municipalised, sewage disposal improved and massive urban reconstruction schemes inaugurated. Behind these practical schemes lay the belief that the improvement of their surroundings would facilitate the intellectual and moral uplifting of the masses. R. W. Dale, another prominent Nonconformist exponent of Birmingham's 'Civic Gospel', expressly included in it 'harmless public amusement' along with good drains, schools and streetlighting. The cultural dimension of the 'Civic Gospel' therefore aimed to utilise leisure to promote the pursuit of personal fulfilment and social control, with the energies and aspirations of the working class directed into approved channels which would result in civilisation, uplift and improvement. These objectives were shared by churches and religious organisations, temperance groups and voluntary bodies, and 'Rational Recreation' was provided by means of libraries and art galleries, parks and sports fields, public baths and lecture courses.

The 'Civic Gospellers' and the 'Rational Recreationists', however, reckoned without two developments which were to undermine their earnest endeavours. One was the stubborn resistance of certain elements in the working class to being 'improved'. The other was the development of commercial enterprises which aimed to provide leisure activities which offered entertainment rather than 'improvement'.

These two developments coincided in the last decades of the nineteenth century, with the masses using their increased spending power and leisure time to patronise the activities promoted by the new leisure industries. Pre-eminent among them was the music hall, increasingly controlled by large national circuits with massive capital investment. The power of these commercial interests can be seen in the changes which overtook music hall during these years. Moralists had consistently attacked the music halls for their association with drunkenness, sexuality and rowdiness. But reform came at the behest of music hall proprietors and theatrical entrepreneurs, anxious to broaden their appeal and make yet more money up-market. They remodelled their buildings, banned drink from the auditoria, dispensed with the chairman, cleaned up song lyrics and kept out the obviously rougher elements. In the process they created a bastard form of music hall called 'variety' to which the working class continued to flock, though now joined by middle- and upper-class audiences. The same pattern developed in the cinema industry, where the control of film content and improvement of cinema facilities were instigated by the commercial interests themselves.[32]

The cinema, with its avowed desire to entertain rather than improve, was soon seen by the moralists as the new threat to their leisure aims, a threat symbolised in Birmingham by the conversion of George Dawson's own Church of the Saviour into a cinema in the early years of the century. The potential for physical, moral, social, psychological and intellectual danger which the cinema was deemed to constitute had already provoked the wide-ranging enquiry into the cinema undertaken in 1917 by the National Council for Public Morals. The members of the Commission of enquiry, teachers, churchmen, doctors, magistrates and youth workers, were precisely those groups which were to provide the most vocal critics of the cinema throughout the 1930s.

In Birmingham the arguments for and against cinema crystallised around two *causes célèbres* – the debate about Sunday opening and the Birmingham Cinema Enquiry Committee. The Sunday opening debate reached its climax in the early 1930s. There had been sporadic demands for Sunday opening throughout the 1920s and since 1912 there had been specially licensed Sunday shows occasionally for charitable purposes. But the opening of cinemas in neighbouring Smethwick prompted *The Birmingham Gazette* (5 January 1929) to ask 'why not in Birmingham?' Both the Birmingham City Justices ('The general opinion is held that there is no public demand for regular opening of entertainment houses on Sunday') and the Birmingham branch of the Cinematograph Exhibitors Association ('In towns where the picture houses were open on Sunday proprietors usually found that takings during the week suffered') opposed Sunday opening. But their statements provoked a flood of letters to the local newspapers and the revival of the slumbering Sunday opening issue. Churchgoers and churchmen wrote to protest against the desecration of the traditional Sunday. But a comprehensive argument for Sunday opening came from a youth signing himself 'Honi Soit' of Kidderminster:[33]

I am aged 18 and I know many of both sexes and all of them are in favour of Sunday opening. Why should cinemas be open? In the first place, youth will not stay at home on Sunday night. I myself have (with many more) walked about town in pouring rain. If we were told by the police to go home (which generally happens when it rains at night), did we? No – the nearest public house. Youth must have excitement. If it cannot have it one way, it will another. If shifted off the streets we go into public houses, at first for lemonade and for someone to talk to. One thing leads to another. We take to beer. I myself (although ashamed to say so) have got to drinking whiskey. All because there is nowhere to go on Sundays. Another thing. Let anyone take a walk around any 'monkey run' and (they wont need to listen; they'll hear all right) pass their opinion on the language they hear. Now if the cinemas were open, the streets would be deserted, the police would have an easier time and youth would be satisfied.

It is interesting to note that this view was shared by the Chief Constable of Birmingham, Sir Charles Rafter.[34]

Throughout 1930 the debate hotted up. The movement for Sunday opening, calling itself the 'Brighter Sunday' movement, gained the backing of the Trades and Labour Council and its campaign reached the national press.[35] Alderman William Lovsey, a Birmingham justice and vocal champion of the 'Brighter Sunday' movement, told *The Daily Express* (6 March 1930): 'There is a great demand for a brighter Sunday. Hotels have their entertainment, the city orchestra gives concerts, and the theatres often open for charity performances. One can boat and fish and play golf on the municipal links, but the cinemas remain closed. What is the difference between these entertainments and a picture show? A brighter Sunday evening in Birmingham must come sooner or later. We shall win through yet.'

The Cinematograph Exhibitors Association, responding to the evidence of public demand, declared its willingness to open on Sundays, and on 3 January 1930 the Birmingham licensing justices were formally petitioned for permission to open cinemas on Sundays.[36] The Anglican and Free Churches in Birmingham, headed by Dr Barnes, the Bishop of Birmingham, issued a lengthy manifesto summarising their reasons for opposing this move: that Sunday was needed as a day of rest, that it was undesirable to commercialise Sunday, that there was a danger of imposing a seven-day working week on those working in the cinema trade, that church organisations and social clubs already provided enough Sunday entertainment for the young, and that Sunday was in danger of being exploited for profit by the cinema trade. It was a combination then of concern for the workers, concern for the sanctity of Sunday and, implicitly, concern for church attendance.[37]

The Justices rejected the request for Sunday opening, giving as their reasons the fact that no other public body apart from the Trades Council advocated Sunday opening, that there was plenty of other Sunday entertainment available, that all other cities comparable to Birmingham forbade it and the evidence from places where it was allowed came mainly from seaside towns, which had different aims and outlooks from big cities.[38] But there was underneath all this an essentially moralistic objection: the belief that Sunday cinema opening – indeed even the cinema itself – was potentially both immoral and demoralising. This view was clear from the speech made by one of the justices and reported by *The Birmingham Post* (27 May 1930):

> Brigadier General W. R. Ludlow said that he was not a bigot or a spoilsport. He believed in *rational recreation* [my italics] on Sundays because it was the only day on which they could take some rest from the incessant strain of life. He recognised that a great change had taken place towards the observance of

Sunday, particularly since the war. He had an open mind in regard to all outdoor games on Sunday afternoons in public parks and other places which did not entail Sunday labour; but he drew the line very strictly between what was recreation and what was pure amusement. There was far too much amusement at the present day and too little work six days out of seven. It was idle to say the opening of cinemas would keep the young people off the streets. The great majority of films exhibited were not such that would *elevate* or *improve* young people or their elders; they mostly dealt with crime or sex problems, and scenes were enacted that would not be tolerated in any theatre in the land. The cinema in his opinion was a modern institution which was doing a great deal of harm. A great many cinemas were not paying their way and this was purely a commercial move on the part of the trade to make a greater profit by working seven days a week.

This comprehensive tissue of prejudice highlights a fairly common upper-middle-class view about the essential idleness of the workers, the moral worthlessness of films and the greedy commercialism of the cinema trade.

However, the next stage came with the passage through Parliament of the Sunday Public Entertainment Bill of 1932. A spate of prosecutions of cinemas for Sunday opening had emphasised the problem and after a debate which rehearsed the familiar arguments on both sides, Sunday film shows by local option were legalised, so long as safeguards for labour were established and a charitable levy imposed.

During the course of the parliamentary debate, the situation in Birmingham was cited by Mr E. Doran (Unionist, Tottenham North) in support of national Sunday opening:

Has it ever been any honourable member's experience to be stranded in Birmingham on a Sunday? I have had that most unfortunate experience. A few weeks ago, to my horror and consternation, I was left entirely alone and unattended in the great city of Birmingham. I looked at that city and it struck me as a city of the dead. Hardly a light was burning. I went to the hotel porter and said: 'Where can I go to kill the time because if I cannot kill the time, the time will surely kill me?' He said, 'I am very sorry, sir. There is only one thing you can do, and that is to jump on a tramcar and go to West Bromwich.' In a spirit of recklessness and devilry, I invested three pence and went to West Bromwich. To my profound surprise, I saw a town full of glittering lights and happy and merry looking people walking along the streets. I was like little Alice in Wonderland, for the picture houses were open and the girls and boys were going in to see the shows. The funny part about it is that the majority of them were the unfortunate people of Birmingham, who had gone on the same excursion as myself.[39]

Armed with the new act, the Cinematograph Exhibitors Association petitioned the justices for permission to open on Sundays, and despite the opposition of the Christian Social Council, representing the Anglican and Free Churches, this permission was granted. After much negotiation, the conditions laid down were that the opening hours would be 7 p.m. to 10 p.m., that the entertainment was to be 'healthy and elevating', that ten per cent of the profits should go to charity and that no employee should work more than one Sunday in four. The Association argued that the last condition would mean then trebling their staff, which would make Sunday opening uneconomic.[40] After further discussions, the justices, amended the condition to read that 'no worker should be employed more than three Sundays in four'. But the Association decided that this condition was also too restrictive. With attention focused on this point, the Churches now concentrated their opposition on the defence of workers' rights.[41]

The matter became the subject of a debate in the Lower House of Convocation. Dr Woods, the Bishop of Croydon, moved that in view of the Sunday Entertainment Act 'This House is of the opinion that the Church should approve the opening of cinemas on Sunday evenings provided that in addition to the safeguards provided in the Act the hours of opening should not be before 6 p.m. and that the pictures should be of a wholesome character.' In support of his motion, he made an enlightened speech calling on the Church to recognise the changing nature of leisure. But the Dean of Canterbury clearly spoke for the majority of churchmen when he replied that 'the average man in a workshop is against Sunday cinema. His idea of Sunday was to stand at his door with his coat off to hear the church bells, to see his children well dressed, to see the whole family at home for Sunday meals and to see nothing break up the family unit. The Sunday cinema was just another step to rob such of their leisure on Sunday'. But the main opposition to the Bishop's motion came from two of the leading Birmingham sabbatarians, Canon Guy Rogers, the Rector of Birmingham, and the Venerable J. H. Richards, the Archdeacon of Aston. Canon Rogers proposed an amendment urging that where Sunday opening was allowed, they should seek to defend the rights of workers to their Sundays off and to oppose the exploitation of Sunday for private gain. Canon Rogers said that his motion did not oppose Sunday cinema shows in principle, though he thought in fact that the opening of clubs and occupational centres on Sundays was preferable and that the much-attacked 'Sunday parades' were harmless ('it is usually of a very jolly character, although it sometimes gets a little boisterous'). Archdeacon Richards, seconding the amendment, said that young people wanted fellowship not cinemas on Sundays, adding that he had observed 'Sunday parading' for thirty years in Birmingham and it was not a problem ('If there is a danger, it is very often through the sexual excitement produced by what is so often purveyed to them at the local theatres'). The amendment was passed almost unanimously.[42] This view of the benign nature of 'Sunday parades' contrasts strongly with the Church's view of them in a previous generation. The Reverend H. S. Pelham, Domestic Chaplain to the Bishop of Birmingham, had written of them in 1914: 'It is a heartrending occupation to walk about the centre of Birmingham on a Saturday and Sunday night, and to witness the thousands of boys and girls ragging about and engaging in perfectly filthy conversation. This goes on in the poorer parts of the city as well, and is largely responsible for the terrifying spread of immorality.'[43] Evidently this evil had now paled beside the lure of the silver screen.

The deadlock over Sunday opening was eventually resolved by the commercial interests. Twenty-one of the eighty-two cinemas in Birmingham were controlled by the big circuits, chiefly Gaumont and Associated British, and they had the reserves of staff to supply Sunday service on the terms laid down by the Justices, so they declared their intention of opening on Sunday 5 February, and the independents fell into line.[44] On the agreed day, five city centre cinemas and fifty-one cinemas duly opened for the first city-wide Sunday showing. It was officially declared a success, with central and inner suburban cinemas full and the outer suburbs reporting thinner attendance, suggesting that the working class responded with greater alacrity than the middle class to the new leisure opportunity. An estimated forty to fifty thousand people attended the second Sunday opening and it was absolutely clear that there was sufficient public demand for the Sunday shows to continue. At the same time, the Churches reported no decline in the size of the congregations and the 'Sunday parades' of young people appeared equally undiminished, suggesting that cinemagoing was added to rather than substituted for existing activities.[45] On 2 November 1933 the licensing justices renewed permission for Sunday shows for a further year and by the end of 1933 the number of cinemas open on Sunday had risen from fifty-six to seventy.[46] *The Birmingham Mail* (22 December 1933) concluded: 'it is a fair assumption that a very large section of our people have been innocently entertained on Sunday evenings'. The battle had been won, and Sunday cinema shows became an established part of local leisure-time activities.

Behind the opposition to Sunday cinema, apart from the fear of desecration of the Sabbath and concern for workers' rest, lay a clear moral disapproval of the cinema and particularly of film content. It was this feeling which animated the other movement in Birmingham in the 1930s – the Birmingham Cinema Enquiry. Birmingham was not alone in its concern and similar enquiries and investigations were held by civic bodies in Edinburgh, London, Sheffield and Birkenhead. But the Birmingham Enquiry attained a national eminence which resulted in its being consulted as an authoritative source on matters cinematic and was widely quoted both inside and outside parliament.

It grew out of a conference held in Birmingham in 1930 by the National Council of Women on the subject of film content. To investigate further it was decided to set up the Birmingham Cinema Enquiry Committee, headed by the Vice-Chancellor of Birmingham University, Sir Charles Grant Robertson. Its membership included interested and concerned magistrates, doctors, teachers and clergymen. Its stated purpose was to try to persuade the Home Office to hold an enquiry into film content. But the committee's lack of objectivity was clear from the outset; its members had already made up their minds about the link between films and deviant behaviour. *The Birmingham Gazette* (7 November 1930) reported of the Enquiry: 'It is not antagonistic to cinemas as an institution but merely to the standard of films, the chief objection to which is what is said to be "vicious sensationalism" that portrays an unreal idea of the values of life.'

A public meeting was held on 7 October 1930 to launch a petition for an enquiry by the Home Office, its object according to Dr W. A. Potts, psychological adviser to the Birmingham justices, being 'to find out how far unhappy homes, divorce, illegitimacy and disease were due to the pictures'.[47] To support their demands the Birmingham Committee launched an enquiry into the effect of the cinema on children by circulating a questionnaire to 'a number of representative elementary, secondary and private schools in Birmingham'. Twenty-four schools were circulated and 1439 children questioned. Only thirty children never went to the cinema and 780 went once a week. Asked why they went, the majority declared 'to pass the time', though a number went 'to see my favourite stars'. Comedies were most popular and detective stories and adventure stories, second favourites. But when the report lists what individual children got out of the films, it turns into a highly impressionistic case for the prosecution. For example: ' "One child said that she would show me how to strangle people" remarks one commissioner. There is a boy who revels in burglar films and says "Only potty children are frightened." "The pictures taught me how to shoot" says another boy. Many describe in detail gory incidents. There are several remarks which indicate that "The Yellow Peril" has bred a fear of Chinese.'[48]

There was criticism of this enquiry from *The Birmingham Mail* (3 June 1931), which in a perceptive editorial observed: 'it cannot be said that the attempt ... to study the influence of the cinema on children scientifically has yielded very definite or very enlightening results'. *The Mail* thought the Committee was unduly exercised about the unsuitability of films:

Personally we think they are exciting themselves unduly. It is the old story of the child and literature over again. It used to be the 'penny dreadful' which was corrupting our young innocents, now it is the pictures. Many 'classics' were considered as not at all suitable for the youthful mind. The truth is that the child approaches these things from a very different angle to the adult ... the cinema is the most wonderful and most potent educational force yet evolved, and children probably get a great deal more good than harm from it. It undoubtedly could do with improvement in many directions, but even were all the ideals of the committee carried out, children would still go on misunderstanding and misinterpreting many things they saw and also learning lessons which the committee would never suspect. In the words of a good many of the children examined, they would 'learn what life is like', and learn it all wrong, but it would be an essential stage in their development through which they must pass before they arrive at a maturer judgement.

The committee's petition ('a strong protest against the harmful and undesirable nature of many of the films shown in picture houses') with eighteen thousand signatures was handed in to the Home Secretary, Mr J. R. Clynes, by a deputation from the Birmingham Enquiry Committee, headed by Grant Robertson, in May 1931. They called for stricter censorship and a public enquiry into the production, classification and exhibition of films, citing the petition and questionnaire as evidence. Mr Clynes declared himself sympathetic and agreed to consider the proposal.[49]

After a busy first year, the Committee published its first annual report on 1 July 1931, summarising its reports on 285 films shown in the city. It pronounced seventy-nine of them unsatisfactory. Sir Charles Grant Robertson declared:

We are not 'prohibitionists', 'killjoys' or 'cranks'. We believe that this great instrument which modern science has given us can be, indeed is bound to be, a tremendous and inexhaustible source of recreation and education. For this very reason we are determined to persist in our endeavour until the abuse and dangers – intellectual, physical and moral – particularly for children and adolescents, which are present make what might be an instrument of untold good into an instrument of incalculable and irreparable harm have been extirpated.[50]

Not surprisingly, the trade was foremost among the critics of the Enquiry Committee. Oscar Deutsch, Chairman of the Midland Branch of the Cinematograph Exhibitors Association, declared it 'composed of the blindest class known to mankind – the class determined not to see unless it suits their own purpose'. He said that there was too much interference in the cinema business by local bodies which 'continue to give much cause for mirth to the general public but add very considerably to the difficulties of cinema owners'.[51] But the committee's work was defended by Mr G. A. Bryson, deputy chairman of the Birmingham justices. He declared that Birmingham had a reputation for clean entertainment of which they might be proud and there was a danger to children from films of which they needed to be aware: 'We don't want our children to go about saying "Oh yeah" and "O.K. kid" and there is no doubt a tendency to Americanize the English language throughout the film that is, I think, deplorable.' He concluded: 'We are satisfied that the members of the Cinema Enquiry are in earnest; that they are not killjoys or busybodies, but wish to keep the films clean and healthy and wholesome.' But a minority of the justices dissented from this view; Mr W. A. Dalley called them 'an interfering lot of old women of both sexes' and the redoubtable Alderman Lovsey called them 'troglodytes'. But the majority of the justices endorsed Mr Bryson's view.[52]

The Birmingham Enquiry next held a national conference on problems connected with the cinema at Birmingham University on 27 February 1932. It was attended by representatives of forty-two social organisations, twenty-two educational bodies, nineteen religious bodies, four medical bodies and forty towns and cities. There was a call for State censorship to replace the informal system operated by the British Board of Film Censors. Miss Cottell, ex-President of the NUT, drew loud applause when she declared: 'We have come to the conclusion that in many respects we cannot entirely trust to the responsibility of parents, particularly since there is no regular preparation for parenthood, and while that is so we have felt in many ways that we must protect the children even from their own parents.' Mr J. A. Lovat-Fraser M.P. (National Labour, Lichfield), Joint Honorary Secretary of the State Children's Association, attributed much juvenile delinquency to the influence of the cinema. Dr W. A. Potts, representing this time the National Council of Mental Hygiene, attributed the ninety per cent increase in indecent assaults on boys and the sixty-two per cent increase in assaults on young children in recent years to the sex content of films. The conference resolved once more to call for a government enquiry into the cinema and Grant Robertson once again headed a deputation to the Home Office. Sir Herbert Samuel, the Home Secretary, received them on 6 April 1932 and listened sympathetically. Samuel thought however that the Board of Censors was doing a good job and since he had just set up a liaison committee to maintain links between them and the local licensing bodies, he wanted to await the outcome of their discussions.[53]

The Enquiry Committee persisted and in March 1933 Grant Robertson presided at another meeting at the University, which once again called for tighter censorship. Mr Sidney Dark, Editor of the *Church*

Times, gave full rein to the sense of moral outrage that many must have shared. He declared that:

> The large proportion of the people who filled the picture theatres were young, comparatively unintelligent and with untrained judgement. This vast army of the least intelligent and least morally equipped members of society were allowed to have all sorts of intellectual and moral poison pumped into them without any kind of interference. Judging by the output of Hollywood, to describe that city as a cesspool, would be complimentary. A considerable proportion of the films imported into this country were dangerously false. They accentuated the trivial and neglected all that was important and vital in life. In this complex age it was race suicide to allow foreigners to impregnate falsehood into the lifeblood of this nation.[54]

The climactic assault of the cinema's moralist critics came on 15 January 1935, with a delegation presented to Mr Ramsay MacDonald, the Prime Minister, by the Archbishop of Canterbury. The speakers included Sir Charles Grant Robertson and the deputation included the President of the NUT, the Chief Rabbi, the General Secretary of the National Council of Evangelical Free Churches, the Director of the NSPCC, the President of the National Association of Schoolmasters, the President of the Mothers' Union, the Chairman of the Parents' National Educational Union, the Vice-Chairman of the Public Morality Council and the Editor of *The Methodist Times*. Introducing the speakers, the Archbishop said that they were concerned about the current state of the cinema and wanted a government enquiry into it. Grant Robertson summarised the reasons for instituting such an enquiry: the large number of children and adolescents in cinema audiences, the 'undesirable and disquieting character of films', the fact that the Board of Censors was a trade-financed organisation and by implication therefore *parti pris*, the fact that the Home Office consultative committee had proved disappointing and that local licensing laws permitted too wide a leeway in the showing of undesirable films. Mr MacDonald agreed to look into the situation. But no enquiry was forthcoming.[55]

Although the Birmingham Committee constantly stated that they valued the cinema as means of education, they appeared in reality to regard it as the source of virtually all ills in society. Professing their concern for the young, they and similar groups pressed for stronger censorship. It is interesting to observe that both in argument and in tone the Committee represent a continuity with the similar moralistic group which worked for the suppression of wakes and fairs in nineteenth-century Birmingham. An alliance of Nonconformist conscience and 'civic gospel' had attacked wakes and fairs for providing entertainment that was morally inferior and not 'improving' enough and because drunkenness and immorality were stimulated by these events. Although the cinema was not accused of promoting drunkenness, its role as a source of immorality and crime was constantly reiterated. As in the cinema debate, so in the fairs debate, opposition to suppression came from the commercial elements, who thought fairs economically important, desirable and profitable, and from those radical and liberal elements who defended 'the innocent diversion and recreation of the common people'. The parallel is exact and makes it clear that the attack on the cinema was part of a longstanding concern about working-class leisure.[56]

But the Birmingham Cinema Enquiry, like similar bodies, faded away in the second half of the 1930s. There had never been general public concern about the content of films, as Home Office statistics reveal. In February 1931, the Home Office sent out a questionnaire to all local licensing authorities to establish the precise scope of the content problem. Of the 603 licensing authorities, only twenty-one had received any complaints from the public about the films exhibited in their areas in the previous three years. The total number of films complained of in those years was thirty-eight. Of the 603 authorities, 586 stated that they had not during the three years prohibited exhibition of any film passed by the Board of Censors. Eight authorities had prohibited whole films, nine authorities parts of films. A total of twenty-seven films had been banned by those eight authorities, mainly on grounds of sexual immorality, and a total of thirty-six films previously passed by the Board had been banned in whole or in part by the local authorities. It was this evidence which convinced the Home Office that there was no need to launch a national enquiry.[57]

Nor did the Home Office accept the oft-argued link between cinema and juvenile crime. Sir Herbert Samuel, the Home Secretary, told the Commons on 15 April 1932: 'My very expert and experienced advisers at the Home Office are of the opinion that on the whole the cinema conduces more to the prevention of crime than to its commission. It keeps boys out of mischief; it gives them something to think about ... In general, the Home Office opinion is that if the cinemas had never existed, there would probably be more crime than there is, rather than less.'[58]

The object of the moralists' collective antipathy was the British Board of Film Censors, which, they constantly asserted, was not stringent enough in its censoring and was in fact an organ of the cinema trade. But although set up and financed by the trade, it was wholly independent of it in its judgements and worked in effect more as an unofficial agency of the government. Its presidents were retired public officials; in the 1930s successively the former Home Secretary, Edward Shortt, and the former Ambassador to Paris, Lord Tyrrell of Avon. Its censorship rules were extremely strict and specifically designed to purge the screen of anything offensive or controversial. Home Secretary J. R. Clynes declared in December 1930 that he 'had no reason to believe that any alternative system so far proposed would produce better results or command general support, or that the standard of censorship in this country was not at least as high as in any other'.[59]

The Board was as concerned as its critics to remove anything immoral and its annual reports singled out disturbing trends in films which it wanted to see curtailed. The coming of sound undoubtedly did lead to an upsurge of gangster films and 'sex' films, coming out of Hollywood. The Board sought to check the flow and similar moralistic movements in Hollywood to those in Britain, particularly the Catholic Legion of Decency, brought so much pressure to bear that Hollywood's own censorship code, the Hays Code, was rewritten and strictly enforced. Under its pressure, the studios in 1934–5 turned away from contemporary themes to dramatisations of Victorian novels and historical dramas. By 1935 therefore there was comparatively little to complain of in film content, even for the moralists. The President of the Board noted with satisfaction in his annual report for that year that 'a very satisfactory feature of the past year has been the marked diminution of hostile criticism of the cinema and films, and of adverse comment on the work of the Board'.[60]

In the late 1930s there were other positive developments to deal with the perceived needs of the child. The recommendations of the Birmingham enquiry – specifically the need for greater censorship to combat the evils of films – had been almost wholly negative. In the mid-1930s a movement developed with the more positive aim of providing special shows and indeed special films for children which could entertain, educate and improve their audiences. Various educational and religious bodies and local authorities sponsored children's film shows in places like Bath, Bristol and Glasgow. Conferences were held on 'children and the cinema' and considerable unanimity emerged between parents, teachers, psychologists and cinema exhibitors about what sort of films they wanted children to see. The trade co-operated enthusiastically and the result was the setting up in 1937 of Odeon children's matinées, a concept rapidly followed by the other circuits, which provided wholesome films, charitable activities and road safety training. In due course, the Children's Film Foundation was set up to provide specific films for these shows.[61]

What is clear from this study of the cinema in Birmingham is that the old nineteenth-century desire of a vociferous section of the middle class to impose on the masses the kind of leisure deemed good for them by their betters was still very strong and active in the 1930s. It had found a new enemy, a new scapegoat for all the moral and social ills of the age. But despite all the concern about and distaste for films expressed by middle-class moralists, by the latterday proponents of 'Civic Gospel' and 'Rational Recreation,' the cinema took an ineradicable hold on the popular imagination. When reform came, as for instance in the establishment of film censorship or children's matinées, it came about because the commercial interests willed it in the interests of greater respectability and thus wider audiences for their product. Thus the cinema followed more or less the same pattern of development as has been traced in the evolution of its immediate predecessor, music hall. The experience of cinema confirms that in the last resort the combination of the popular will and the acumen of big business leisure industries was unbeatable.[62]

NOTES

1 P. Morton Shand, *Modern Theatres and Cinemas* (1930), pp. 9–10.

2 N. Pronay, 'British newsreels in the 1930's (i) audience and producers', *History* 56 (October 1971), pp. 412–13.

3 A. Aldgate, *Cinema and History* (1979), pp. 54–5.

4 National Council of Public Morals, *The Cinema: its Present Position and Future Possibilities* (1917), p. xxiv.

5 D. C. Jones, *The Social Survey of Merseyside* (Liverpool, 1934), vol. 3, p. 281.

6 J. P. Mayer, *British Cinemas and their Audiences* (1948), p. 252.

7 On the general picture see A. Field, *Picture Palace: a Social History of the Cinema* (1974).

8 E. W. Bakke, *The Unemployed Man* (1933), pp. 181–3; C. Cameron, A. Lush and G. Meara (eds.), *Disinherited Youth* (Edinburgh, 1943), pp. 100–9.

9 Commission on Educational and Cultural Films, *The Film in National Life* (1932), p. 10.

10 P. Stead, 'Hollywood's message for the world: the British response in the nineteen-thirties', *Historical Journal of Film, Radio and Television* 1 (1981), pp. 19–32.

11 H. C. Deb. vol. 266, cols. 741–2; on attitudes of the Establishment to the cinema see N. Pronay, 'The first reality: film censorship in liberal England', in K. R. M. Short (ed.), *Feature Films as History* (1981), pp. 113–37.

12 T. J. Hollins, 'The Conservative Party and film propaganda between the wars', *English Historical Review* 96 (April 1981), pp. 359–69.

13 H. Llewellyn Smith et al. (ed.), *New Survey of London Life and Labour* (1934), vol. 9, p. 47.

14 A. J. P. Taylor, *English History 1914–45* (Harmondsworth, 1976), p. 237.

15 National Council of Public Morals, *op. cit.*, pp. 175–7, 333–69; B. Seebohm Rowntree, *Poverty and Progress* (1941), pp. 469–70.

16 *The Birmingham Mail* 24 December 1934.

17 The best account of the development of censorship in Britain is N. M. Hunnings, *Film Censors and the Law* (1967). But see also N. Pronay, 'The first reality: film censorship in liberal England', *op. cit.*, and J. Richards, 'Content control: some aspects of the work of the British Board of Film Censors in the

1930's', *Historical Journal of Film, Radio and Television* 1, 2 (1981), pp. 95–116, & 2, 1 (1982), pp. 39–48.

18 R. Winnington, *Drawn and Quartered* (n.d.), p. 123.

19 G. Orwell, *The Road to Wigan Pier* (Harmondsworth, 1962), p. 80.

20 There is as yet no comprehensive history of the cinema in Birmingham. But the early years are well covered in D. Mayall, 'Leisure and the working class, with special reference to the cinema in Birmingham 1908–18', unpublished M.A. thesis, University of Warwick, October 1977. There is a sketch of the cinema's development in three articles by Leonard Rose entitled 'Cavalcade of the cinema in Birmingham' in *Birmingham Weekly Post*, 24 July 1953; 31 July 1953; 7 August 1953. The career of Birmingham's leading cinema pioneer, Waller Jeffs, is discussed in J. H. Bird, *Cinema Parade* (Birmingham, n.d.), pp. 43–54. On the fate of Birmingham's theatres, see D. Salberg, *Ring Down the Curtain* (Luton, 1980). On the date of the first film show in Birmingham, see *The Birmingham Mail*, 4 May 1966.

21 *Films* I.i. (12 August 1915), p. 1. The fifty-seven cinemas are listed in *Films* 7.i (23 September 1915), p. 6.

22 For the history of cinema-building and architectural styles see D. Sharp, *The Picture Palace and other Buildings for the Movies* (1969) and D. Atwell, *Cathedrals of the Movies* (1980). We badly need individual regional surveys of cinema building. But as yet only one has appeared, Stephen Peart, *The Picture House in East Anglia* (Lavenham, 1980).

23 All figures for Birmingham cinemas are taken from *Kinematograph Year Books*.

24 *Birmingham Gazette*, 4 November 1931.

25 *Evening Despatch*, 15 May 1936.

26 *Evening Despatch*, 22 December 1928.

27 *Birmingham Post*, 1 January 1932; 20 March 1937; *Birmingham Mail*, 18 January 1932.

28 A. Eyles, 'Oscar and the Odeons', *Focus on Film* 22 (autumn 1975), pp. 38–57.

29 For a parallel development in suburban London, see A. A. Jackson, *Semi-detached London* (1973), pp. 176–80.

30 *Birmingham Post*, 7 March 1929.

31 *Birmingham Gazette*, 1 January 1930.

32 On the development of the 'Civic Gospel' in Birmingham, see E. P. Hennock, *Fit and Proper Persons* (1973). On attempts to direct leisure into approved channels, see H. Meller, *Leisure and the Changing City* (1976); P. Bailey, *Leisure and Class in Victorian England* (1978) and S. Yeo, *Religion and Voluntary Organizations in Crisis* (1976).

33 The letters are contained in *Birmingham Gazette*, 8 January 1929; 26 February 1929.

34 *Birmingham Post*, 19 March 1930.

35 *Birmingham Post*, 13 January 1930.

36 *Birmingham Gazette*, 5 February 1930.

37 *Daily Express*, 8 March 1930; *Birmingham Mail*, 8 March 1930.

38 *Birmingham Post* 18 March 1930; 19 March 1930; 27 May 1930.

39 H. C. Deb. vol. 266 col. 750.

40 *Birmingham Gazette*, 3 November 1932; 4 November 1932; *Birmingham Mail*, 12 November 1932; 14 November 1932; *Birmingham Post*, 16 November 1932; 18 November 1932.

41 *Birmingham Post*, 26 November 1932; 23 January 1932; 24 January 1932; 7 January 1932; *Birmingham Gazette*, 2 December 1932; 9 December 1932; 17 January 1933; *Birmingham Mail*, 10 January 1933; 16 January 1933. One cinema, Lozells Picture House, which was not in the C.E.A. actually opened on Sunday 8 January 1933 but the manager reported that attendance had not met expectations.

42 *Evening Despatch*, 19 January 1933; *Birmingham Post*, 20 January 1933.

43 H. S. Pelham, *The Training of a Working Boy* (1914), p. 51.

44 *Birmingham Gazette* 24 January 1933.

45 *Birmingham Gazette*, 4 February 1933; *Birmingham Post*, 4 February 1933; 6 February 1933; *Birmingham Mail*, 6 February 1933; 13 February 1933.

46 *Birmingham Post*, 3 November 1933; *Birmingham Mail*, 3 November 1933; *Birmingham Gazette*, 3 November 1933.

47 *Birmingham Gazette*, 8 November 1930.

48 *Birmingham Mail*, 25 March 1931; 2 June 1931.

49 *Evening Despatch*, 8 May 1931.

50 *Birmingham Mail*, 2 June 1931; *Evening Despatch*, 1 June 1931.

51 *Birmingham Mail*, 20 January 1932.

52 *Birmingham Post*, 9 January 1932.

53 *B.B.F.C. Verbatim Reports*, 1932–5, Report on National Conference on Problems Connected with Cinema; *Birmingham Gazette*, 29 February 1932; *Evening Despatch*, 7 April 1932.

54 *Birmingham Mail*, 22 March 1933; *Birmingham Post*, 22 March 1933.

55 Notes on a deputation received by the Prime Minister in relation to the Film Industry, 15 January 1935, *B.B.F.C. Verbatim Reports*, 1932–5.

56 On fairs and wakes, see D. Reid, 'Popular culture and the march of progress: the wakes and fairs of Birmingham', in R. D. Storch (ed.), *Popular Culture in Modern Britain: Persistence and Change* (1982).

57 Home Office Questionnaire, February 1931, *B.B.F.C. Verbatim Reports*, 1930–1.

58 H. C. Deb. vol. 264 col. 1141.

59 H. C. Deb. vol. 246 col. 517.

60 *B.B.F.C. Annual Report*, 1935, p. 1.

61 R. Ford, *Children in the Cinema* (1939). For the story of the C.F.F. see Mary Field, *Good Company* (1952).

62 I am grateful to Miss Dorothy McCulla and the staff of the local History Section of Birmingham Central Library for their generous co-operation and help.

4 KATHLEEN BARKER
The performing arts in Newcastle upon Tyne, 1840-70

If there is one thing more than another which the people of this country stand in need of, it is the means of obtaining cheap and innocent amusement. (*Tyne Mercury*, 25 October 1842)

Recent studies of provincial leisure in the nineteenth century have concentrated on audiences rather than entrepreneurs or performers. They have also focused mainly on the working classes. Moreover, despite the general contemporary significance of music hall and theatre, historians of those institutions have overwhelmingly concentrated their attention on the metropolis at the expense of the provinces.[1]

There were, however, developments of considerable importance in the provision of professional entertainment outside London between 1840 and 1870, and nowhere are these more apparent than in those urban, mainly industrial, areas which were most affected by the 'flight to the towns' of the nineteenth century. The period saw a revival of theatre, following some decades of ruinous disorganisation, peak provision of touring circus, and the emergence of music hall as a professional institution. There was tremendous growth in choral and orchestral music, and the availability of grand opera; it was the heyday, too, of a genre most often known as 'dramatic' or 'drawing-room' entertainments, defined by the *Newcastle Chronicle* as 'entertainments given by one or two persons who imitate with more or less success various characters, and tell stories or sing songs for the amusement of the audience'.[2] Finally, and not least, the period saw the provision of specialised buildings for most if not all of these arts.

Newcastle upon Tyne provides a good example of the development of provincial entertainment. In common with almost every similar area, Northumbria had suffered from the slump after the Napoleonic wars ended, the returning servicemen without a trade, the bad harvests. Northumberland and Durham were prominent in the attempts at unionisation among the miners, in movements for Parliamentary reform (for example, in the setting up of the Northern Political Union) and in Chartist activities generally. This political awareness and restlessness, together with general economic uncertainty, were factors affecting both the willingness and the ability of the public to support professional entertainments.

They were not, however, the only factors. The theatre, once the principal performing art available in the provinces, had steadily declined since 1820 with changes in public attitudes, brought about not only by a generally stricter public morality[3] but by both physical and artistic decline. Population shifts had left to decay the once-fashionable areas in which many Georgian theatres had been built: the St Mary Gate Theatre in Nottingham was by 1840 in the midst of the worst slums of the town, while the Theatre Royal, Bristol, backed on to the Rackhay, a rookery which was the nursery of a major cholera outbreak in 1849. In newer buildings, such as the 1807 Brighton Theatre Royal, the 'popularisation' of theatre had led to the inclusion of large galleries which held as many playgoers as the rest of the theatre put together. The 'Gods' came to dominate the house both in point of behaviour and repertoire, setting up a vicious circle in the discouragement of the 'respectable paying audience' which managers so much needed to survive. Increasingly it was the context rather than the text of the acted drama which attracted the attacks of moralists.

Newcastle did, however, have certain advantages. It was not, in 1840, so dependent either on one or two trades as were, say, Sheffield and Nottingham; or on a particular section of the community as were Bath and Brighton; the most numerous groups in the 1841 Census, apart from labourers and domestic servants, were boot- and shoe-makers, carpenters and tailors. Regional rail transport was developed early, with links west, south and east, enhancing the sense of belonging to a region rather than being a self-sufficient community, and correspondingly enlarging the potential entertainment audience, with special trains after concerts or major theatrical attractions. For the Polytechnic Exhibition of 1840 the Carlisle Railway authority provided cheap day returns; while for a concert by Giulia Grisi it was said that parties came from nearly one hundred miles away.[4]

But Newcastle had the (pre-eminent) advantage of the great town replanning scheme devised by John Dobson, built by Richard Grainger and steered through the local Council by its Town Clerk, John Clayton, between 1834 and 1839, at a cost said to be in the region of £2 million. The scheme affected all the arts, and particularly the theatre, for one of the new roads planned by Dobson and Grainger involved the demolition of the existing theatre in Mosely Street. Grainger therefore offered to build a new theatre, paying the proprietors £500 for the materials of the old one, and receiving a contribution of £1000 (borrowed by the proprietors from Clayton) towards the cost.[5] Designed by Benjamin Green and opened on 20 February 1837, it had a classical frontage which was a focal point for anyone looking up the sweep of Grey Street, a richly-ornamented horseshoe auditorium, and a stage as large in surface area as the pit. Altogether it was an imposing structure, estimated to hold 250 in the lower boxes, 250 in upper boxes, 200 in the pit and no fewer than 1,200 in the gallery, at prices of 3s for boxes, 2s for pit, and 1s for gallery.

The Assembly Rooms, near the old theatre, which had been the usual venue for concerts, still remained, but a new music hall was built in Nelson Street, with a lecture hall beneath, so that the 'new town', too, could have its concerts. It was, however, several years before it became much used, for it seems, unlike the theatre, to have been a rather spartan affair and it was not large enough for grand occasions, for which the Theatre Royal was usually hired. Additionally, new and old hotels, particularly the Turk's Head, contributed their long rooms to the stock of halls available for entertainments, so that in the important matter of accommodation Newcastle was exceptionally well off.

Unhappily this did not prevent the contemporary provincial pattern of theatrical bankruptcy being repeated in Newcastle between 1835 and 1845 in particular. Like most towns of its size, it had become separated from the country circuit to which it had once belonged, when Sampson Penley became lessee of the Mosely Street Theatre in 1830. His brother Montague took over management in December 1835, and was reinstated in the new Theatre Royal on its opening, but by 1839 he was £100 behind with his rent. His successor, Thomas Lawless Ternan, had one good season, but by February 1842 his debt was £200, and he was succeeded that autumn by Henry Hall, a popular low comedian and former manager of the (London) Strand Theatre. At the end of a year he in his turn was bankrupt, his financial guarantors declining to help, and James Munro, who had partnered Mercer Simpson in Birmingham in one of the most stable provincial managements of the century, was appointed after some dissension. But Munro was even less successful. He quarrelled with the local press; his standards were, to put it kindly, erratic; and during the third season he failed to appear at all and left the management to William Rignold senior. To no one's surprise he gave up in 1846.

This catalogue of disasters cannot entirely be blamed on 'the depression of the times' so often quoted by managers in excuse, although that certainly contributed. For example, in July 1841 the local situation was such that the Mayor set up a Distress Fund, and the *Newcastle Journal* reported two thousand unemployed and 'a very serious amount of destitution is general amongst them'.[6] Yet just previously Macready and Charles Kean, carrying out successive 'starring' engagements, drew excellent houses, knowledgeably (and vocally) critical of cuts in the latter's version of *Hamlet*.[7]

The quality of fare offered seems genuinely to have been the major determinant of success or failure. Newcastle managers themselves reiterated this,[8] whereas in other cities they were more likely to blame the taste of the town for an inferior repertoire. Henry Hall found this out: when he produced *The Tempest* in February 1843 he was able to run it for ten nights; an attempt to capitalise on the pictorial effects in the nautical melodrama of *The Pilot* lasted just four performances (with two more at half price). Since Newcastle had an exceptionally low percentage of educated professional inhabitants, and of men and women of independent means, this is no small tribute to the intrinsic intelligence and taste of the audience in Newcastle.

The Patent Theatre was supplemented, rather than rivalled, by a still strong tradition of travelling theatre, and while much of this activity was the casual accompaniment of 'hoppings' and other fairs, booth managers sometimes ran quite lengthy seasons in temporary structures, usually in St Nicholas Square. Thomas Thomas set up his 'Adelphi Theatre' in the Cornmarket and ran programmes of melodramas, songs and farces right through the summer and early autumn of 1843. He would have continued through the winter had not a gale blown the roof off his booth and so given the Theatre Royal Proprietors, opposing his licence application when his season threatened to overlap theirs, an excuse to claim that it was no longer a building within the meaning of the 1843 Act.[9] The next year Thomas's booth was taken over by Billy Purvis, and yet another strolling manager, Thorne, set up a marquee on the Forth. During the winter of 1845–6 Purvis actually leased the Music Hall till his summer booth in St Nicholas Square was ready.[10] But these timber and canvas constructions, with entry prices of 6*d* and 3*d*, or even lower, in all probability catered for a different audience than that of the Theatre Royal, perhaps one more likely to be affected by trade depressions. Purvis indeed mentions that during his season of 1844 'on account of the strike among the colliers, business was but dull'.[11]

The other great performing art, music, seems to have been provided on a very limited scale at this time. There was no continuous tradition of singing, such as we find in, for example, Nottingham; the only local choir of the 1840s, the Newcastle and Gateshead Choral Society, performed but rarely. The occasional attempt to reach a wider public – Concerts à la Musard in the Theatre in the summer of 1840, and an imitation of the Three Choirs Festival in September 1842 – both ended in financial disaster. On the other hand, a local musician and concert organiser, Carte, brought the greatest names in vocal and instrumental music to Newcastle: Grisi, Mario, Adelaide Kemble, Liszt, Thalberg and the violinist Sivori; and these almost invariably drew crowded audiences at seat prices double and treble those of the theatre. It was normal to have a matinée performance for the leisured and for country families at the Assembly Rooms, and in the evening move to the far larger Theatre Royal. The only 'popular' concerts, normally priced at 2*s* and 1*s*, were provided by ballad recitals, often of folk music. John Wilson, with his Scottish programmes, and Samuel Lover in *Paddy's Portfolio*, were frequent visitors, as were the concert tenor Henry Phillips and the ballad writer and singer Henry Russell.

In the second half of the 1840s, however, much of this pattern began to change. Most importantly, in 1846 the Theatre Royal management passed into the hands of the man whose name became synonymous with Newcastle Theatre for the next twenty-four years, Edward Dean Davis. Davis was not an obvious choice. Somerset-born, his managerial experience had been of a scattered and rather precarious small-town West Country circuit, extending over Wiltshire, Dorset and North Devon. It is likely that he obtained the preference because he offered generous shares in the takings instead of a set rent – an offer which, in a particularly successful first season, cost him more than he anticipated, and thereafter he reverted to negotiating an annual rent.

Davis's managerial principles may be summed up in two statements of his own, one at the beginning and one near the end of his career in Newcastle. In an early letter to the Proprietors, he asserted:

> I *never* engage an inferior Star, deeming it much better to make an additional outlay in procuring a really good Stock Company – indeed I am altogether opposed to the Star system, as I have found by experience that Stars who are really attractive take so large a portion of the receipts, that the profit is at best questionable, while inferior Stars are a certain loss.
>
> When, however, such as Macready and Charles Kean are to be had, then we must submit to the prejudices of the public and engage them.[12]

And regarding his repertoire, he told his audience at the end of the 1864–5 season: 'This was an age of sensation, and they brought forward a number of sensation pieces; but he was proud to acknowledge that in spite of such a taste, he never forgot the legitimate drama, and from that he derived his greatest support.'[13] Circumstances did not always permit Davis to adhere strictly to these admirable principles, but he certainly tried to do so. Since so few new plays of any merit were available, respectability lay mainly in the classics, particularly Shakespeare. In his very first season Davis was responsible for a remarkable revival of *A Midsummer Night's Dream*. It has to be admitted that what appeared upon the stage was a truncated (three-act) operaticised and Victorianised fairy spectacle, but it quite caught the taste of the town, and played for fourteen nights, a most unusual run for the period. He took equal pains with the staging of *Hamlet*, and his production of the Ghost scenes in particular was praised for the heightening of atmosphere it created. Another piece of enterprise was the bringing out, again in his first season, of a new ballad opera by the Theatre Royal's composer and musical director, Henry Deval, called *The Rival Clans*, based on the Huntley–Murray feud, which ran for five nights in the latter half of the season.

Besides encouraging the musical talent in his company in this way, Davis repeatedly engaged groups of London singers to mount both ballad and grand opera in English. More than this, he took an early and active part in promoting visits from Italian opera companies. Jenny Lind sang in *Sonnambula* in September 1848; a company led by Signora Montenegro sang a series of six operas in August 1849,[14] and they were closely followed by Mme Sontag and the Lablaches in *Il Barbiere* and *Don Pasquale* in September. In 1850 Davis gave an engagement to Mme Charton's French Opera Troupe, and advertised party rates for schools and large families wishing to improve their French.[15]

The Theatre Royal, therefore, had an important role in the development of music as well as of the drama in Newcastle, and no doubt this helped in Davis's all-important aim of establishing the respectability of theatre among the middle and upper classes. It was necessarily a long process, and it was some years before Davis felt secure financially, but he steadily built up a repertoire of exceptional enterprise, both with the help of stars and by encouraging new plays from members of his company and from the public.

Davis's greatest asset in the first case was Isabella Glyn, who had been Samuel Phelps's leading lady in his most successful seasons at Sadler's Wells – 'the great gun, Glyn', as Davis described her in one season's rhymed epilogue. Phelps's eclectic repertory enabled her to reintroduce to the provinces a number of plays no longer stock pieces. On her first visit to Newcastle, in the autumn of 1851, the list included *The Winter's Tale*; during the second, Webster's *Duchess of Malfi*. In 1853 the attraction was *Antony and Cleopatra*;[16] this ran for seven successive nights, and it became quite a favourite play in Newcastle, being revived not only for Miss Glyn but later on two occasions for Charles Calvert. *King John* was yet another Shakespearian rarity featured by Miss Glyn with success from 1856 onwards. Her mentor Samuel Phelps was another regular visitor, and again did much to enlarge theatregoers' horizons. He introduced Beaumont and Fletcher's *The Bridal* with some success in March 1856, and included *Julius Caesar* and *King Lear* in his Shakespearian revivals, while Macklin's *Man of the World* was always well received.

Among local writers, William Charlton of Hesleyside provided Davis with a new translation of *Ingomar*, under the title of *The Son of the Wilderness*, which received great praise, while in the spring of 1856, Davis brought out in a revised form the historical tragedy *Caius Marius*, written by Thomas Doubleday, soap manufacturer, radical Quaker, and prominent member of the Newcastle Political Union. Towards the end of the 1850s there was a positive spate, not only of fresh dramatisations and translations (both by members of the Davis family and by local writers) but of original farces, interludes and dramas. Henry Shield, a talented local amateur actor, was particularly prolific, ranging from pantomime to a quite remarkable full-length play, far ahead of its time, called *A Dream and a Reality*. This was the story of a man who dreamed so vividly 'that he on many occasions, acted upon what he had dreamed as though that which he had done in his vision had actually happened'. Under such a delusion he came to believe he had committed a murder, and actually killed his brother, who in his dream had been a witness of the crime.[17] At Christmas 1860 the local press was able to point proudly to the fact that both main piece and pantomime had been written by 'Newcastle gentlemen'.[18] While it was much more common than is often realised for provincial managers to encourage original contributions, the extent and range of the dramatic works produced in Newcastle seem greater than in other comparable cities.

As the Theatre Royal began to play, once more, the dominant part in local entertainment, the visitors of the booth theatres gradually dwindled, and except for casual visits for 'hoppings' disappeared by the mid-1850s.[19] There were, however, many other competitors, particularly for the pit and gallery audiences, as the prosperity of Tyneside increased with the river improvements which followed the repeal of the Navigation Laws in 1849, and the growth of engineering firms, particularly Armstrong's works at Elswick, where a huge suburb sprang up in the 1850s.[20]

There was, for example, the gradual rise of the music hall. There are traces of a Free and Easy Society at the Cornmarket Tavern in October 1842[21] and of singing entertainments at the Phoenix Inn, Newgate Street, the following year. Some time in 1848, perhaps the best known music hall outside London, 'Balmbra's', began at the Wheat Sheaf in the Cloth Market.[22] John Balmbra was a man of some standing in the community; for many years he was an official of the local Licensed Victuallers' Association, and Quartermaster of the Northumberland Yeomanry Cavalry. He must also have been a very shrewd provider of entertainment, for his proved to be the only consistently successful tavern saloon in Newcastle – indeed there were comparatively few attempts at rivalry even in the 1850s, when singing saloons were proliferating in most provincial towns.[23] The names on his bills are those found in many other similar saloons: good sound entertainers of the second rank, with few of any 'star' pretensions, though Jenny Hill, 'the Vital Spark', was a great favourite at Balmbra's in her early days.

There were more single- and double-handed entertainers, too, and their programmes were becoming more varied and sophisticated. Ballad recitalists, especially Scottish singers, were still popular, but artists like John Parry, pianist and buffo bass, and the Sisters Sophia and Annie in programmes of character sketches and songs started to visit Newcastle. It began to be worthwhile for actors and singers from the regular stage to concoct an entertainment and set up on their own. William Gourlay, a favourite Scottish comedian in the Newcastle Theatre Royal company, having received a legacy of £2,000 from his former colleage James Mungall, used it to start independently in this way, and with his wife devised a most popular entertainment under the title *Mrs M'Gregor's Levee.*[24] But whether because of distance, or for reasons of local taste, such entertainments (which from content and price seem to have been aimed principally at the middle classes) were appreciably less common in Newcastle than in towns like Brighton and Bristol.

There was, however, a great increase in circus entertainment, especially compared with the 1840s, which is directly contrary to the tendency in most provincial towns. In many places during the 1840s it was the rival entertainment most feared by the theatres: in Brighton it was the prime instrument of at least two managerial bankruptcies. But in Newcastle there were only two seasons of any length, though the first of these, by Price and North (who ran up a wooden amphitheatre in St Nicholas Square in December 1843) was successful enough for the Theatre Royal Proprietors to bring forward their annual Bespeak 'in consequence of the Circus being opened during the Theatrical Season'.[25] In the 1850s however, whereas elsewhere equestrian novelties had become tame from repetition, the circus had more appeal in Newcastle. There came to be (as there was in Nottingham, and other towns lacking a permanent structure for circus use) a recognised site for these troupes, near the west end of Central Station. Since every successful circus proprietor had his own architect and foreman, he was able, with the help of local labour, to erect in a matter of weeks a quite substantial wooden amphitheatre with stage, equestrian ring, boxes and gallery, lit by gas throughout. The adaptability of these amphitheatres often kept them in use for years: that erected by James Cooke in Newcastle in 1852 was used as a booth by Billy Purvis in July that year, reverted in August to a circus for a nine weeks' season by Franconi, and early in 1853 was adapted by Robert Howard as a music hall under the name of the Royal Olympic.

One of the most important advances for the arts came in the improvement of buildings. The gargantuan demands made on capital by the construction of railways were almost over, and everywhere civic pride was growing and expressing itself in improvements and new building. The arts, though not yet a priority, were not excluded: the acquisition of the Royal Pavilion by Brighton Corporation gave that town two very pleasant halls for small scale entertainments, while theatre proprietors in Sheffield, Nottingham and not least Newcastle gutted their buildings and remodelled them on up-to-date lines. In the summer of 1857 the whole dress circle of the Newcastle Theatre Royal was removed, the pit being extended to the back of the house so as to seat four hundred more spectators, and a new 'dress tier' was constructed over it. Sight lines everywhere were improved; the stage was extended by five feet, the ceiling raised, refreshment rooms added and the whole redecorated at a total cost of some £1,300.[26]

Even more important to Newcastle was the provision for concerts made during the decade, and brought about through the same blend of private pressure and civic initiative as had given the city its new Theatre Royal in 1837. There had been a gradual revival of music-making, the Newcastle and Gateshead Choral Society resuming rehearsals in the autumn of 1850, when a Philharmonic Society (chiefly orchestral) was also founded. Both began to give regular concerts, and soon found out the drawbacks of the existing halls. The Music Hall had been smartened up, 'but the want of room, the want of ventilation and the want of seats, make it most uncomfortable ... The Theatre and the Assembly Rooms are both so expensive, that people will not hire them, and the Lecture Room down stairs was tried once, to the horror and dismay of the musicians, and the disgust of the audience'.[27] During 1852 the Sacred Harmonic Society was also formed, adding more pressure on accommodation, for this meant two societies giving regular oratorio performances with large choirs and orchestras.

Opportunity came by way of disaster. On 6 October 1854 a fire in a worsted factory in Gateshead spread to an adjacent chemical store, which exploded, showering burning debris over several square miles on both sides of the river, and causing devastation in the closely-packed quayside area of Newcastle. Part of the cleared site, on one side of St Nicholas Square, was selected by the Council for its new Town Hall, and, after the pattern of Bradford and Leeds, it was decided to include in the new building a hall seating over three thousand. In February 1855 the plans were published,[28] and on 1 September 1858 the New Town Hall was opened, in the best Victorian tradition, with two oratorio performances by the Sacred Harmonic Society.

The availability of the New Town Hall gave a tremendous boost to all kinds of entertainments, but especially, as was intended, to the musical life of the town. This was further encouraged when the Council engaged William Rea as organist, for Rea was an enthusiast, a missionary for good music, and his impact went far beyond the recitals and lectures he was engaged to give. He was soon drawn into the music-making activities of the town as conductor or organist for the choral societies, and spread a knowledge of the finest composers of the eighteenth and nineteenth centuries; additionally he was himself a composer of some merit. But his most outstanding contribution was to organise seasons of promenade concerts, lasting a month at a time, from 1867 onwards, with a professional orchestra of nearly forty and programmes regularly including a complete symphony or sonata, vocal and instrumental solos, one or two overtures, and operatic selections. There were Beethoven, Mendelssohn and Mozart nights, and several evenings were given over to oratorio. Rea had guarantees from philanthropic townsmen, but every series up to and including 1870 broke even, despite the fact that the subscription rate was only a guinea for the earlier seasons, $1\frac{1}{2}$ guineas later on. The size of the hall enabled a number of seats to be priced at only 6*d*, thus bringing first-class concerts within the range of a large number of citizens.

The size of the New Town Hall naturally attracted also leading entertainers in other genres, temporarily impoverishing managers of the smaller halls and hotel assembly rooms. However, since it was rarely feasible to book the Town Hall for any extended period, owners of dioramas, mechanical exhibitions and the like benefited from the increasing availability of, in particular, the Music Hall. Some solo entertainers, including Dickens in his readings, found the Town Hall too large and unsympathetic acoustically, and returned thankfully to the greater intimacy of the smaller rooms.

The managers of such halls were not slow to take initiatives of their own in providing 'entertainments for the people'. H. Smith, manager of the Victoria Rooms in Grey Street, which had been used for a miscellany of shows since 1845, advertised in July 1857 'Saturday and Monday evening concerts' and invited 'Professionals, travelling to and fro from Scotland' to write for engagements. The programmes bore less resemblance to standard concerts than to those of a good music hall, including comic sketches, dancing and conjuring; and Smith also played host to the earliest of the concert parties led by London music hall stars like Sam Cowell and Arthur Lloyd. But it was Adam Donald, manager of Grainger's Hotel, who took the next step and announced that as from 24 December 1860 he would run his premises as a Song and Supper Room; Smith followed his lead in September 1861.

The most outstanding contribution to this sudden expansion of music hall in Newcastle, however, was made by George Stanley, a former member of the Theatre Royal company, who had left to manage a circuit of small theatres in the area – what was left of the old border circuit to which Newcastle itself had once belonged. An amphitheatre put up by the Sanger brothers in Neville Street in 1857, and subsequently adapted, as was commonly done, by a variety of other entertainers, was available, and Stanley leased it in the summer of 1860, applying for a theatre licence. Repeatedly blocked by the opposition of the Theatre Royal Proprietors, he opened it instead as the Tyne Concert Hall ('Licensed by public opinion, not by the Magistrates'), on 24 August 1861. It had a capacity of nearly two thousand five hundred, at prices ranging from 1*s* to 3*d*. Stanley was fortunate in catching the local music hall boom at its peak, and the Tyne, bigger and with better facilities than any of its rivals, rapidly became acknowledged as the leader in this field. He was even more fortunate in being backed by Joseph Cowan, Newcastle builder and proprietor of the *Newcastle Chronicle*, an association which had important consequences.[29]

Thus within two years the number of professional halls in Newcastle had risen from one to four. Smith's policy was to recruit 'star' names, while Balmbra and Stanley concentrated on a sound, varied bill with considerable use of local talent. No other region seems to have thrown up quite such a group of original song writers and singers, giving expression to the humour and sadness of life around them.[30] Most were amateurs, so are to be found on the bills only within their own area, but Ned Corvan, a former colleague of Billy Purvis, toured all over the north-east, keeping alive the tradition of his master with his imitation of Billy's old sketch 'Whae stole the bundle?'[31] Just as popular on Tyneside were Joe Wilson, 'The Gallowgate Lad', a printer by trade, and Geordie Ridley, the ex-miner, best remembered now as author of 'Blaydon Races.'

This flowering of music hall proved as brief as it was rapid. First to drop out was the Grainger Hotel, not heard of again in that capacity after January 1866; then, having at last obtained his theatrical licence, Stanley gave up the Tyne Concert Hall in September 1867. It is noteworthy that, eminently successful and well equipped though it was, no one was prepared to take over the building. By the end of the decade, only the Wheat Sheaf (by now renamed the Oxford, and under new management) and the Victoria were left.

Probably some part of the demand was by now being met by the concert parties to whom Smith had earlier given engagements, and who were now visiting Newcastle in increasing numbers. With the availability of the new Town Hall, the great names of the London music hall, backed by three or four supporting artists, could in a night earn much larger sums than if they took an engagement in any of the halls, though Harry Liston did also accept several engagements at the Victoria.

Unlike the music hall, the circus maintained and even increased its popularity, as the number and length of visits by high quality troupes grew during the 1860s in accordance with a national trend. Thomas Barlow erected in November/December 1863 an amphitheatre near the Cattle Market, Marlborough Street, which was used again by Pinder in April 1864. In 1866 Newsome opened a circus in Percy Street, Haymarket, for four and a half months, and from then until the end of the decade no year was without a circus season.

The Theatre Royal too was highly successful in the early 1860s. In addition to a long stock company season, it became increasingly possible to obtain a miscellany of touring attractions during the summer; not only dramatic companies (usually organised to support a particular star) but conjurors, Christy Minstrels and panoramas. Grand opera companies visited at least once every season, and a four-week stay was common. Again, one finds in Newcastle not only a high standard of repertory (*Fidelio* and *Don Giovanni*, for example, occur more frequently than in any similar town), but evidence of a very large supportive audience. To be able to play three consecutive performances of *Rigoletto*, five performances of *Lurline* in ten days, or run *Faust* for a whole week, argues a remarkable number of keen operagoers. Undoubtedly the work of Rea helped to stimulate and extend the taste for opera in the town.

More attractive new plays were now becoming available. Tom Taylor's *Ticket-of-Leave Man* and the sensation pieces of Falconer and Boucicault repeated their London successes – and where the genuine article was not available, a house dramatist could often adapt the same original story under a similar title.[32] Davis continued to encourage members of his family, his company and the public to supply him with new pieces, and even secured the premiere of *Griffith Gaunt*, adapted by Charles Reade to display the talents of Avonia Jones, a great favourite in Newcastle.[33]

The prosperity of the Theatre Royal inevitably brought moves to break its monopoly, in the sacred name of free enterprise. In Newcastle as elsewhere, the proprietors of the town's Patent Theatre fiercely opposed any other attempts to obtain a dramatic licence, and being well represented on the magistrates' bench, usually succeeded. It was not surprising, therefore, that George Stanley encountered such difficulties, but he refused to be discouraged, backed as he was by Joseph Cowan who compaigned against monopoly in the columns of the *Newcastle Chronicle*.[34] Eventually in October 1863 Stanley received a broad hint from the magistrates that 'they think it most desirable that if a second Theatre is to be established in this town, it should be one of a permanent character', and the same night, at the Tyne Concert Hall, Stanley announced his intention of providing just that.[35]

This personal enterprise was very much the contemporary pattern. Successful lessees who wished to be their own masters for both financial and artistic reasons, increasingly built up and borrowed capital, and put up their own theatres, either in rivalry (as in Bristol) or as a replacement (as in Brighton). It was rarer for the initiative to come from the community, but the Bath Theatre Royal was rebuilt by public subscription, and the new Nottingham Theatre by private funds (it was turned into a joint stock company within a year). Stanley's capital was very probably provided by Cowan, though the Tyne had been successful enough for him to have amassed some means of his own. It may have been difficulties in finance which led to the delay of four years before the new building was ready, whereas ten months to a year seems to have been the usual period, but on 23 September 1867 the Tyne Theatre in Westgate Street (still standing, and recently reclaimed as a working theatre) was finally opened.

Loud were the choruses in praise of the benefits of competition, as each manager strove to outdo the other in the production of novelties and the engagement of stars. In the event, as Sheffield had found in the 1850s and Bristol was about to find, though populations had risen, and attitudes towards and support for the theatre had improved, there turned out not to be room for two competing theatres of a similar type. There was a national downturn of the economy in the last years of the 1860s, while on Tyneside itself the great impetus of the 1850s was almost spent and new initiatives were as yet lacking. In a speech at the opening of his 1869–70 season Stanley admitted the impact of the 'great and prolonged depression of trade': 'The commercial panic of 1866 injured business in all departments, but it completely paralysed Theatricals, and the last three years have been, without comparison, the worst the Theatrical Profession has experienced since I have known it.'[36] But Stanley had the attraction of novelty, the capital backing of Cowan, and the energy of a man in his prime, while Davis was over sixty, and the most active members of his family, on whom he had very much relied in the past, had by now set up for themselves elsewhere. Within two years of the opening of the Tyne Theatre, Davis was bankrupt, and when his lease ran out in the spring of 1870, the proprietors felt bound to look elsewhere for a manager.

The feeling aroused by this decision was considerable. Davis was no paragon; he had a quick temper, and his career was studded with uproarious and not always very creditable personal disputes. More damagingly, he had twice been manœuvred into seeming money-grabbing and vindictive in the matter of charity benefits,[37] and Cowan, through the *Chronicle*, did his best to exploit the complaints. When in the spring of 1862 Davis appeared to slight his very popular leading lady, Juliet Desborough, the audience was actively against him,[38] and again the *Chronicle* made the most of it. George Stanley went one better, and engaged her to give dramatic readings at the Tyne Concert Hall.

But despite such episodes, Davis had been identified with the theatre in Newcastle for twenty-four years, and no one who could remember the state, and status, of the Theatre Royal when he took over management was likely to underestimate his achievements. He may reasonably have felt a certain grim satisfaction when his successor, W. H. Swanborough, was declared bankrupt even before the season started; while by the time he completed his one year's lesseeship the Royal had lost almost every major attraction to the Tyne.[39]

For the Theatre Royal this was a sad ending to the decade; but it should not obscure the tremendous advances made over the previous thirty years. In 1840–1 Ternan at the Theatre Royal had run a stock company season four nights a week only between 16 November and 30 April; in 1869–70 there were two theatres, both running six nights a week. Davis's stock company played from 6 September to 1 April (the previous year, touring engagements had extended the season into June); while Stanley at the Tyne had engaged touring companies from 30 August to 18 September, run a stock season till 2 May, and then continued visiting attractions with only short breaks till 25 June.

In music the increase of provision was just as startling: in 1840 there was one piano recital, a series of financially disastrous popular promenade concerts in the summer, and one grand subscription concert in November. In 1870, a large concert hall was available, with weekly organ recitals, several oratorios, at least half a dozen grand concerts, a four weeks' season of orchestral and choral performances organised by Rea, and almost innumerable amateur and charity affairs.

The contrast is no less marked in popular entertainments. From 1840 to the end of 1842 the sole visitors were conjurors; in 1870 they ranged from leading members of the music hall profession to a diorama of Ireland with accompanying entertainments; two troupes of Japanese acrobats; three sets of Christy Minstrels, and James Doughty with his performing dogs. Music hall had developed from tavern sing-songs to professional independence, while the circus had become an annual tradition with a long season. From 1840 to 1848 there had been only five circus visits to Newcastle, and their total duration added up to less than Newsome's one season in 1870.

This is a pattern which in outline is typical of the performing arts in the expanding towns of the mid nineteenth century: improvement of premises during the 1850s, new buildings in the 1860s; steadily rising quantity and quality of both dramatic and musical performances, and with them the implication of a greatly enlarged 'reservoir' of both participants and audience. Population increase (Newcastle's rose by eighty per cent between 1841 and 1871) accounted for much; increasing national and regional prosperity for even more. Less quantifiable, but still undoubtedly important, was the improvement in official attitudes towards the arts, making the utilisation of capital for their housing, and support for their performance, publicly acceptable. Inextricably mixed with this was the growing provision of 'improving' leisure opportunities for the 'lower classes', expressing itself in civic and private expenditure not only on parks and reading rooms but also on concert rooms and Mechanics' Institutes with their large halls bookable for all types of entertainment.

Nor should the contribution of the individual manager or entrepreneur be overlooked. Davis's achievements in raising the standard of the theatre in Newcastle can be paralleled by, for example, those of Henry Nye

Chart in Brighton and J. H. Chute in Bristol, Rea's services to music by those of Kuhe in Brighton and, pre-eminently, Hallé in Manchester.

No two cities are identical in development; the paucity of circus visits to Newcastle in the 1840s, and their great increase in the 1850s, is, as we have seen, a reversal of the pattern found in most large towns. The development of music hall seems to have been more sluggish, and its flowering shorter, than in other large industrial towns. The discovery and exploitation of local talent, whether as performers in the saloons or as writers for the stage, was possibly unique. Generally speaking, Newcastle's dramatic and musical taste seems to have been of exceptional standard,[40] and since no manager, however high minded, can force a classical repertoire on an unwilling public, one might postulate a better educated, more 'middle-class' audience in Newcastle.

This however, runs counter to the statistics, for the proportion of professional and leisured inhabitants in the town, even by 1870, was very low. Both percentages are closely comparable with those for Nottingham, where by contrast the dramatic repertoire at the St Mary Gate theatre was pedestrian, and at the new Theatre Royal 'everything by starts and nothing long'; while the very lively musical life of the town was centred almost entirely upon the various glee clubs and concerts of what would now be classified, at best, as 'light music'. There is, in fact, very little hard evidence as to the constitution of Newcastle audiences; reports tend to use such bland clichés as 'attended by a numerous and respectable audience', or, in the case of fashionable occasions, 'the élite of Newcastle and neighbourhood'. The evidence of seat prices for most types of entertainment is that they maintained a middle level and were remarkably stable throughout the three decades, though the theatre reduced its gallery price to 6*d* and the size of the new Town Hall enabled a proportion of seats to be offered at the same low price, both of which must have extended potential audiences appreciably, even if still leaving out large numbers of the lowest paid.

It should not be forgotten that there were many other ways in which the members of that audience might have used their money and their leisure time. As the *Sheffield Telegraph* pointed out to the lessees of the theatre in that town at the end of an unhappy season,

> Managers must now look about them ... With libraries, reading rooms, museums, lectures, schools of art, public meetings, cheap concerts, and innumerable public houses, all calling upon the public for support; with cheap literature of a first-class character, country houses, low-priced pianos and music for the million, penny banks, mechanics' institutions, people's colleges and temperance halls – dividing the interest, time and thought of the people – a theatre must be conducted with great spirit, tact, and discretion ...[41]

The clear implication of the expansion of professional entertainment in towns like Newcastle, in the face of all these competing calls, is that there was a genuine and widespread increase in support and appreciation of the performing arts in the provinces, and they suggest a very much more cheerful picture of regional culture in the first thirty years of Victoria's reign than is usually painted.

NOTES

1 An honourable exception to both criticisms is Peter Bailey's *Leisure and Class in Victorian England* (1978).

2 *Newcastle Chronicle*, 25 December 1857.

3 The changes of outlook are perceptively discussed in Muriel Jaeger, *Before Victoria* (1960).

4 *Newcastle Chronicle*, 16 May 1840 and *Newcastle Journal*, 25 September 1841.

5 Theatre Royal Proprietors' Minute Book in Tyne & Wear Archives; *Newcastle Advertiser*, 14 July 1846. The plans of the theatre are now in the Metropolitan Museum of Art, New York, and are reproduced in R. Southern, *The Georgian Playhouse* (1948), pls. 51-4 and *Theatre Notebook* 1, ii.

6 *Newcastle Journal*, 24 July 1841.

7 H. Oswald, *The Theatres Royal in Newcastle upon Tyne* (Newcastle, 1936), p. 99

8 See, e.g., reports in *Tyne Mercury*, 8 February 1842 and 30 May 1843.

9 *Ibid.*, 17 October 1843.

10 J. P. Robson, *Life and Adventures of the Far-Famed Billy Purvis* (Newcastle, 1849), pp. 228-9.

11 *Ibid.*, pp. 222-3.

12 Letter quoted in Minutes of Proprietors' Committee Meeting, 12 June 1846.

13 *Newcastle Daily Chronicle*, 13 May 1865.

14 The operas were *Norma, Lucia di Lammermoor, Lucrezia Borgia, Il Barbiere di Siviglia, L'Elisir d'Amore* and *I Puritani*; quite a formidable repertory for that or any day.

15 *Newcastle Chronicle*, 1 March 1850.

16 Her leading man on both occasions was John Coleman, who gives a very partial, but very funny, account of the clashes between them in *Fifty Years of an Actor's Life* (1902), vol. 11, pp. 567-8 and 570-2.

17 Playbill, 11 April 1859.

18 *Newcastle Chronicle*, 5 January 1861; the first piece was *The Fairy*, adapted from Octave Feuillet's *La Fée* by Baxter Langley, a reporter on the *Chronicle*, while the pantomime, *Harlequin King of the Peacocks*, was written by Alfred Davis, one of E. D. Davis's sons.

19 In a pleasant gesture, Davis gave the veteran Billy Purvis a farewell Benefit on 19 April 1852.

20 The 1861 Census, recording an increase of population from 3,539 to

14,345 in this district, notes that it 'is attributable to the operations of the ordnance and engineering works of Sir William Armstrong, at which about 3,000 men are employed; and to the facilities afforded for building'.

21 *Tyne Mercury*, 18 October 1842.

22 Balmbra took the Wheat Sheaf in 1840; the first notice of a singing room there is in the *Era* of 27 August 1848, and implies that it had been open for some little time.

23 As late as 1859, for instance, I can find mention of only two other music halls in Newcastle, one a very temporary affair, while in Sheffield there are notices of ten.

24 *Newcastle Daily Chronicle*, 28 January 1842.

25 Proprietors' Committee Minutes, 2 January 1844; Price and North's prices slightly undercut those of the theatre, ranging from 2s 6d to 6d.

26 *Newcastle Chronicle*, 24 July 1857.

27 *Ibid.*, 21 March 1852.

28 *Ibid.*, 9 February 1855.

29 The four halls, and those of the adjacent towns, are sympathetically described in *Newcastle Daily Chronicle*, 18 January 1865, though nowhere does the writer indicate their clientèle beyond insisting that they were respectable and well-behaved.

30 See D. Harker, *Geordie Ridley, Gateshead Poet and Vocalist* (Newcastle, 1973); R. Colls, *The Collier's Rant* (1977), pp. 38-45; M. Vicinus, *The Industrial Muse* (1974), pp. 238-80. Both the latter see the music hall songs as a continuation of earlier working-class culture, channelled into a particular genre.

31 Described in *Newcastle Daily Chronicle*, 31 March 1862; see also D. Mayer, 'Billy Purvis, Travelling Showman', *Theatre Quarterly* I, iv, 27-34.

32 For example, a close imitation of Boucicault's *Flying Scud*, made by Henry Roxby Beverley, under the title of *Flying Jib*, was played by Davis in September 1867.

33 *Newcastle Daily Journal*, 15-24 April 1867; *Era*, 28 April 1867. Avonia Jones and G. V. Brooke had on a previous visit succeeded in running a double bill of *Medea* and *East Lynne* for a fortnight; a tribute as much to the staying power as to the classical taste of the Newcastle public.

34 For the relationship between Cowan and Stanley see Harker, *op. cit.*, p. 5.

35 *Newcastle Chronicle*, 21 October 1863; *Era*, 25 October 1863.

36 *Era*, 26 September 1869.

37 *Newcastle Chronicle*, 10 and 24 December 1859; *Newcastle Daily Chronicle*, 17, 19 and 24 February 1862.

38 *Ibid.*, 5 April 1862.

39 See letter from Glover and Francis to the Proprietors, quoted in Committee Minutes, 1 May 1871.

40 A typical 'popular night' in Rea's promenade season, including two overtures and the Andante from the Surprise Symphony, drew a crowded hall, and the *Newcastle Daily Journal* of 28 October 1867 commented that 'if [such items are] to be considered as popular, it shows that the popular standard in this town is a very lofty one'.

41 *Sheffield Daily Telegraph*, 20 February 1858.

5 ROBERT POOLE
Oldham Wakes

I

The wakes holiday was in origin a religious festival, probably grafted on to earlier pagan observances by the early Christian missionaries. Taking place on the anniversary of the dedication day of a church, which was usually also the day of its patron saint, this essentially lower-class festival survived attacks by the puritans in the sixteenth and seventeenth centuries to become part of the eighteenth century's flourishing calendar of customary leisure.[1] The late eighteenth century saw a 'quite sharp attack upon popular customs, sports and holidays' but, like Josiah Wedgwood who complained that 'the Wakes must be observed though the world was to end with them', Lancashire millowners found themselves often unable to prevent their workers from 'running off' at wakes time.[2] Cunningham concludes that 'in nearly all cases employers had to settle for some form of compromise, had to submit in some degree to the force of custom'.[3] The Lancashire wakes survived with surprising vigour into the middle of the nineteenth century, and subsequently evolved into great cotton holidays with which the term is now most usually associated.

In the early nineteenth century, the survival of wakes in England was most marked in the north of England and the Black Country; within Lancashire, they were found mainly in the more economically advanced south and east of the county.[4] The connection between a prosperous craft-based economy and a strong attachment to customary leisure is well known.[5] Yet in Lancashire, where the factory system developed so early and so extensively, the wakes developed into a mass industrial holiday faster and farther than anywhere else in the country. It might, then, broadly be argued that the county's early and rapid industrialisation tended not so much to obliterate the customary holiday as to incorporate it within the new order. Oldham provides a useful testing-ground for this idea.

The Oldham area probably had the strongest wakes tradition in Lancashire. Foster notes, but does not pursue, 'a vigorous survival of certain peasant customs (like the annual wakes and rushcarts)'; in fact, this had more to do with a thriving handicraft economy than a stubborn peasantry.[6] Oldham's industrialisation, and its transition from being a centre of coarse weaving to one of spinning, was rapid. Between 1789 and 1851 the population of the township of Oldham rose from about eight thousand to 52,818, and that of the parish, including the out-townships of Royton, Chadderton and Crompton, rose in the same period from 13,916 to 72,354. In 1788 there were eleven cotton mills in the town; in 1825, there were forty-six, housing 139 firms, while the engineering industry grew in proportion. Throughout the century, the cotton industry employed thirty to forty per cent of the labour force.[7]

This industrialisation, though, did not involve a break with 'traditional society' in the form of the arrival of the self-made innovator. Most of Oldham's millowners came from wealthy or landed backgrounds, and were usually locals; 'all the gentlemen of Oldham are concerned in the manufacture of the town', said a magistrate in 1828. These gentlemen manufacturers had rejoined 'the Anglican–Tory world of county society' well before 1850. On the other hand, there was a rapid turnover of firms, and there were also, noted Reach in 1849, 'a great number of small capitalists renting floors or small portions of factories. These employers have themselves generally risen from the mule or the loom, and maintain in a great degree their operatives' appearance, thoughts and habits'. They would 'drink and sing in low taverns with their own working hands'. Employers such as these were unlikely to be fatally hostile to customary holidays.[8]

On a similar theme of continuity, the urban growth of Oldham corresponds to Thompson's assertion that 'most of the new industrial towns did not so much displace the countryside as grow over it'. In 1802–7 the thinly populated and marshy commons around the then 'large village' of Oldham were enclosed 'without any allotment for recreation'. The local historian Edwin Butterworth remembered that 'the advantage of these moors as places of recreation and exercise had rendered them spots deeply endeared to successive generations', and the enclosure caused deep popular resentment. Although Northmoor and Greenacres Moor were built over at an 'astonishing' rate, we shall see that their inhabitants, and those of other recently built-up areas, were still parading their identity by bringing the customary 'rushcarts' to Oldham Wakes until after mid-century. Crompton, Royton and other townships in the Oldham area kept up their own separate wakes throughout the nineteenth century.[9]

Oldham had a long-standing reputation as a town of rough, independent and traditionalist character. An early Wesleyan preacher who experienced 'heavy persecution for a season' there described it as 'a place famous throughout all that country for daring and desperate wickedness'. The breaking-up of a reform meeting in 1794 long had a place in local folklore as 'Royton Races', and Butterworth recalled of the period that 'the demeanour of the mass of the population was characterized by a freedom that was regarded by the inhabitants of more polished places as bordering on rudeness, and sometimes extending to what they conceived to be insolence and brutality'. He added: 'there are still traces of the coarse unpolished manners which marked the population of the last and the early part of the present century, but such repulsive exteriors generally possess a flow of substantial kindness'. Around the same time, Lord Ellesmere wrote, Oldham people were, despite their political militancy, 'remarkable for their hearty spontaneous sociality of disposition to all sects and descriptions of men'. Oldham's famous radicalism had a robust traditionalism about it. The town's first two members of Parliament were William Cobbett and John Fielden; not until 1847 did a Liberal reformer sit for Oldham.[10] The independent-mindedness and social conservatism of fifty years before were still strongly evident in 1879–82 when the wakes were successfully defended against an attempted reform.[11] By this time, people were investing on a large scale for this annual spree in wakes savings clubs; in the 1830s, they had invested in shilling-a-week 'shaking clubs' in the hope of purchasing the occasional windfall on a throw of the dice.[12] Both could be seen as either prudent or profligate, but the wakes savings clubs earned praise for their method of thrift. How much had really changed?

It is difficult to make any direct connection between the social and economic condition of the Oldham area and the remarkable consistency of wakes observance there, but its social remodelling was by no means as drastic as might at first appear, and there was much about it that was conducive to the survival of popular customs such as the wakes. These seem to have survived almost intact, if somewhat changed in character, to the middle of the nineteenth century, when the coming of the railways transformed them in several important respects but ensured their survival into the age of mass commercial leisure.

II

The wakes season in the Oldham area began with Mossley Wakes towards the end of July and continued at the rate of one or two a week throughout summer with Hollinwood, Royton, Shaw, Crompton, Lees, Newton Heath, Milnrow, Middleton, Saddleworth (Uppermill), Saddleworth (Delph and Heights) and finally, on the last Saturday in August and the first few days in September, Oldham Wakes. The centrepiece of the old-style wakes was the annual renewal of the rushes on the floor of the parish church. Within a twenty-mile radius of Manchester the custom had evolved of bringing them to the church in the form of a rushcart; that is, arranged on a cart in a pyramidal shape anything up to twelve feet high and decorated with oak branches, flowers, mottoes and, draped over the front, a white 'packsheet' hung with silver and other valuables.[13] The flagging of church floors and the rise of evangelical attitudes in the late eighteenth and early nineteenth centuries brought a general withdrawal of church patronage. The wakes or rushbearing, however, survived as a secular festival, celebrated on the Saturday rather than the Sunday but still extending over the following few days. In the townships of Lees and Hey, Hollinwood, Royton and Mossley, new chapels were

built in the mid eighteenth century to cope with the rising population
produced by the growing domestic economy, so the wakes in these places
were probably much more recent in origin than those in Oldham, Shaw,
Crompton and Saddleworth, where the religious foundations were much
older.[14] There were also unofficial 'wakes' which appeared from time to
time in populous suburbs such as Lydgate and Sholver, no doubt owing
much to the enterprise of local publicans and tradesmen but kept up over
some years with surprising consistency. The link between the area's
flourishing wakes tradition and its growing economy is also demonstrated
in Samuel Bamford's account of the wakes as it existed during his boy-
hood in the early nineteenth century in the mining and weaving village
of Middleton. Weavers worked desperately hard to earn money for the
wakes, dashing off to Manchester with their cloth on the Saturday
morning to return in time to see their village's rushcart move off. The
cart was a symbol of local pride and prosperity, 'arrayed [with] silver
watches, trays, spoons, sugar tongs, teapots, snuffers or other fitting
articles of ornament or value, and the more numerous and precious the
articles were, the greater was the deference which the party that displayed
them expected from the wandering crowd'. The cart paraded noisily to
the church from the hamlet where it was built, pulled by young men in
colourful costume, accompanied by morris dancers, fife and drum, fiddle
and whip-cracker, and joined by friends visiting from other villages.

> Arriving at the village, other parties similar to their own will be found
> parading their cart on the highroad. The neighbouring folds and hamlets,
> having been nearly deserted by their inhabitants, are there concentrated
> seeing the wakes and partaking in the universal enjoyment. The highway is
> thronged by visitors in gay attire, whilst shops, nut stalls, flying boxes,
> merry-go-rounds, and other means of amusement are rife on every hand.
> Should two carts meet, and there be a grudge on either side, a wrangle, and
> probably a battle or two, settles the question, and they each move on; if the
> parties are in amity, they salute each other with friendly hurras, the drawers
> holding their stretchers over their heads until they have passed. Each cart
> stops at the door of every public-house, which the leaders enter tumultuously,
> jumping, jingling their bells, and imitating the neighing of horses. A can of
> ale is then generally brought to the door, and distributed to the drawers and
> attendants; those who ride on top not forgetting to claim their share ... After
> disposing of the rushes, either by gift to the church ... or by sale to the best
> bidder, the lads and their friends, sweethearts and helpers, repaired to the
> public-house at which they put up for the wakes, and there spent the night
> in drinking and dancing.

A rushcart, then, was very much a collective enterprise, involving both
men and women, old and young, in its construction, decoration and
display. On the next day, Sunday, the villagers extended open hospitality

to friends, relatives, and even passers-by. On Monday, there was a fresh influx of crowds for the main day of the fair, and the celebrations continued (on a dwindling scale) for the rest of the week. Bamford also remembered a great deal of hard drinking and fighting.[15]

In Oldham itself, with its large juvenile factory population and high rate of in-migration, community ties were weaker. The rushbearing here had by the 1820s become the culmination of two months of gang warfare in which the youth of the mills played a leading part. Butterworth's description of the end of a rushcart procession in his own town is somewhat different from Bamford's: 'the rushcarters now become half drunk, the sheet is torn off, and the *men-horses* becomes as wild as but more fearful than hares, the respective carts when meeting terminate the proceedings when fighting, and the pile of rushes becomes a prey to the crowd of gazers who accompany the carts ...'. 'These contests', remembered one 'B. Grime', 'always ended in bruised and broken heads or limbs'.[16] Six men were gaoled after one such fight in 1800; another was accidentally run over and killed in 1840. It is difficult to generalise about the character of rushcarts in town and country, or at one time or another, since so much clearly depends on the opinions of the observers. To Bamford, men acting like horses were a lively rustic frolic; to Butterworth, they were bestial. But as the domestic weaving economy declined and the bonds of traditional society became weaker, the rushcart became more particularly the concern of the youths and men who drew it to collect beer money, and the attendant violence and disorder became more conspicuous and less acceptable to authority. Yet the same Oldham rushcarts that prompted Butterworth's disparaging account of the custom in 1831 were collecting 'money at the houses of the principal inhabitants'. The pride of individual communities and the fighting between their respective rushcarts were two sides of the same coin in both town and country throughout the first half of the nineteenth century. In Saddleworth in the 1810s and 1820s, five or six rushcarts was the usual number at the wakes, each having its own place in the order of precedence when they drew up in front of the church. In Bamford's Middleton, there were six hamlets which customarily got up rushcarts. The diarist William Rowbottom (whose eccentric spelling has been retained in quotations throughout this chapter) noted some twenty-five different places which sent rushcarts to Oldham Wakes between 1793 and 1829. Carts from Northmoor and Greenacres Moor were particularly consistent in their appearances, both before and after their enclosure and sudden urbanisation, and other places also prided themselves on their long tradition of rushbearing to Oldham Wakes.[17]

Rushcarts could be symbolic of more than just local identity, and they often appear as vehicles of social or political protest—sometimes reactionary, sometimes radical, but always traditionalist. One famous local rushcart builder, 'Dick o' Joshua's', 'formed them to the state of the times, and his carts were like the caricatures of print-shops, expressive of the public feelings of the day'.[18] In 1793, 'the people of Cowhill strove to show their detestation of Jacobins by decorating their rushcarts with emblems of loyalty'; patriotic symbols were a very common ingredient of rushcart design. At the 1826 wakes, following outbreaks of power loom smashing in north Lancashire in the spring, 'There was a cart from Shaw in wich was placed a pair of looms, on wich a person was weaving, and another was winding another pair of looms of a similar description, wich came from Saint Hellens, Northmoor. They had a very novel appearance and attracted a deal of admiration.' Handlooms were also displayed on Oldham rushcarts in 1861 and 1862, a focus by now, perhaps, of sentiment rather than of protest. At the wakes of the 1820s and 1830s there also appeared a number of 'coal carts', 'carrying immense pieces of coal' and 'dragged by blackened collier lads'. There were alarms for the peace of the town as the miners sought to provoke 'a regular set-to in the up and down style' with the rushcarters. In 1837, though, they were 'admired for their neat and becoming aspect'. Here, we see again the two complementary sides to rushcart display.[19]

Oldham Wakes suffered very badly during the downswings of the trade cycle. In 1811, for example, 'there were but few company, and in consequence of the times there was only one rushcart, wich came from Hollinwood, wich was never the case before in the memory of the oldest person living . . . They took the rushes back, so that there was not a single rush in Oldham Church to preserve the old people's feet from cold during the winter.' Similarly, there was 'not a solitary rushcart' at the depressed wakes of 1842.[20] At Christmas 1811, Rowbottom reported, 'the old English hospitality is nearly extinguished in every family . . . and a deal of families have not left off work at all'. Christmas was more readily sacrificed than the wakes, but at both festivals, high food prices could destroy the traditional open hospitality.[21] The crowds at the pubs grew smaller as home brewing took over in bad years, and the high price of malt might preclude even that. Factory workers suffered much less in these years than craft workers, but it was the state of the latter which largely governed the success or failure of the wakes. Scarcely able to afford to leave off work, they were unable to get up rushcarts or to afford any celebration. The French wars added another persistent frustration as the appearance of vulture-like recruiting parties reduced the sex ratio to 'two nymphs to one swain' or even (in Rowbottom's words) 'three nymphs to one swain. Oh, the blessed effect of this accursed war!'[22]

Economic depression put a tremendous strain on customary holidays, but it did not, as has sometimes been supposed, eliminate them.[23]

Reviving trade was quickly marked by their rejuvenation, as in 1797 when 'owing to the briskness of the fustian trade there were eight rushcarts' and 'plenty of brewing with families wich a short time since were verey poor'. When the wars ended in 1815 there was 'the most grand and splendid wakes wich as been in the memory of the oldest person living', with feasting, entertaining and 'rustic sports' on a large scale. 'High spending and much fighting' generally went together, and appeals to orderliness and thrift on such occasions fell on deaf ears.[24] The return of relative prosperity was not to go unmarked, for it meant a great deal to the strength of communities, exemplified most clearly at the wakes by the scale of entertainment and rushcart building. It is even possible that the disastrous effects of the war and the trade cycle in the early part of the century intensified popular sentiment in favour of wakes and rushbearings, despite the decline of handloom weaving communities. In defying respectable logic and progressive morals to keep up these customs, people were in a definite way 'defending a culture, a whole way of life, against the demands of capitalism'.[25]

Violence and blood sports, particularly bull-baiting, were for long a usual ingredient of wakes, as Samuel Riley, a visitor to Saddleworth Wakes in 1773, was shocked to discover:

> He went into an alehouse that was crowded with men and women rolling about drunk and singing indecent songs. Then he went into a barn where two half naked men were fighting on the floor like wild beasts, and when the victor got up he stepped back and, taking a kick at his prostrate opponent, drove in three of his ribs. He saw a bull baited by a crowd of men that were little less than savages. Its nose was hanging in bloody shreds, and while some men were twisting its tail, others were beating it with clubs. As it was licking the blood from its nose a part of its tongue was bitten off by a dog, to the howling joy of the mob.[26]

Bull-baiting was a central feature of many Lancashire wakes up to, and even after, its prohibition in 1835. It took place at wakes in the out-townships and villages round Oldham into the 1830s, and possibly as late as 1849, but there is no mention of its having taken place in Oldham itself, where it was banned under the 1826 Improvement Act.[27] Oldham, though, was notorious for its dog-fighting, which was widely encouraged by publicans and was still 'common amongst the lowest orders' in 1849; a champion fighting dog was displayed atop one rushcart in 1834. 'Rustic sports' were another long-standing wakes amusement. Hollinwood Wakes in 1833 saw, as well as bull-baiting, 'Duck Swimming, Races in Sacks, Climbing a [greasy] Pole for a hat, Ass Races, Running for Caps, Tea Drinking matches &c.', no doubt put on by publicans.[28] The point to these sports was that there was something for everyone – watching dogs chase ducks in a pond for the less active, the 'tea drinking matches' for old women, straight races for the more athletic, and comic races to cater for just about every type of person – old men, wives, maidens, butchers, carters and people with wooden legs. There was a democratic, participatory form of competitiveness about such events, where the main virtue was often not to mind looking foolish, which contrasts with the striving for orders of merit and spectator–competitor division marking the athletics festivals of future decades.[29] The fairs which accompanied every wakes in the area had a similarly wide appeal. Until 1850 these, though extensive, consisted of basically small-scale attractions. Simple hand-operated roundabouts, 'swing-boats' and 'fly-boats', travelling theatres (performing Shakespeare in record time), penny shows, a circus, Wombwell's menagerie, mountebank shows and dozens of stalls selling crockery, cutlery and sweetmeats were typical ingredients of an Oldham Wakes fair in the 1830s. Although it was part of the same travelling circuit, Oldham's was already bigger than those of other towns and villages of the area, but it was a long time before they were supplanted.[30]

Middle- and upper-class attitudes to Oldham Wakes seem, from scanty evidence, to have been surprisingly favourable. Hey Wakes was actively encouraged by a sympathetic minister and attended by prominent local families as late as 1810. The patronage given by Oldham's resident gentry to rushcarts in the 1830s has already been noted; in the 1860s, the liberal *Oldham Chronicle* vigorously defended the revellers and their rushcarts from the encroachments of authority.[31] Temperance organisations were active from the 1830s in putting on meetings, tea parties and processions at Oldham Wakes, and there was a 'social festival' organised by 'the Socialists' in 1838 and a festival at the Mechanics' Institute in 1840. In contrast with Rochdale, though, where radicals, Sunday school teachers and the strongly pro-temperance *Rochdale Observer* were united in their disapproval, there was no discernible opposition to the wakes as an institution.[32] Edwin Butterworth, a radical with traditionalist sympathies, saw the wakes as 'a period of rustic pleasure and artless amusement ... now little else than an occasion on the part of some operatives for indulging in an extra degree of intemperance, and for practising brutal sports'. He wavered in his opinion of rushcarts: sometimes he saw them as 'rural ornaments', at others as 'monuments of childish barbarism'. He blamed 'the fallen character of the factory operatives', and ultimately the factory system itself, for 'the visible decline of the more innocent diversions and customs of the South East Lancashire population at these feasts, and the increase of the grosser and more vicious portion of the practice of such times'. There was some sentimentality here, as with Bamford, but he was genuinely moved to despair at the sight of 'the laborious swains' of Hollinwood 'drinking themselves into the midst of distress for the sole purpose of supporting the disgraceful, useless wake'.[33] Accounts of eighteenth-century wakes, such as Riley's, undermine the plausibility of allegations of moral decline made by more morally sensitive nineteenth-century observers, who saw perhaps only the surface turbulence of these festivals from their distant cultural bunkers. The violence and indulgence of wakes was, however, probably becoming less acceptable generally. The old handloom weaving communities which provided the intimate and tolerant social background which sanctioned these annual releases of energy were in decline, and in Oldham, at least, rushbearing was left more to the excitable youth of the factories, although it undoubtedly retained a much wider social base. By 1850, though, the overall level of riot at wakes everywhere had declined. The festival had survived successive trade depressions and had grown roots in the social life of the urban population, ready to find its place in the increasingly commercial working-class leisure pattern of the second half of the nineteenth century.

III

'The railway excursion and consequent rise of the holiday resort killed the Lancashire wake and civilized the local fair', writes Brian Harrison.[34] This was far from true; the coming of the railways in many ways enhanced the wakes as a local celebration, and the real decline of this side of the festival did not appear for several decades.

The linking-up of the Manchester stations in 1844 gave Oldham a direct rail route to the coast at Liverpool, and already in 1846 several hundred people went there on an excursion on wakes Monday. Although the Lancashire working-class custom of sea bathing does not seem to have reached as far inland as Oldham, the cheap trip to the seaside was soon an established part of Oldham Wakes. The town's railway link to Blackpool was completed in 1848 and that to Southport in 1855. In 1858 nearly fourteen thousand people left Oldham on special trains over the five days of the wakes, and in 1860 the total traffic was over twenty-three thousand, ordinary trains included. This proved to be a peak year, and although numbers recovered after the cotton famine, the excursion traffic remained at a similar level during the 1870s.[35] The surrounding towns and villages followed the trend set by Oldham, at a few years' distance. Churches, Sunday schools and temperance bodies already had experience in organising trips and field days, and these were among the earliest organisations chartering trains for excursions. There was a strong element of counter-attractionist ideology here, for the seaside was seen as more physically and morally healthy than the degenerate domestic wakes. Ticket sales, however, were fairly indiscriminate (usually to 'teachers, scholars and friends') and the trips were run, except in the case of children, for profit rather than for moral improvement. Controlling behaviour on these trips was in any case impossible, since passengers travelled in closed compartments and dispersed on arrival – Sunday school teachers were no match for them. Passengers in Middleton would pay 'little regard to politics' in choosing between the excursions offered by the local Liberal and Conservative parties. The cheap trip was too popular an institution to remain a reformers' monopoly for long, and organisers in Oldham in the 1860s and 1870s included political groups, mutual improvement societies, literary institutes, bands, cricket clubs, friendly societies, factory workers, tea dealers and 'Cowhill rushbearers'. By 1882, even the seasonally overworked police were able to get away to the seaside, although their excursion had to wait until the end of wakes week. Other Lancashire towns had similar experiences, and so the surviving wakes holiday system in the county, combined with the rising living standards, brought about the rise of the working-class seaside holiday.[36]

This exodus had a marked effect on local wakes in the Oldham area. In 1858, for example, the Saddleworth district 'became nearly depopulated' on Delph Wakes Monday, 'most of the adults having left on cheap trips' which, complained the showmen, 'take all the money out of the district'.[37] There were, however, several mitigating factors which prevented such sudden changes from becoming general or permanent. Until the later 1870s, nearly all the trips were day trips, which left local people free to entertain guests and visit their own fairs on other days. They also had the effect of extending the wakes, in many cases, for an extra day. In 1842, two days had been the normal holiday round Oldham – that is, Monday and Tuesday. The elastic demand for excursions meant that in good years like 1860, the Wednesday traffic increased enormously (producing a spectacular crush of several hours' duration at Oldham Mumps station), and the Wednesday slowly became an established, if unofficial, extension to the holiday. Employers had little defence against this form of holiday extension on the upswing of the trade cycle.[38] Furthermore, these trips had the effect of evening out local trade as between good and bad years; thus, at Mossley Wakes at the start of the cotton famine, 'business was improved by the entire absence of cheap trips'.[39]

The railway network made the growing population of industrial Lancashire more mobile. Families and communities broken up by the pattern of short-distance migration which characterised the early industrial town could now be re-united more easily and over longer distances. The wakes was still the obvious time for this, with rising living standards making it ever more possible, although the traditional type of 'open house' hospitality must by now have declined, particularly in large towns like

Oldham. The third quarter of the nineteenth century might be viewed as the golden age of wakes hospitality in Lancashire, with huge local movements of population every week throughout the summer. Already in 1846 there were so many people trying to leave Oldham to return home on wakes Sunday evening that the railway company was 'utterly unable to provide them with accommodation'.[40] In preparation for the wakes, houses were limed and whitewashed, and linen and crockery were renewed. 'Chair bottomers and tub thumpers' were much in demand, and in Saddleworth it was usual 'to find all the painters, plasterers, tailors, dressmakers and cordwainers in the district busily engaged for a full month before wakes Sunday'. In Oldham, 'iron bedsteads, wool and cotton flocks, feathers, &c.' were advertised as wakes purchases, and for 'clothiers, hatters, drapers, boot makers and such like' the wakes marked the climax – and the end – of the summer season. On wakes Saturday evening the town was filled with 'lively groups of operatives effecting their purchases of clothing and provisions'.[41] At the start of Mossley Wakes, 'Twenty-six cow heads and as many hearts are hung up like criminals outside the butcher's shops because they happen to be too lean and bony for a wakes time'. Next week, there would be 'a great rush on the boiling and stewing pieces'. 'Were it not for the wakes', it was said, 'many a young boy and girl would have to be absent from Sunday School, Church and Chapel, in consequence of not having what they consider suitable clothing.'[42] The press approved this sociable and thrifty side of the wakes, and took an idealised view of it:

> Families that have been broken up by marriage and otherwise are brought together under the old paternal roof, and quaint stories are told of by gone days as they quaff their home-brewed ale amid fumes of tobacco. The little offspring gather round the good old folks, and count their halfpence in Gronny's lap, whilst they revel in the gleeful expectation of wakes festivities.[43]

The same newspaper, though, contained a report of a housewife who attempted suicide following an argument over 'wakes brass, rum and tea, and pawn tickets'. The wakes was by no means reserved for the thrifty, respectable artisan with a comfortable home and the money to 'go off' to the seaside.

From about 1850 to 1880 a pattern was established at Oldham Wakes and others in the area. Celebrations began on Saturday night; Sunday was the main day for entertaining friends and relatives; Monday was the main day for locals and visitors to attend the fair; Monday or Tuesday was the day for an excursion; and on Wednesday there was another trip, if circumstances allowed, with the expanding range of seasonal attractions at Manchester's Belle Vue Gardens and zoo a favourite resort. In this period of growing mobility, the smaller district fairs suffered by comparison as purely commercial attractions with the growing extravaganza on Oldham's Tommyfield. However, cheap trips from these places were not so firmly established as in Oldham itself, for many people observed Oldham Wakes too, and took their excursion then, and the overall effect may well have been to preserve these district wakes as occasions of domestic sociability rather than of commercial pleasure-seeking. The range of wakes attractions was, however, expanding throughout this period. As well as Belle Vue, there was Marple in Cheshire ('a delightful summer retreat' – 1*s* return), Hollingworth Lake (with its pleasure boats and regattas), 'Bill's o' Jack's' (a popular country pub in Saddleworth), the Volunteers' annual muster, and a growing calendar of brass band contests and athletics festivals.[44] In Oldham itself, there were Glodwick Strawberry Gardens, as well as other pleasure grounds which opened later on, the skating rink and the theatres and music halls, which often opened, redecorated, for a season at the wakes. Innovations at the fairground in the 1850s and 1860s included photographers, steam-powered rides, naphtha burners for better night trading, shooting galleries, donkey rides and 'locomotives for roasting potatoes'.[45] Races on Greenacres Moor at Oldham Wakes attracted such vast crowds (up to twenty thousand) that they had to be stopped for public safety after a jockey was killed. Pub entertainments proliferated, and the Sunday ban on all music except the sacred was liberally interpreted to allow hotted-up hymn tunes and other performances 'which could not by any possibility confine themselves to the region of the sacred'. This was for the entertainment of visitors, who were also likely to be treated to 'rough music and astounding songs improvised on the spot' by impromptu bands armed with frying pans and penny whistles.[46]

In the Oldham area, at least, alternative amusements and 'rational recreations' were no match for all this, and were on the whole conspicuous by their absence. Religious and other improving bodies, like other less elevated entrepreneurs, came to use the wakes to raise money and win publicity. The Salvation Army's mock battles of Good versus Evil, the evangelical and socialist speakers who took over the deserted fairground on Sunday, and their occasionally hilarious conflicts, all became an appreciated part of the background to the wakes. 'The only topic that rivals teetotalism on our Wakes Sunday is Tichbornism', remarked the *Oldham Chronicle* in 1879.[47]

Oldham Wakes, then, was in the mid-Victorian period a rich and diverse festival where traditional and modern elements flourished together. The wakes in the surrounding area were beginning to look relatively pale, but were generally healthy enough in their own right. Before moving to consider later developments, we must, however, return to examine the fate of that durable and 'fantastical recreation of rushcarts'.[48]

IV

The Oldham authorities for long fought an unequal battle to control the annual rushcart processions. The town acquired a force of four constables under the 1826 Improvement Act, with orders to act against blood sports, disorderly persons, 'sundry nuisances' and carts blocking the streets for no good purpose. In 1829 an attempt to ban rushcarts from the town on wakes Saturday because of the crowds on that day was defied by the rushcart from Greenfield (part of rural Saddleworth), and 'a terrible conflict ensued, in wich the authoritys and their assistances were totally defeated'. The ban was none the less made to stick in 1830, and the rushcarts thereafter paraded on the Monday; apart from this episode, 'the police never interfered' with the rushbearers.[49] Dog-fighting remained widespread in Oldham, cock-fighting also persisted, and the situation elsewhere in the area must have been even less satisfactory. When the constable at Hey entered the arena to prevent his fellow-operatives from baiting a bull at Acorn Mill, his wooden leg sank into the mud and he had to be rescued by a spectator.[50] For many years, Oldham's radicals controlled the police commission and blocked moves to strengthen the force or to introduce the county police, but in 1847–9 they lost control. At the 1847 wakes, following the election riots when the Liberals were victorious the previous month, there was a severe fight between rival groups of rushcarters which required 'the utmost exertions' of the police to restore order. The next year, though, 'the "rush cart" exhibition was remarkable for quietness and order'. The same was true in the following year, when the magistrates had managed to bring in the county police. In November 1849, following the radicals' defeat in the municipal elections, a borough police force of twelve was finally established; the next wakes saw a carefully-managed 'procession of fourteen rushcarts, many of them beautifully adorned with flowers, and displaying in front a profusion of silver plate', preceded by the fire brigade and accompanied by fourteen coal wheelers, each with a barrow of coal. The following year there were eighteen 'rushcarts' and an impressive teetotal procession incorporating twenty gentlemen on horseback and floats depicting 'the drunkard's home' and 'the happy home'. Whether this was an attempt to challenge or to civilise the rushcart procession is not clear; nor is it clear whether there was any political reason for wanting to suppress rushcarts. The pageants of 1850 and 1851, however, accorded with respectable sentiment about restoring the custom to its 'original purity'.[51]

From here on, each rushcart was usually accompanied by a policeman 'to preserve order', and although the single procession model did not last, elaborate plans were made to ensure that the routes of individual rushcarts did not clash. When the magistrates sniffed rumours that Anglo-Irish fighting had been arranged at the 1861 wakes, all rushcarts were banned and the police successfully threatened one landlord that 'they would remove his licence if he had anything to do with rushcarts'. Rushcarts appeared none the less, and one was only deterred from keeping an appointment for a battle by a burly constable who barred its way at a toll-gate and 'threatened to break the skull of any man amongst them who passed through. The rushcart therefore turned back.' All turned out peacefully in the end. The Mayor, a cotton spinner and a prominent Wesleyan, who had himself signed the ban, slipped the rushbearers some money, in solidarity with tradition or, at least, with the English side of the argument. ('What's t'mayor gan thee lad?' asked a spectator, and came the reply: 'He's gan half-a-crown like a felly, instead o' five shillings like a gentleman.') The *Oldham Chronicle* was eloquent in its support for the rushbearers: 'If rushcarts are obstructive, so are Whit processions. Whether they are immoral is irrelevant. The bench has no business with morals, and will not be allowed to ride roughshod over the people's pastimes and their ancient customs, without protest, so long as there is a free press in the country and a free spirit in its people.'[52] The borough police in Oldham, as elsewhere in Lancashire, were limited in their effectiveness by their general unpopularity. With their own often lowly social origins and unreformed personal morals, they were short on the necessary respect; they were subject to another scathing attack by the *Chronicle* in 1864 for 'despotism' in their action against illegal wakes drinkers – 'frivolous interferences with the simple pleasures of the people'. A reporter in 1879 summed up the changes of sixty years in the policing of Oldham. The retiring local constable in 1819 had been a keen pugilist and would watch or even join in any fights he came across; the modern police would 'quietly wait around the corner until the row is over, and then, as quietly, capture one or both of the breathless combatants, and "run 'em in"'.[53]

Despite, then, this marked but essentially limited success with the rushcarts, other factors were more important than the police force in bringing order to the mid-Victorian Oldham Wakes. These included the growing exodus of locals on cheap trips, the improving standard of behaviour in a settled industrial society, and the decline in the vitality of the rushcart tradition itself. This last was obvious by 1864:

Instead of – as in former times – a muster of fifty grown men pulling at the 'waiges', it is only the youths that will turn to the work now. The shafts of the carts, or waggons, are not now, as formerly, held up by some half-dozen men, but a horse is made to serve instead. Instead of the cart sheet, as in former years, being covered with watches, silver plate, and all the other valuables that can be mustered, the cart is now ornamented with materials of less value. The rivalry of display on the part of the rushcarts is now apparently a thing of the past. This is not much to be regretted, but more than once it has resulted in fighting . . . Now the greeting is a nod or a shake of the head.[54]

In addition, it was by this time 'no easy matter to get up a rushcart'. In Bamford's Middleton, free materials and communal effort were drawn upon, but all over south-east Lancashire, would-be rushbearers found these commodities harder to come by. Horses and cart might have to be hired; rushes became scarce as marshland was drained, and then farmed or built over, and youths were paid to go long distances to collect them, even in relatively rural Saddleworth; and the services of the declining number of skilled rushcart builders became harder to come by, their fees rising to £1 or more.[55] With the customary patronage of local gentry dead now that most had left the area, getting money from wealthier patrons in Oldham meant putting on a display which would appeal to respectable sentiment.[56] The black-faced grotesques and the fife and drum were replaced by neatly-turned-out morris dancers and brass bands, and the 'men-horses' by real horses. Whip-cracking also seems, oddly enough, to have been a dying art, and a new whip and expert cracker could also cost money. All the participants expected their share of the takings, while the cost soared. A rushcart at Hebers in 1867 cost £7, one at Uppermill in 1890 cost £9, and one otherwise successful rushcart at Hollinwood 'cost so much money that no further attempt at a revival was ever made'. As with other leisure activities, the publican became an important figure, offering money, organising ability, and space in which to build the rushcart. The policing arrangements for Oldham Wakes in 1864 show that at least six out of the eight carts started out at pubs, all of them coming from built-up areas within about half a mile of the town centre.[57]

One reaction to the cost and difficulty of getting up rushcarts was to build smaller ones. Known as 'Adam and Eve carts' or 'grove carts', these had modest traditional precedents, and became increasingly common in the Oldham area as the true rushcart died out during the 1860s. At Oldham Wakes in 1870, for example, there was only one decent attempt at a rushcart – 'all the others were mere abortions'. All the same, this demonstrated the strength of a custom which was kept up even when the means were lacking. Morris dancers increasingly went about collecting money on their own, like those at the Volunteer Inn when their rushcart was banned in 1861, and by the 1890s all that was left of the custom in Oldham itself was the groups of children displaying garlands and decorated handcarts for money to spend at the fair.[58]

Overall, then, the rushcart became an object of commercial display, the product of specific initiatives rather than communal organisation, and embodying traditionalist sentiment rather than living custom. Its symbolism remained popularly understood, and continued, as with the old loom and coal carts, to be put to use, apparently by the town's upper classes as well as its workers. The initials of Sir Robert Peel appeared on one Oldham rushcart in 1850. In 1863, during a controversy over the workhouse test, there appeared 'a "dirt cart"', attended by men employed in the removal of earth under the directions of the famine relief committee'. Six years later the town's cotton waste dealers exhibited a 'Willower's and Mixers' flock cart', made of cotton waste – custom moving with the times indeed.[59] In 1864, when it seemed that Hollinwood Wakes was losing support before the superior pull of Oldham Wakes, 'the publicans ... subscribed handsomely' for a rushcart to restore interest in the occasion, and there was similarly a revival of rushcarts at local wakes all round Oldham in 1879 when it was feared that a change in the date of Oldham Wakes would result in a more general absorption.[60] In Saddleworth, the old–style rushbearing still flourished in the 1860s, and was documented as it survived in the 1880s by the folklorist Alfred Burton. By this time, the custom was suffering from the decline of the old skills, but it continued unbroken into the twentieth century, and there are still occasional revivals today.[61] The survival of an enthusiastically-supported rushcart tradition in industrial Lancashire for long after it had lost its original social context must surely count as an outstanding example of 'the defence of custom'.

V

It was not the coming of the railways but the rise of the prolonged seaside holiday which brought about the decline of the locally-based wakes in the Oldham area. The number of trips lasting from four to seven days at Oldham Wakes slowly overhauled that of day excursions in the 1870s, and in 1896 some eighty thousand people were returning to the town at the end of wakes week. The range and extent of holidays on offer multiplied: Hargreaves the travel agency started three-day trips to London in 1871 and trips to Paris in 1878; special tickets to all parts of the country were regularly available in the 1880s; in 1896 'almost all the European capitals were visited by the ubiquitous Wakes tripper'; and in 1910 one agent, perhaps more in search of publicity than of custom, advertised 'Pekin in 14 days; Tokyo in 17 days; passengers leave Oldham (Clegg St) 2.42pm'. For the great majority, though, seaside resorts remained favourite, and dozens of trains departed for the coast, the first ones soon after 3 a.m. For one week every year Blackpool became 'Oldham-by-the-Sea'.[62] Oldham Wakes spread still further afield; they were celebrated by local troops at Cawnpore in 1879; and in a well-organised manner by cotton famine migrants in New Jersey as late as 1888.

The rise in the number of tourist class bookings in the 1870s was the result, in the first instance, of the 'going-off club system', whose rise in Oldham was concurrent with that of the week-long wakes trip.[63] Oldham was a town where real wages were well above the Lancashire average, where the institutions of thrift – building societies, friendly societies, 'permanent money clubs' and Co-operative societies – were particularly well-developed, and where 'everybody who could afford it' was a shareholder in the limited liability movement.[64] Although 'the vast majority of the juvenile proletariat' were attending Sunday school by 1850, the level of religious observance remained low, reflecting, perhaps, a tendency for the working class to adopt respectable values and institutions as it suited them. In 1888, according to *Co-Operative News*, Oldham had 'a well-employed and stable population. Independence and self-respect abound'; there are echoes here of the more turbulent independence of three generations before.[65] The informal 'shaking clubs' of the 1830s, as mentioned above, may have provided a precedent of sorts for the going-off clubs, the first of which in Oldham began at Werneth Spindle Works in 1871 or before. Employees saved for fifty weeks at 6*d* a share for a 25*s* per share payout at the wakes, totalling over £1,000. Clubs on this principle appeared in their hundreds after this, organised by factories, workshops, clubs, schools, political societies, pubs and streets. The estimated total payout at Oldham Wakes rose to £10,000 in 1877, £60,000 in 1884 and £175,000 in 1900 – roughly £1 per head of the population. The average payout of the clubs grew from £200–£300 in 1884 to £600 in 1900, with little difference in size on the whole between the various types of club.[66] Small local clubs played an important role throughout, and the size and number of those run from pubs, streets and small workshops relative to those run from mills and large institutions actually increased during this period. This was partly because strikes in the engineering industry in 1885 and 1897 set workers against saving directly with their employers; the massive club at Platt's engineering works, whose payout of over £19,000 in 1884 required thirty secretaries to administer it, never really recovered from this double setback. Employers encouraged the clubs, with Platt's allowing loans during the year against the amounts invested, but nearly all the clubs, large and small, paid dividends. Very many reinvested their money in the companies, though by 1895 the town's three major breweries were getting over half the total.[67]

London reporters observing this phenomenon complained that Oldham people saved only to spend, which was 'thrift of a sort, but hardly of the right sort'. The *Oldham Chronicle* defended its readership, enthusing about 'the power of the penny'. Although payouts of £20 or even £30 to individuals were not uncommon, much of this was spent on the seasonal renewal of clothes and furniture; 'many a thrifty wife' invested in the going-off clubs, as well as brides-to-be. The wakes savings clubs clearly represented a great advance in financial prudence over the profligate habits of earlier in the century. Their basic effect, however, was to increase the scale of spending on both pleasures and processions, and increasingly to insulate it from the effects of the trade cycle. The going-off clubs institutionalised the annual wakes spree.[68]

The extended cheap trip also lengthened the wakes holiday. The Werneth Spindle Works, home of the town's first going-off club, was giving a week as early as 1872, and this became general in the area in the later 1880s, with official recognition lagging behind actual practice because of the prevalence of 'running-off'. The extra days seem to have been gained during depression years and held during good ones, with the new limiteds being more inclined than the private companies to close to limit production. The views of the limiteds became irresistible, and a fortnight's break became increasingly usual between 1890 and 1910.[69]

Another result of this prolonged exodus was the decline of local celebrations at the various wakes in the Oldham area. The wakes fair on Oldham's Tommyfield was becoming 'more popular by the year' in 1895 by virtue of the trainloads of visitors who came from all over the country. Smaller wakes fairs (such as that in Delph, whose date clashed with that of Oldham) suffered by comparison.[70] Tommyfield was (and still is) Oldham's central market ground, preserved by virtue of the tolls it brought to the council, but in other places, such as Delph, Hollinwood and Newton Heath, fairs were moved from place to place, as their sites were built over and as local boards imposed restrictions on street stalls.[71] The attraction of Oldham Wakes took its toll. In the 1880s, mills at Hollinwood, Lees, Failsworth and Newton Heath began to close for Oldham Wakes rather than their own.[72] People were increasingly less likely to find their friends at home at their own wakes and increasingly likely to find them on a cheap trip at Oldham Wakes, so the centralising process fed itself, but local wakes survived as holidays all the same.[73] In Royton, Shaw, Saddleworth and Middleton these were kept up past the end of the century, and the going-off clubs timed their payouts accordingly. In Hollinwood, the ever-durable local side of the wakes seems actually to have revived once the town started taking its trips with Oldham a month later.[74]

VI

The continuing place of the locally-based wakes was demonstrated in 1879–82 by the successful popular resistance to an attempt to amalgamate them all with Oldham Wakes.[75] The moving force behind the change was Edward Ingham, an engineer and freethinker who had been involved in the Young Oldham movement, part of the Liberal resurgence which had ousted the radicals from power in 1847–9. He was chairman of the School Board, and a leading figure in the Co-operative movement, in Henshaw Street Mutual Improvement Society, and no doubt also in the local branches of the Amalgamated Society of Engineers; all of these bodies pressed for the wakes reform, along with the Oldham Master Cotton Spinners' Association and a number of trade union branches, friendly societies and mills.[76] The reasons for the change were straightforward enough. The School Board initiated it, for the staggered wakes in the Oldham area made enforcing school attendance in the summer almost impossible. Children playing in the street lied to the inspectors about which wakes they were supposed to be observing, and 'large grants of money now depended on the regular attendance of scholars'. Employers had problems with workers continually running off to out-township wakes, either to visit friends and relatives or simply to keep each other company; this was said to be particularly damaging in large modern factories which drew their labour force from a wide area.[77] It was hoped that moving Oldham Wakes from the last to the first Saturday in August, thus placing it in the middle of the wakes season rather than at the end, would enable it to absorb the surrounding wakes and so establish a single summer holiday for the whole area.

The public arguments of the reformers, though, were less than open. The agitation proceeded by means of a petition representing (and misrepresenting) the views of the twenty-six thousand people who were members of the organisations which signed it. A town meeting carried a motion 'to change the time of holding the annual wakes from the last to the first Saturday in August each year'. The arguments of the reformers about economic efficiency were disguised under a general appeal to 'progress'. 'The entire social system', and with it 'the object of the Wakes holiday', 'had changed . . . The people of Oldham were too busy building mills instead of building rushcarts', and the wakes was now 'essentially a going-off season'. Much was made of the social value of the whole area going off on holiday together, and of the better weather in early August. The Council agreed and, citing as its authority the clause in the 1865 Improvement Act which allowed it to vary the date of fairs within the borough, voted to move the wakes forward a month.[78]

The new wakes took place as planned; and it poured. There was a widespread feeling that 'the School Board Wakes wur as weet as every Owdham Wakes had bin' and that 'the wakes has been removed to suit the convenience of a few'. But the mills closed on the new date, the going-off clubs paid out accordingly, and so the change was a qualified success. At Crompton, Lees and Royton, the local wakes clashed with Oldham's new wakes and were 'a dead letter'. At Shaw, Mossley and Hollinwood, where the mills closed for Oldham Wakes, local festivities supported by publicans and traders were vigorously kept up on the customary local dates; 'Bill's o' Tom's', the old Heyside rushcart builder, found his services in heavy demand. Taking place further afield and later in August, Saddleworth Wakes and Newton Heath Wakes were unaffected. The new Oldham Wakes might have stuck and the old local ones might, as they eventually did, have withered but for the extraordinary decision of the Finance Committee, greedy for extra rent, to let the fairground to showmen on the date of the old wakes as well. This effectively scuppered their earlier commitment to the new wakes, but they pretended not to notice. 'They knew nothing about the Wakes; they only let the stalls' said one alderman. 'We don't object to receiving £250 ground rent' added another. Although only a few mills closed, the old wakes was observed on a large scale in 1879 and, despite record railway traffic on the new date, in the two following years as well.[79]

It was becoming clear to even the most committed of reformers that the old wakes were socially entrenched; all they had done was to create a problem bigger than the one they were trying to solve. In June 1882 the Council received another petition 'very well signed by influential gentlemen' and was forced to call a town meeting to restore the old wakes. 'If they retained the new wakes they would always have two wakes, because the majority of the people of Oldham would keep the old Wakes whatever time was fixed', said one councillor. 'If the new wakes were wet, people would certainly fetch up with the old Wakes when it was fine', said the Mayor, adding gloomily that 'there were very many people in the town who were anxious to have two holidays'. A week later, in a town hall overflowing with an excited working-class crowd and positively bursting with traditionalist feeling, the reformers publicly conceded defeat. 'People in the outlying districts ... had not been as complaisant as expected' explained one, apologetically. Speaker after speaker derided the earlier arguments about better weather and rational family recreation. Many people, it was insisted, could not afford to go off, especially with only two months to save up after Whitsun, and those that could found the boarding houses packed at the height of the season;[80] Lancashire's resort facilities had evolved because of the wakes system to meet a holiday demand staggered over the whole summer. Besides, local traders lost nearly a month off the end of their summer season – no one bought new things after the wakes.[81] The meeting consigned the contemptuously termed 'School Board Wakes' to oblivion by 750 votes to 50.

The importance of this episode, whose many and complex ingredients can only be hinted at here, was that it demonstrated that the functions of the old system of staggered local wakes were still very much alive, and that they were most vigorously alive in the collective mind of those who celebrated them. Although the wakes in the townships round Oldham were already starting to decline before the demand of thousands of individuals for seaside holidays, they were strongly defended against any attempt at control or abolition from above. The *Oldham Standard* (always traditionalist but, like the *Chronicle*, an initial supporter of the abortive change) shared these sentiments: 'Dear old Tommyfield, with its crowds of noisy joyous revellers! May its attraction never diminish! May its shadow never grow less!' The reporter might almost have been crying into his beer.[82]

All this should warn us against supposing that because their local attractions eventually succumbed before the superior temptations of the seaside, the Lancashire wakes were thus somehow 'killed'. On the contrary, they flourished in their new setting as the fairground amusements of the wakes migrated to the coast with their patrons, bringing with them many familiar nuisances. Lancashire's working class found Blackpool's character as a town 'friendly and homely', and whole streets of people from the cotton towns transported themselves there *en bloc* at the wakes, entertaining each other in turn at their respective boarding houses, just as they had once done at home: 'when Oldham goes abroad at Wakes Week, it is Oldham still'.[83] It has been suggested that occasions such as Lancashire's wakes were 'carnivalesque'; that is, that they represented a temporary inversion of normal values.[84] This may have been true relative to the values of respectable observers, but such judgements surely underestimate the degree of colour in ordinary working-class culture. 'Oldham operatives do not change their characteristics because they turn their backs on the mills for a week ... The vigour they have previously thrown into work they immediately fling into play.'[85] At Oldham's wakes, the more positive and joyous features of working-class life were magnified, and this expression was achieved using the infrastructure of everyday life, whether in the communal enterprise of the rushcart or in the communal enterprise of the going-off club. The wakes was a release of energy, certainly; not, however, a negative but rather an affirmative one. The *Oldham Standard*'s description of Mossley Wakes in 1866 might almost equally have applied to Oldham in 1800 or 'Oldham-by-the-Sea' in 1900:

A wakes is something like a medley on singing – a confused mass. Everybody is clever, from the street sweeper to the parish beadle. What makes people so clever but the libations they take: a sort of false glory. It is a rendezvous for the maimed, the halt and the blind; it is a sort of natural almshouse, where everybody gets relief who is worthy, and many who are not pass in the multitude of sinners.[86]

NOTES

1 J. Porter, *History of the Fylde of Lancashire* (Blackpool, 1876), pp. 98–9; D. J. Clark, 'Annual holidays in Puritan England', unpublished dissertation, University of Kent, 1971, p. 24 and chapter 5; E. P. Thompson, *The Making of the English Working Class* (1963; Penguin edn 1968), pp. 41–56. The word 'wakes' is both singular and plural.

2 E. P. Thompson, 'Time, work discipline and industrial capitalism', *Past and Present* 38 (December 1967), pp. 76, 84; H. Cunningham, *Leisure in the Industrial Revolution* (1980), pp. 61–2; Royal Commission on the Employment of Children in Mines and Manufactories, *Parliamentary Papers* 1842, XV, p. 123; J. K. Walton, 'The demand for working-class seaside holidays in Victorian England', *Economic History Review* 2nd series, XXXIV (1981), pp. 253–8; N. McKendrick, 'Josiah Wedgwood and factory discipline', *Historical Journal* 4. I (1961), p. 46; J. K. Walton, *The Blackpool Landlady* (Manchester, 1978), pp. 33–6.

3 Cunningham, p. 58. This observation, and the argument of this paper, conflict, however, with the statement on p. 62 that 'By mid-century, custom was only dimly, if nostalgically, remembered'.

4 North and west Lancashire were not without their annual festivals, but they tended to be fewer and took place more on fairs or 'club days'. In north-east Lancashire, the wakes were known as 'rushbearings', after the wakes custom described below.

5 Cunningham, chapter 2; Thompson, *Making*, pp. 441–51.

6 J. Foster, *Class Struggle in the Industrial Revolution* (1974), p. 24.

7 E. Butterworth, *Historical Sketches of Oldham* (Oldham, 1847), pp. 160–1, 218–28; E. Butterworth, *Historical Sketches of Oldham* (2nd edn, Oldham, 1856), p. 243; R. N. S. Angus, 'The Co-operative Movement in Oldham, 1850–1900', unpublished M.A. dissertation, University of Lancaster, 1979, p. 4.

8 P. Joyce, *Work, Society and Politics* (Brighton, 1980), pp. 8 and 20; Foster, pp. 8–13; D. Foster, 'Class and county government in early nineteenth century Lancashire', *Northern History* IX (1974), p. 51; E. Butterworth (1847), pp. 220–1; A. B. Reach, *Manchester and the Textile Districts in 1849*, ed. C. Aspin (Helmshore, 1972), pp. 79–80.

9 Thompson, *Making*, p. 446; E. Butterworth (1847), pp. 174, 192; J. L. and B. Hammond, *The Age of the Chartists* (1930), p. 112; J. Butterworth, *History of Oldham* (Oldham, 1826), p. 84.

10 E. Butterworth (1847), pp. 149, 166–7, 252; R. A. Sykes, 'Some aspects of working-class consciousness in Oldham, 1830–1842', *Historical Journal* 23. i (1980), pp. 173–6.

11 See section VI below.

12 'B. Grime', 'Oldham fifty years ago', part VI, *Oldham Chronicle* (henceforth *OC*), 30 August 1884.

13 Joseph Bradbury, *Saddleworth Sketches* (Oldham, 1871), p. 256.

14 G. Perry-Gore, *St Mary's, Oldham* (Oldham, 1906), pp. 27–8, 31, 50; G. Shaw, *Local Notes and Gleanings: Oldham and Neighbourhood* (Oldham, 1877), vol. I, p. 79; *A Souvenir of the Bazaar Held at St John's Schools, Hey . . . 1905* (Oldham, 1905), p. 39. Oldham Church was floored with rushes until 1801, Newton Heath Church until 1808, and Saddleworth Church until 1826: H. Bateson, *A History of Oldham* (repr. Dewsbury, 1974), pp. 70–1; 'Rushbearing at Newton Heath', undated cutting, Oldham Local Interest Centre (henceforth OLIC); A. J. Howcroft, *History of the Chapelry and Church of Saddleworth* (Oldham, 1915), p. 38.

15 Samuel Bamford, *Early Days* (1848–9; repr. London, 1967), pp. 146–56.

16 E. Butterworth, diary (OLIC), August 1831; 'B. Grime', *op. cit.*; William Rowbottom, diary (OLIC), August 1800 – editor's comment; *Bolton Chronicle*, 11 September 1840.

17 Bradbury, *op. cit.*, pp. 253–4; Bamford, *op. cit.*, p. 147; Rowbottom diary, *passim*.

18 J. Butterworth, *History of Oldham* (2nd edn., Oldham, 1826), p. 98. There is unfortunately no room to reproduce here his account of one satirically conceived rushcart produced by the bell-ringers of Oldham in protest against an unfair decision in a contest against those of Ashton.

19 Rowbottom diary, August 1793, August 1826; *OC*, 7 September 1861, 6 September 1862; E. Butterworth diary, August 1835, August 1836, August 1837. 'Up and down fighting' was the Lancashire method of fighting with both fist and clog.

20 Rowbottom diary, August 1811; Butterworth diary, August 1842.

21 Rowbottom diary, December 1808, December 1811, December 1812.

22 Rowbottom diary, August 1800, December 1800, August 1811, December 1808, August 1801, May 1809 (Oldham Fair). (Oldham's fairs were of very little recreational importance beside the wakes.)

23 E.g. M. Hodgson, 'The working day and the working week in Victorian Britain', unpublished M.Phil. thesis, University of London, 1974, p. 242; K. Allan, 'The recreations and amusements of the industrial working class in the second quarter of the nineteenth century, with special reference to Lancashire', unpublished M.A. thesis, University of Manchester, 1947, pp. 104–11.

24 Rowbottom diary, August 1797, August 1815, August 1809.

25 Cunningham, *op. cit.*, p. 72.

26 Samuel Riley in *The Itinerant*, quoted by Ammon Wrigley, *Those were the Days* (Stalybridge, 1937), p. 65.

27 Butterworth diary, August 1830 (at Hollinwood and Royley, during Oldham Wakes), July 1833 (Hollinwood Wakes); Shaw, *op. cit.*, pp. 78–81 (Mossley, Lees and Hey 1835, Lydgate 1833); A. Holt, *The Story of Mossley* (Manchester, 1926), p. 117 (Lydgate 1849); *An Act for Paving . . . etc. Oldham, 1826* (OLIC), p. 65.

28 J. Butterworth, *op. cit.*, p. 86; Reach, *op. cit.*, p. 79; E. Butterworth diary, August 1834, July 1833. 'Duck swimming' was a sort of substitute blood sport

which involved sending dogs into a pond to catch ducks, usually without success.

29 Compare Mass Observation's conclusions about 'the democracy of drinking' and the uncompetitive pastimes which characterised Bolton pub life in the 1930s; Mass Observation, *The Pub and the People* (1943, repr. Welwyn, 1970), pp. 301–2, 312–13.

30 Butterworth diary, August 1834, August 1835, August 1837.

31 'Notes and Queries' (OLIC), 17 June 1879; Butterworth diary, 1831; *OC*, 7 September 1861, 3 September 1864; and see below.

32 Butterworth diary, August 1834, August 1835, August 1838, August 1840. There was clearly working-class involvement in some of these alternative wakes campaigns, but how much can only be speculated. Radicals in nearby Rochdale opposed the Tory-organised 'Nudger Sports' as debasing, and an attempt to defuse unrest; twenty years later, Milnrow's Sunday school teachers campaigned against rushcarts with missionary fervour. In Oldham, the (Chartist) 'Socialist Institution' had 'wholesome recreation' as one of its purposes (T. R. Tholfsen, *Working Class Radicalism in Mid-Victorian England* (1976), p. 131). In the late 1840s, there was the progressive, reforming 'Young Oldham' movement; one of its leaders was Edward Ingham, a skilled engineer and prominent Co-Operator, who later led the unpopular attempt to 'rationalise' the area's wakes in 1879–82 (see below).

33 Butterworth diary, July 1831 (Hollinwood Wakes), August 1834 (Oldham Wakes), August 1835 ('Provincial Rushbearings'), August 1836 (Oldham Wakes).

34 B. Harrison, *Drink and the Victorians* (1971), p. 330.

35 T. A. Fletcher, *The First Railway to Oldham* (1972); J. Marshall, *The Lancashire and Yorkshire Railway* (Newton Abbot, 1971); *Manchester Examiner* (henceforth *MEx*), 5 September 1846; Walton, *Blackpool Landlady*, pp. 15–16; *OC*, 4 September 1858, 1 September 1860.

36 *OC*, 31 August 1872 (Middleton Wakes); *Oldham Standard* (henceforth *OS*), 4 September 1869, 26 August 1882; *OC* 6 September 1862, 3 September 1864, 1 September 1877, 2 September 1882; Walton, 'Holidays', pp. 252–8.

37 *OC*, 14 September 1858.

38 Royal Commission on the Employment of Children in Mines and Manufactories, *Parliamentary Papers* 1842, XV, p. 124; *OC* 1 September 1860; Walton, 'Holidays', p. 255.

39 *OC*, 1 August 1863; see also *OC*, 9 June 1862 (Lees and Hey Wakes), 1 August 1885 (Hollinwood Wakes).

40 M. Anderson, *Family Structure in Nineteenth Century Lancashire* (Cambridge, 1971); *MEx* 5 September 1846; compare P. Bailey, *Leisure and Class in Victorian England* (1978), pp. 14–15, for a similar effect in Bolton.

41 *OS*, 28 July 1860; *OC*, 31 August 1861 (Saddleworth Wakes), 28 August 1869, 16 August 1879 (letter); *MEx* 5 September 1846.

42 *OC*, 28 July 1866 (Mossley Wakes), 31 August 1888 (Saddleworth Wakes), 28 August 1858.

43 *OC*, 30 July 1864 (Hollinwood Wakes); see also Ammon Wrigley, *Old Saddleworth Days* (Oldham, 1920), pp. 100–10, for a rather romantic account of an 'old-style' wakes in a semi-rural parish.

44 W. Bates, *The Handy Book of Oldham* (Oldham, 1877), pp. 39-41; *OC*, 7 September 1861, 3 September 1870, 4 September 1875, 1 September 1877 (Volunteers camps at Oldham Wakes).

45 I. Stansmore, *English Fairs* (1975), pp. 46-51; *OC* 11 August 1866 (Lees Wakes), 3 September 1864. This may mark the introduction of chips, which had become an inseparable part of Saddleworth Wakes in the 1880s, when they were sold as 'A1 potato chips, fried in the London style': *OC*, 1 August 1883, 24 August 1886.

46 *OC*, 5 September 1863, 5 September 1868, 5 September 1859 (Oldham Wakes), 1 August 1855 (Lees Wakes).

47 *OC*, 29 July 1872 (Mossley Wakes), 26 August 1882 (Newton Heath Wakes), 30 August 1887 (Oldham Wakes - socialists *v.* missionaries), 6 September 1884, 9 August 1879.

48 Butterworth diary, August 1836.

49 *OC*, 11 May 1946; Rowbottom diary, August 1829; Butterworth diary, August 1830; 'B. Grime', *op. cit.*

50 Reach, *op. cit.*, p. 79; *MEx* 12 January 1850; *A Souvenir of the Bazaar Held at St John's Schools, Hey*, pp. 35-6.

51 Foster, *op. cit*, pp. 56-61; *Oldham Jubilee of Incorporation Souvenir* (Oldham, 1899), p. 15; *MEx*, 31 August 1847, 2 September 1848, 3 September 1849, 4 September 1850, 3 September 1851. When large numbers of rushcarts like this appear at the wakes, it is unlikely that they were all full, traditional rushcarts; most were probably smaller and merely symbolic in character.

52 *OC*, 1 September 1855, 5 September 1863, 10 August 1861 (Town Council), 7 September 1861.

53 R. D. Storch, 'The plague of blue locusts', *International Review of Social History* XX (1975), pp. 61-90; 'The problem of working class leisure', in A. P. Donajgrodzki (ed.), *Social Control in Nineteenth-Century Britain*, pp. 138-62; *Oldham Jubilee Souvenir 1899*, p. 5; D. Taylor, *999 and all that* (Oldham, 1968), chapters 5 and 7; *OC*, 3 September 1864; OLIC News cuttings, vol. III, p. 118 (n.d., 1879).

54 *OC*, 3 September 1864.

55 *OC*, 3 September 1870 (Oldham Wakes), 24 August 1878 (Saddleworth Wakes); 'Rushbearing at Hebers', *OS*, 26 August 1865; Alfred Burton, *Rushbearing* (Manchester, 1891), p. 90.

56 Foster, *op cit.*, p. 82.

57 See e.g. Butterworth diary, August 1835; Wrigley, *Old Saddleworth Days*, pp. 104-6; Burton, *Rushbearing*, pp. 81-8; Ben Brierley, *Home Memoirs and Recollections of a Life* (Manchester, 1886), p. 46; *OS* 26 August 1865; *OC*, 3 September 1864.

58 *OC*, 5 September 1863, 3 September 1870, 7 September 1861, 2 September 1905.

59 *MEx*, 4 September 1850; *OC*, 5 September 1863; *OS*, 4 September 1869.

60 *OS*, 30 July 1864, 3 September 1864; see also *OS*, 23 July 1870, 30 July 1870, 13 August 1870, 27 August 1870, with Shaw Wakes threatened; and see below.

61 *OC*, 31 August 1861 carries a good account; Burton, *Rushbearing*, pp. 81-8.

62 *OC*, 1 September 1877, 7 September 1896, 7 September 1872, 7 September 1878, 14 September 1878; *OS*, 2 September 1896; *OC*, 20 August 1910, 2 September 1895; *OS*, 3 September 1898; T. Webb, *Memorable Dates of Long Ago* (OLIC cuttings, n.d.); *OC*, 27 August 1888.

63 *OC*, 1 September 1877.

64 Angus, *op. cit.* (note 7), pp. 9-10, 47; Bates, *op. cit.*, p. 120; Foster, *op. cit.*, pp. 221-4. Perhaps Bates had the going-off clubs in mind when he made his statement about popular shareholding in limited companies.

65 C. E. Ward, 'Education as social control: Sunday schools in Oldham 1780-1850', unpublished M.A. dissertation, University of Lancaster, 1975, p. 52; Angus, *op. cit.*, pp. 11-12; *Co-Operative News*, 7 April 1888, quoted in Angus, p. 10.

66 *OC*, 7 September 1872, 25 August 1877, 30 August 1884, 25 August 1900. These averages do not include the two giant clubs run at Platt's and Lees', the engineering works, which were exceptional. Platt's in particular seems to have acted both as a large going-off club and as an investment bank for small going-off clubs.

67 *OC*, 26 August 1886; *OS*, 3 September 1898; *OC*, 30 August 1884, 31 August 1895.

68 *OC*, 30 August 1890, 26 August 1899, 3 September 1889 (Milnrow Wakes), 25 August 1900; compare Walton, *Blackpool Landlady*, p. 33.

69 *OC*, 14 August 1886; 18 August 1900 (Middleton and Shaw Wakes); Walton, 'Holidays', p. 256. This conflicts with the suggestion that the extra days were won by 'running off' in good years and held on to by extended stoppages in bad years. The point is perhaps academic; both factors must have operated.

70 *OC*, 7 September 1895, 7 September 1861, 5 September 1863 (Delph Wakes).

71 *OC*, 1 September 1883, 29 August 1885 (Delph Wakes); *OS*, 29 July 1882; *OC*, 31 July 1886, 2 August 1890 (Hollinwood Wakes), 25 August 1877, 24 August 1889 (Newton Heath Wakes).

72 *OC*, 27 August 1887 (Hollinwood Wakes), 11 August 1883, 4 August 1886 (Lees Wakes), 18 August 1888 (Newton Heath Wakes). By 1890, Newton Heath, midway between Oldham and Manchester, had switched to the Manchester system of Bank holidays – *OC*, 30 August 1890.

73 *OC*, 25 August 1900 (Royton, Shaw, Saddleworth and Middleton Wakes), 5 August 1905, 6 August 1910 (Royton Wakes), 19 August 1905, 13 August 1910 (Shaw Wakes).

74 *OC*, 27 July 1905, 30 July 1910 (Hollinwood Wakes).

75 Stockport underwent a similarly abortive experiment in 1884-7, but the amalgamation of Tunstall, Burslem and Hanley Wakes in the Potteries succeeded in 1879. In Birmingham, the suppression of the Birmingham fairs in 1875 was only partially successful, but revealed 'the repressive underside of the "civic gospel"'. *Stockport Advertiser*, 1884-7, *passim*; Walton, 'Holidays', p. 261; D. Reid, 'Popular culture and the march of progress: the wakes and fairs of Birmingham', in R. D. Storch (ed.), *Popular Culture and Custom in Nineteenth-Century England* (1982).

76 *OC*, 12 November 1888 (obituary); Foster, *op. cit.*, pp. 222, 228; Angus, *op. cit.*, pp. 42-4, 48; *OC*, 8 March 1879.

77 *OC*, 7 December 1878, 8 February 1879, 3 August 1879; *OS*, 10 August 1862.

78 *OC*, 1 March 1879, 18 January 1879 (editorial), 8 March 1879; *Oldham Borough Improvement Act, 1865*, pp. 47–8.

79 *The General Advertiser* (Oldham), Nos. 6 and 9 (August/September 1879); *OS*, 9 August 1879, 16 August 1879, 30 August 1879, 16 September 1879, 23 September 1879, 7 August 1880, 14 August 1880, 21 August 1880; *OC*, 19 July 1879, 9 August 1879, 30 August 1879, 7 August 1880, 14 August 1880, 21 August 1880, 4 September 1880, 11 August 1881, 30 August 1881. The decision to let Tommyfield for the old wakes was also made in 1881 – *OC*, 12 August 1881.

80 Walton, *Blackpool Landlady*, pp. 35–40.

81 *OC*, 16 August 1879, 23 August 1879, 6 September 1879; *OS*, 10 June 1882.

82 *OS*, 28 August 1896. There has recently been an interesting postscript to this story. A move by the education committee of Bolton Corporation to amalgamate the schools' two summer holidays into one by staying open during the July 'wakes' fortnight (and thus save on money and administration) has failed, in the face of 'tremendous public pressure to hang onto the traditional trade holiday pattern'. *Bolton Evening News*, 11 July 1981.

83 Walton, *Blackpool Landlady*, pp. 52–7 and chapter 7, *passim*; *OC*, 8 September 1883.

84 Reid, 'Popular culture', *loc. cit.* The distinction postulated here between 'wakes' and 'fairs' in Birmingham is not appropriate to Lancashire, where fairs served as holidays where there were no wakes, as in Blackburn and Burnley, and where the wakes attracted major fairs.

85 *OC*, 29 August 1896.

86 *OS*, 4 August 1866.

6 DAVE RUSSELL

Popular musical culture and popular politics in the Yorkshire textile districts, 1880-1914

THE FAMOUS MELTHAM MILLS BAND, 1878,

With their Set of "Prototype" Instruments

Manufactured by BESSON & CO., 198, Euston Road, London.

In 1897 Count Guiseppe Franchi Verney was sent by the Italian government to investigate musical education in English schools. Verney returned home, impressed not simply by what he had witnessed in the classroom, but by the enthusiasm which the population in general showed for music. He reported that 'there are few countries in the world where music is made the object of such enthusiastic worship. It might almost be said that music is a vital and indispensable element of English life'.[1]

Late Victorian England was indeed, at every social level, an intensely musical place. The concert hall, the music hall, the public house, the parlour, the church, the park and the street were all centres of musical activity. Five hundred thousand copies of Sullivan's ballad *The Lost Chord*, published in 1877, were sold in the next twenty-five years; the number of 'musicians and music masters' recorded in the census returns increased from twenty-five thousand in 1871 to forty-seven thousand in 1911; seventy thousand people watched the 1907 Crystal Palace Brass Band Championships. These bare statistics fail to capture the musical atmosphere of the period, but they help illustrate the enormous contemporary appetite for music.[2]

A substantial part of this enthusiasm for music stemmed from the Victorians', particularly the middle class's, tendency to invest music with an enormous amount of moral and political significance. Music was viewed, amongst other things, as a method of promoting Christianity, temperance, patriotism, even Socialism, as well as being a way of strengthening family ties and developing the character. Certainly, by the Edwardian period, an 'art for art's sake' mentality was beginning to emerge, but the old attitude was still strong. In 1907 supporters of a proposed series of free chamber music concerts for the working class of Bradford justified their case not simply on musical grounds, but because they agreed with local shoe manufacturer William Riley that such concerts would limit the excesses of local courting habits. They would clear the streets of 'the young life of the city ... no one can pass along Market Street and Manningham Lane without feeling that something should be done to correct the evil influences of these parades'.[3]

This chapter, through study of the brass band and choral movements in one area of England, investigates both the relationships between popular music and popular culture, especially *political* culture, that contemporary theorists supposed to have existed, and those relationships that actually emerged. It is by no means easy to establish direct links between leisure experience and political culture and much of the ensuing attempt to explore the connections between popular politics and popular music is tentative but worthwhile speculation. Historians are only just beginning to contemplate the possibility of links between the two subject areas, preferring for the most part to see overtly political and industrial happenings as the key factors in the structuring of working-class consciousness. There is, however, a serious need to investigate the relationship between leisure and politics, which, after all, are not discrete entities but integral parts of the individual's life experience. Recreation, and in this instance popular musical life, was a central part of people's life-style, and the opinions, interests and loyalties that it fostered must have played an important role in shaping their political stances and beliefs, and indeed, in shaping many other aspects of their life.[4]

The bands and choirs of nineteenth- and twentieth-century Britain, along with most aspects of popular music, have been largely ignored by academic historians, yet these organisations occupied such an important place in popular social life that they demand study.[5] People had grouped together to make music for centuries, but the formal musical society with its concerts, committees, rules and membership subscriptions really dates from the first two decades of the nineteenth century. The number of choirs and bands in Britain grew throughout the century, reaching a peak in the 1880s and 1890s, and then declining slightly in the Edwardian period. The exact number of choral societies and brass bands in the country as a whole is unknown. Contemporary estimates vary alarmingly and are of little value. In 1889, for example, *Wright and Round's Amateur Band Teacher's Guide* claimed there were forty thousand amateur wind bands in Britain. However, a few months later, the *Brass Band News*, a weekly journal also published by Wright and Round's, put the number at thirty thousand, thus eliminating ten thousand bands and perhaps two hundred thousand bandsmen![6] All that can be said is that most towns and larger villages had at least one amateur musical body combining to produce a popular musical tradition of great depth and variety.

Certain areas came to enjoy particularly well-developed band and choral traditions, with Yorkshire, Lancashire, Durham, the Potteries and south Wales being the areas most frequently cited by contemporaries as centres of excellence. The West Riding textile district, which forms the focus of this chapter, was an area thought by many to be the musical centre of the nation. Writing in 1834, George Hogarth claimed that 'The spirit of music pervades the people of this district in a manner unknown and unfelt in the rest of our Island'. Throughout the century, singers, composers and music journalists came to similar conclusions.[7]

The Yorkshire textile district forms a distinctive area, roughly six hundred square miles in extent, bounded approximately by Keighley in the north, Leeds in the east, the villages of the Holme Valley in the south and Hebden Bridge in the west.[8] By 1901 it had a population of one and a half million, but although the region contained the large cities of Leeds and Bradford, it should not be viewed as a solidly urban area.

Small towns and industrial villages were more typical of the locality than these cities, and indeed in many of the communities in northern and western parts of the area, the inhabitants, surrounded by desolate Pennine moorland, viewed themselves far more as 'country folk' than as members of an industrial district.

The region's highly-developed musicality seems to have resulted from the interrelation of three factors: the high population which provided a 'market' for local musicians' talent; the presence of many philanthropic and paternalistic employers looking for methods of offering their workforce 'useful' recreation; and perhaps most important of all, the strength of nonconformity in the area. Methodists in particular, with their emphasis upon music as a crucial part of the religious process, did much to elevate its place in local social life. The area produced approximately 240 brass bands and 260 choral societies between 1800 and 1914.[9] Some of these, such as the Black Dyke Mills Band from Queensbury, and the Huddersfield Choral Society, are to this day household names and bywords for musical excellence. In general, it was in the smaller communities where lack of alternative commercial leisure provision, coupled with an intense local pride, created a particularly propitious musical climate, that bands and choirs flourished best. Nowhere was this more apparent than in the industrial villages of the Colne and Holme Valleys, south of Huddersfield. These two areas, with a combined population of only fifty-five thousand people in 1901, produced fifty-six musical societies in the nineteenth century, including some of the most famous organisations of the day.

It is impossible to estimate the exact number of people actively involved in the local musical community. But even if such a task could be undertaken, mere membership figures would tell an incomplete story. Music was not a minority pastime, indulged in only by the active members of the musical societies. Local choirs and bands could generate enormous levels of commitment and enthusiasm. In 1891, for example, a crowd estimated at ten thousand gathered at the village of Denholme to witness a performance by the celebrated Black Dyke Mills Band, and although this was exceptional, audiences several thousand strong were fairly common at open air performances in the late nineteenth century.[10] Moreover, local musicians often became celebrities as a result of their achievements. Saltaire Prize Choir, returning home at 1.30 on Sunday morning after winning a choral competition at Morecambe in 1896, found hundreds gathered at Saltaire Station to welcome them back.[11] The people of Meltham, a village in the Holme Valley, illustrated their appreciation of John Berry, a woollen milner, warpdresser and eventually a small farmer, who had played the cornet with Meltham Mills Brass Band, conducted Meltham Choral Society and founded the Meltham

Philharmonic Orchestra, by presenting him with his portrait in oils, a cloak and an illuminated address.[12] Such respect was perhaps most obvious at death, and crowds estimated at several thousands regularly assembled to mourn the passing of a local musician.[13] Even the street names echoed appreciation of musical culture, as was illustrated by the Handel Streets and Terraces in Bradford, Halifax, Huddersfield and Golcar, Haydn Streets in Halifax and Stanningley, and Mozart Terrace, Slaithwaite.

This vigorous popular musical culture attracted a great deal of moralistic comment and speculation throughout the nineteenth and early twentieth centuries. According to much of the theorising, the brass band and choral movements epitomised the ideal of 'Rational Recreation' and were seen essentially as aiding the creation of a religious, respectable, self-reliant yet collaborationist working population. Choral music had a particular attraction for many reformers of popular social life, because of its very close association with organised religion. Most choirs recruited a large proportion of their members from chapel and church choirs, and thus commentators supposed that choral singers were free of moral taint.[14] More important in their eyes, however, was that much of the choral repertoire took the form of oratorio and cantata, and thus singer and *audience* received direct contact with religious texts. Handel's *Messiah*, the single most popular work in the Victorian choral canon, was held in particular regard. Writing in 1888, the Leeds Borough organist, William Spark, argued that Handel's work, 'has done more to educate musical taste, unclasp the hands of charity, and unfold the mind of God to man, than any other composition, save the Bible itself'.[15]

Political as well as spiritual benefits were expected to flow from the choral movement. In this instance, however, it was the social structure of the choir rather than the content of the repertoire that was held to be important. The choral society, particularly the large bodies of great prestige such as the Huddersfield Choral Society, the Leeds Philharmonic and the Bradford Festival Choral Society, which specialised in performing oratorio before audiences of often over a thousand people, seemed to have considerable success in crossing class barriers. A detailed analysis of the social structure of the Huddersfield Choral Society and the Leeds Philharmonic Society in 1894–5 shows that both choirs attracted a broad-based membership with singers coming from the skilled worker, the lower middle and the 'substantial' middle class in roughly equal proportions.[16] This situation is almost certainly an illustration of the choral tradition's close association with the religious community. Because the majority of societies drew their performing members from local chapel and church choirs they reflected the social structure of contemporary religion, attracting singers along a broad spectrum reaching from the skilled working class to the upper reaches of the middle class. Although by the late Edwardian period the number of upper-middle-class males in the choral movement appears to have been falling rapidly, throughout the period as a whole, the larger societies served as that Victorian ideal – the pan-class recreational institution. Thus in the early twentieth century, J. J. Percy Kent, M.A. (Cantab), private resident of Headingley, one of Leeds's most salubrious suburbs, had amongst his neighbours in the ranks of tenors at Leeds Philharmonic rehearsals and concerts, R. J. Ellis, 'hardware dealer', Benjamin Bray, 'working jeweller', and Edwin Bramley, 'machinist'.[17] Similarly, in the Huddersfield Choral Society, Miss M. B. Sykes of 'Roundfield', Imperial Road, Edgerton, daughter of one of the town's most prosperous woollen manufacturers, rubbed shoulders with Mrs Hartley of 69 Prospect Street, whose husband was a plumber. Great hopes of class reconciliation were built on this situation.[18] Writing in 1907, Samuel Midgley, a Bradford music teacher and chamber musician, claimed that 'those who are aquainted with our West Yorkshire choral societies know how it brings all classes together, making them one of heart and mind; woolcomber and master, scavenger and professional man all meet and rub shoulders together, and by so doing learn to appreciate each other in a way that is good for all'.[19]

The brass band, too, had many supporters amongst the middle classes of the textile region, being, according to the Bingley manufacturer Jonathon Knowles, an institution that 'improved both body and mind.'[20] The middle classes did not become active performing members as they did in the choral movement, but most bands could rely on financial and sometimes organisational assistance from the wealthier parts of the neighbourhood.[21] Of critical importance in this respect were those employers who actually supported bands in their workplace. It is important to appreciate that works bands were not typical of the band movement. There has been a tendency by some writers to view the whole band tradition as the invention of the employing classes, but in fact, even in West Yorkshire, where works bands were fairly common, only forty of the two hundred and forty bands which existed in the nineteenth and early twentieth century were directly connected with a particular workplace.[22] Nevertheless, these bands are of great importance partly because the financial advantages they received enabled several of them to rise to national pre-eminence in the band world, and because they do illustrate the Victorian attempt to use popular music in a political manner.

Works bands tended to emerge in firms which already enjoyed a certain reputation for paternalism, such as Sir Titus Salt's Saltaire Mills at his model village near Bradford, the Ackroyd Carpet Factory in Halifax and John Foster's Black Dyke Mills at Queensbury.[23] It should be stressed that manufacturers rarely elaborated on their decision to fund brass bands. Essentially, the band appears to have been seen as a way of maintaining influence on the local community, through the exercise of benevolence, and as a method of controlling individual members of the workforce. The Edwardian musical writer W. J. Galloway explained how bandsmen were often found jobs: 'with the assumption that misconduct or incompetence meant dismissal . . . [thus] musical proficiency, acquiring a direct economic value, acts as a powerful inducement to commercial industry, efficiency and good conduct'.[24]

To do justice to the majority of employers, it is probable that musical considerations did play a part in the thought of at least some of them. John Foster, for example, had been a French horn player in a village band; William Marriner of Keighley, whose mill sponsored a band throughout the century, was a keen cornetist; Samson Fox, the guiding hand behind the highly successful Leeds Forge Band in the 1880s, was enough of a musical enthusiast to provide £45,000 towards premises for the Royal College of Music.[25] While it would perhaps be rather romantic to claim that the sole aim of these manufacturers was a desire to further music in their locality, their decision to make music a part of their paternalist machinery may have been influenced by their love of the art.

Significantly, this potentially de-radicalising aspect of banding was reinforced from within the band movement itself. By the mid-1890s, the band movement was served by three publications: *Wright and Round's Brass Band News* (1881), the *British Bandsman* (1887) and *The Cornet* (1893). All three of these journals were produced by brass band music publishing houses who, believing that in order to achieve maximum development the movement had to cross social and political frontiers, preached a doctrine of political neutrality.[26] Bandsmen were encouraged to see themselves as 'bandsmen' above all else. Thus, the 1893 coal strike was viewed as a tragedy for the band movement, rather than as an important event in the history of labour.

> The great coal strike has naturally spread its devastating influence among several brass bands in mining districts. From what we hear, the pinch of poverty has wrought sad havoc in many bandsmen's homes. A large number of bands, or at least a portion of them, have been compelled to utilise their musical abilities as a means of procuring the necessities of life for selves and families, causing them to leave home and invade the neighbouring towns and villages, playing about the streets and appealing to a sympathetic public for much-needed assistance. In consequence of this deplorable disagreement 'twixt masters and men', a large number of bands are unsettled and unable to do anything in the way of practice.[27]

Similarly, the editor of *The Cornet*, writing during the 1910 election campaign, attempted to maintain a distance between the musical world and the political world by arguing that 'It was not always good policy for bands to get mixed up in politics – as a band – for someone is bound to be offended. Bands cannot be too careful in this respect; there is so little to gain, and often much to lose.'[28]

In certain instances, even the band repertoire was influenced by the ideal of a non-contentious existence within capitalist society. In 1913 the organisers of the Crystal Palace Brass Band Contest chose as the championship testpiece, a tone poem, *Labour and Love*, by the Midlands composer Percy Fletcher. Fletcher's work was important because it was the first piece by a 'recognised' composer, written specifically for the brass band, beginning a trend that has continued throughout the twentieth century and involved a number of major composers. Historians of music have acknowledged the artistic importance of the work, but have failed to appreciate the political significance of its programme. The piece expresses the changing mood of a working man, initially dissatisfied with a purposeless, physically exhausting job but eventually persuaded by his wife to view his job as a 'labour of love'. In a martial final movement 'He smiles at his troubles, his heart swells with pride at his work ... he throws himself with determination into his task resolved to improve his position by continued devotion to his daily task.' It must be stressed that there is no direct evidence that either Fletcher, or J. H. Iles, the organiser of the contest, saw the work as overt propaganda. But the piece illustrates with great clarity the enormous conservatism that underpinned so many middle-class attempts to encourage the spread of the brass band, and indeed music in general, amongst the working classes. It is fitting that the first major work for brass band by a recognised composer should be a hymn to the joys of hard work, loyalty, self-improvement and contentment.[29]

While the majority of support for popular music was underpinned by an essentially conservative ideology, the defenders of the contemporary order were not alone in their belief that music, and the arts in general, could shape the minds of the labouring population. In the nineteenth century, 'the widening of the human experience through music, drama, reading and entertainment of all kinds' was the goal of many sections of the radical working-class movement.[30]

Criticism of conditions, employers and governments had long since formed the stuff of many broadsides and folksongs. But it was in the late nineteenth century that efforts to harness popular musical culture to the needs of the labour movement reached a peak. This flowering of radical musical life, beginning in the 1880s, was largely an outgrowth of the late Victorian Socialist revival. Music, whether in the shape of the songs sung in country lanes by the socialist pilgrims of the Social Democratic Federation and Independent Labour Party, or of the chamber pieces by Mozart, Mascagni, Haydn and Chopin offered to audiences by Bradford Labour Church in the mid-1890s, was central to the socialist movement of the period.[31] Between 1885 and 1914, almost forty musical organisations grew out of the West Yorkshire radical movement. The majority were choral in nature, probably because they were cheaper to organise and required less specialist talent than bands and orchestras.[32]

The Clarion movement was perhaps the most prolific. In the autumn of 1894 Montague Blatchford wrote a series of articles in the *Clarion*, extolling the virtues of music as a weapon in the socialist armoury, and in the following year established the Clarion Vocal Union to oversee the activities of the handful of choirs that had come into existence.[33] By 1910 the Union contained twenty-three choirs, including nine in the Yorkshire textile region. These choirs, it was hoped, would play a major part in the 'making of socialists'.[34] They would elevate the minds of both singer and audience, helping people 'realise our best selves, to be higher, happier and healthier human beings'. At the same time, choral singing was to provide a lesson in fellowship. 'It is a lesson in discipline and socialism of the most convincing sort. It shows the interdependence of each on all; the necessity of every member doing a given duty in a given way at the proper time to the instant, and gives an excellent feeling of precision, unity and power that would raise and dignify a tailor's dummy.'[35] Socialists of the late nineteenth and early twentieth century, like the pioneers of Methodism almost 120 years earlier, strove to sing themselves to paradise.

Significantly, the Clarion choirs tried to accomplish their task largely within the confines of the existing repertoire, making only a limited effort to create an alternative socialist musical culture. Certainly, socialist works did emerge: *The Comrade's Song of Hope*, Carpenter's *England Arise*, Rutland Boughton's *The City*, a motet 'embodying the composer's vision of the ideal city' and *1910*, a work by the feminist Ethel Smythe, dedicated to the women's suffrage movement, were all overtly political works that found their way into the repertoire. But whether in contests, concerts or street corner rallies, socialist singers seem to have remained well within the mainstream of the Victorian choral tradition. Little did Edward Elgar, Ciro Pinsuti, even Felix Mendelssohn know that they were to be the harbingers of the socialist millennium.[36]

Between 1880 and 1914 the political structure of the textile region altered considerably, although perhaps less fundamentally than is sometimes suggested. This period was to witness the revival of class-based politics, the re-emergence of socialism and the large-scale expansion of trade unionism in the area. In particular, the late 1880s and earlier 1890s, and the period between 1910 and 1913, saw some of the most strongly contested actions in English working-class history.[37] When one looks, for example, at the strike which affected Samuel Cunliffe Lister's Manningham Mills in Bradford between December 1890 and April 1891, with its immense size and scope, the degree of working-class support it attracted, and conversely, the middle-class hostility it aroused, with troops called in by the local Liberal establishment, breaking up a strike meeting and chasing the audience up a city centre street with bayonets drawn, it is almost like delving back into the heady days of the 1790s, 1815-20 or 1832.[38] Again, in late Victorian Yorkshire the historian encounters the language of class war spoken with a fervour and an ideological certainty that had not been present for almost half a century.

But in the final analysis, the threat to capitalist society was tiny. The number of people actively involved in radical politics remained small. Similarly, the political culture of the activists, while radical enough to cause consternation amongst the ranks of capital, was far from revolutionary. Socialism, as opposed to Labourism, remained weak, and in West Yorkshire, the dominant brand of Socialism as practised by the I.L.P. was often, particularly after 1900, almost identical to pre-existing mainstream radical politics, possessing 'a millennial flavour, a revolutionary style oratory, but a programme differing but little from progressive Liberalism'.[39]

In the context of musical life the type of social and political climate that emerged accorded more closely with that envisaged by those seeking to use music in a conservative direction than that championed by Blatchford, and it is at least possible that music itself did play a part in reinforcing, perhaps even creating, this situation. This is not to suggest that the membership of musical societies acquiesced meekly in the demands of the middle classes. It would be wrong to claim, for example, that the wealthy patrons of the brass band movement instructed their bandsmen to adopt a certain political stance and that the band then took up their allotted role. As will be seen there undoubtedly were individuals who, either out of deference or self-preservation, did exactly as they were told, but overall such an interpretation is too crude, too mechanistic. Rather, the argument is that the appeal of radical politics was blunted because many amateur musicians, *through their own musical experience*, discovered that society as it existed had much to offer them.

Obviously, the relationship between music and politics was not clear cut. There were cases in which popular musical life reflected or extended class tensions in local society. Indeed, the solidly working-class membership of the brass band was in itself a reflection of contemporary class division. Again, stern resistance was shown by many working-man musicians to the patronising behaviour of the middle classes. In 1913, for instance, a local correspondent attacked the composer Joseph Holbrooke, in the pages of the *British Bandsman*, for showing condescension towards bandsmen during a report Holbrooke had compiled on the Crystal Palace National Championships of that year. It was nice, the writer claimed,

> that at least one of the members of the great musical aristocracy had looked down in the midst of our humble festivities and smiled benignly upon us ... scores of humble working men, gifted in no little degree with the spark of divine genius (for, we would also say, we do not believe for one moment all the musical brains of the country have been showered upon the student who attends the Royal Academy of Music and similar institutions) have made their lives a living sacrifice for the brass band cause, and are doing it today.[40]

Here wounded artistic pride, coupled with a great sense of popular artistic achievement, produces a heightened degree of class-consciousness.

Moreover, there were instances when the musical society must have furthered the causes of radical reform or helped mobilise the working classes. The Clarion Vocal Unions must have added to the attraction of their cause when appearing at concerts and rallies. Similarly, the brass band, which seems to have developed close links with the labour movement, brought a degree of pomp and dignity to trade union processions. Certain large trade union festivals became major events in the brass band calendar. The annual Yorkshire miners' demonstration, described by one band paper in 1907 as 'one of the great events of the band season', regularly attracted over fifty bands whose playing was then enthusiastically discussed in the band press.[41] As well as performing at these annual rituals, bands were often engaged to lead strike processions, and were in evidence at most major disputes in the period. This close association with the ranks of organised labour called forth many criticisms of the band movement, and even in 1914 there would have been many ready to echo the sentiments of this contributor to the *Yorkshire Orchestra* in 1868: 'I look upon all persons who admire brass bands as possessing a primitive taste. Such music is only suited to precede a mob of inebriated rioters, revolutionists, electioneerists, trade unionists etc.; and I hope the day is not far distant when it will cease to exist and be looked upon as a barbarism of the past.'[42]

However, it is hard to escape the feeling that the thrust of the popular musical movement was in a 'conservative' direction. It would be unwise, for example, to view the brass band movement as a fully-fledged cultural adjunct of organised labour. Trade unions and Socialist societies were not the only bodies to utilise the services of the local musical community. The Liberal Party, the Primrose League, and various Conservative and Unionist associations hired bands to perform at their open-air engagements.[43] Some bands, and indeed some choirs, seem to have developed a strictly businesslike approach to political events. The ultimate achievement in this respect was probably that of the Bramley Band, who during the 1839 election campaign played for both the Liberals and Conservatives on the same day. Late Victorian and Edwardian bands showed slightly more tact, although the Brighouse Borough Band came close to repeating Bramley's disinterested action when in June 1904 they led a demonstration of the unemployed, organised by the relatively militant Brighouse Trades Council, in the same week as persuading Sir Thomas Brooke-Hitching, the Conservative and Unionist candidate for Elland, to become their patron. The Huddersfield Glee and Madrigal Society showed a similar willingness to put art and musical prestige (and money?) before political scruple when in 1900 the choir, which contained a considerable number of manufacturers and their wives, sang before the T.U.C., at Huddersfield.[44]

By the same token, it should not be assumed that brass bands were the inevitable allies of the Labour movement. While willing to give assistance to strikers, if the workers involved had clear support from the working population, bands might refuse to co-operate if the strike had aroused bitterness in the locality. Strikers at a dyeworks in Sowerby Bridge in 1910 were initially rejected by several bands when attempting to organise a demonstration. Only when local opinion eventually hardened behind the strike did Norland Subscription Band agree to perform.[45] Obviously, individual singers and bandsmen may have remained loyal to a certain political or industrial cause, despite the actions of their musical society. But surely the radicalisation of both performers and the local population was retarded by the musical society's need to appeal across the community, if it was to survive financially. The brass band, in particular its playing members unable to support the band from their pockets alone, was highly vulnerable if it chose to pursue a course unpopular with its patrons. Could it afford to upset local benefactors by playing for a local union or Socialist society? Could a works bandsman whose job as well as his banding career depended upon his standing with the employer, risk involvement in radical political activity? A full integration of popular music and political radicalism was a financial impossibility.

The choral society, and the larger bodies in particular, provided a further opportunity through its pan-class membership to reduce class tension. Obviously, the point should not be exaggerated; the fact that a joiner and a mill-owner were members of the same organisation did not necessarily mean that they would converse with each other, or like each other. Furthermore, the very fact that singers from different social backgrounds could come together in their leisure illustrates the existence of a climate already conducive to a degree of cross-class activity, and the musical society must not be seen as the *initiator* of collaboration. However, it is surely possible that mutual respect based on an appreciation of technical skills exhibited by a 'better' or 'inferior', the unity of purpose that existed in most societies, and any social contact that did take place, helped contain class tension in local society. Equally critical was the choral society's tendency to exacerbate divisions within the working class. It helped pull the labour élite away from the semi- and unskilled sectors of the community, and attach them more firmly to men of social substance.

All this is not to suggest that music somehow brought about political passivity. Rather, the potential for pan-class activity and co-operation that much music-making offered should be seen as part of the network of forces which helped a 'popular radical' style of politics to remain so common in West Yorkshire, even after 1890.

At the same time, it is possible that membership of a band or choir did serve to diminish interest and involvement in political or social issues, or lessen the possibility of such interest developing. In an important sense, leisure and politics were rivals fighting for the time, money and commitment of the working population. There were men who managed to straddle both fields, conducting a choir and organising a socialist club, performing as a cornet soloist and standing for the council, but the biographical information available suggests that music was too consuming and absorbing an activity to allow for involvement in much else. Many working people, while perhaps sympathetic to the ideals of trade unionism, independent labour, perhaps even socialism, were clearly devoting the bulk of their time and energy to other pursuits, of which music was undoubtedly one of the most important.

Perhaps most significant, however, was music's capacity to provide compensations, especially for those lacking material possessions and social status, which thus turned people, particularly those not politically motivated in the first instance, away from seeking political solutions to their problems. For the best and most ambitious singers of humble origin, the musical society could provide an avenue for social mobility. Charles Knowles, a bookbinder who sang with the Leeds Philharmonic Society in the 1890s, eventually became a well-established London opera singer. William Todd and Joel Hirst of the Huddersfield Glee and Madrigal Society toured the world with Sam Hague's Minstrels in the 1880s. Samuel Midgley, a miner's son from Bierley near Bradford, eventually became one of the town's most respected and prosperous music teachers.[46] This list could be extended considerably. While clearly only a minority could benefit in this way, numerous members earned valuable sums of money at contests and concerts. On occasion, money earned in this way prevented real hardship. For example, in the summers of 1894 and 1895, six miners who were members of the Emley Brass Band left the pit when work became short and earned their living playing in a dance band at Blackpool.[47]

There were innumerable benefits to be gained, apart from material ones. Music could prove an extraordinarily gratifying social experience, providing the opportunity to travel, whether it be to the United States, Germany and France, or merely to the seaside or the Yorkshire dales, the conviviality that accompanied rehearsals and performances, the thrill of being lionised by the local community, or merely the chance to make music that the individual found pleasing.[48]

Avoidance of organised political activity has traditionally been termed 'apathy' both by contemporary observers and by later generations of scholars. Dr Stephen Yeo has, however, recently made a series of provocative assaults on this concept, and in the process has done much to change our conception of popular political behaviour. Writing of Reading between 1890 and 1914, but clearly believing his idea to have a wider relevance, he suggests

> that there was a kind of apathy few would deny from a 1975 vantage point, even if the reality behind the apathy should not be seen in the terms chosen by those who identified and deplored it at the time. Positive attitudes there were, even if not the attitudes observers wanted there to be. The holders of these attitudes, already emancipated by ties of deference to a local civic leadership, did not turn in new loyalty towards the organised structures of formal nationalised politics. Rather did they turn away from what is usually called politics altogether, towards realistic cynicism about 'them' up there in politics, combined either with settling for satisfaction which could be had without involving 'them', or with deliberate attempts at by-passing politics via different forms of intermittent 'syndicalism'. What is called 'apathy' is often another name for positive, in certain circumstances militant, rejections of current structures and ideologies in politics.[49]

But Yeo's analysis, valuable as it is, is perhaps a little too concerned with the overtly political aspect of the phenomenon. People did not necessarily 'turn away' from politics: many never even contemplated it in the first place, preferring to seek their pleasures and satisfaction from other areas of experience. Leisure, and in this case, musical activity, was surely a major way through which people 'settled for satisfaction' without recourse to the political system and its exponents. The so-called political apathy of many working-class people stemmed to a considerable extent from the fact that they often had 'better' things to occupy their minds.

Speculation of the type undertaken in this chapter, if taken too far, can lead to a profoundly misleading history. Too long an immersion in the annals of popular recreation can, like absorption in any other specialist area, lead to a rather idiosyncratic view of the relative importance of certain areas of Victorian and Edwardian life. There must be no attempt to create a picture of music healing all social wounds; of ill-fed, ill-clothed, unshod children skipping lightly through the middens of central Bradford humming the *Hallelujah Chorus* and thinking only of Black Dyke's forthcoming visit to the local park. There *was* immense poverty and hardship in West Yorkshire throughout the period, and there *were* radical working-class responses to that poverty and the system that created it. But there was also a considerable amount of happiness and contentment, and, except in brief periods of mass consciousness, widespread uninterest in all spheres of political and trade union activity. The musical society clearly played a part in creating that happiness, and it is at least possible that it helped shape the distinctive political culture that accompanied it.

NOTES

1 *School Music Review* (November 1897).

2 For an introduction to the Victorian and Edwardian musical worlds see E. Mackerness, *A Social History of English Music* (1964); R. Nettel, *Music in The Five Towns* (Oxford, 1944); R. Pearsall, *Edwardian Popular Music* (Newton Abbot, 1975) and *Victorian Popular Music* (Newton Abbot, 1973); H. Raynor, *Music and Society Since 1815* (1976); P. Young, *A History of British Music* (1967). The statistics quoted come from R. Pearsall, *Victorian*, p. 89; C. Ehrlich, *The Piano, a History* (1976), p. 97; *Cornet* (October 1907).

3 *Yorkshire Daily Observer*, 20 August 1907.

4 For pioneering attempts to link popular leisure and popular politics, see H. Cunningham, *Leisure in The Industrial Revolution* (1980); R. Q. Gray, 'Styles of life, the 'Labour Aristocracy' and class relations in later 19th century Edinburgh', *International Review of Social History* 18 (1973); D. Read, *The English Provinces* (1964), pp. 228-31; G. S. Jones, 'Working class culture and working class politics in London, 1870-1900', *Journal of Social History* (1974).

5 The bulk of the material in this article is extracted from my unpublished doctoral thesis, 'The popular musical societies of the Yorkshire textile district, 1850-1914', University of York, 1980. For other studies relating to the brass band movement, see J. F. Russell and J. H. Elliot, *The Brass Band Movement* (1936); J. Scott, 'The evolution of the brass band and its repertoire in northern England', unpub. Ph.D. thesis, University of Sheffield, 1970; A. Taylor, *Brass Bands* (1979). There is no work devoted solely to the choral movement, although Mackerness, Nettel and Raynor, *op. cit.*, contain much useful information.

6 *Wright and Round's Amateur Band Teacher's Guide* (1889), p. 2; *Brass Band News* (November 1889).

7 G. Hogarth, 'A village oratorio', reprinted in *Mainzer's Musical Times* (15 November 1842), pp. 131-3. For other hymns of praise to Yorkshire's musical reputation see *Morning Post* (1 September 1853), during the course of its coverage of the Bradford Musical Festival; *The Times* (29 August 1859); *School Music Review* (November 1903 and January 1910).

8 For an introduction to the region see M. Wild, 'The Yorkshire wool textile industry', in J. G. Jenkins (ed.), *The Wool Textile Industry in Great Britain* (1972).

9 See D. Russell, *op. cit.*, appendix 1, pp. 325-42, for a list of 638 brass bands, choral societies, amateur orchestras, concertina bands and handbell teams, traced in the textile region within this period. In the 1890s, in the peak of local musical life, there were perhaps 350-400 musical societies in existence.

10 *British Bandsman* (November 1891).

11 *School Music Review* (June 1896).

12 *British Bandsman* (29 November 1902).

13 See the descriptions of the funerals of Dewsbury Old Band's conductor, Willie Lee, *Brass Band News* (April 1890) and of the band trainer and arranger Edwin Swift, *Cornet* (March 1904).

14 *The Times* (29 August 1859), described the working-class choralists of Bradford as 'raised in the scale of humanity'.

15 William Spark, *Musical Memories* (1888), p. 463. See R. H. Myers, *Handel's 'Messiah'* (New York, 1948), pp. 232-48 for a number of similar statements.

16 D. Russell, *op. cit.*, pp. 69-77. This analysis was based on the societies' membership records and W. White's *Clothing District Directory* (1894).

17 Leeds Philharmonic Society, Chorus Roll Books, 1894-1913, in the possession of the society; Leeds Philharmonic Society, Chorus Roll books, 1894-1909, in Leeds City Public Reference Library.

18 Huddersfield Choral Society Roll Book, 1894-1913, in the possession of the society. I am extremely grateful to Richard Barraclough, the secretary of the Huddersfield Choral Society, for allowing me access to their records.

19 *Yorkshire Daily Observer* (15 August 1907). The 'it' is, of course, music.

20 *British Bandsman* (December 1889).

21 D. Russell, *op. cit.*, pp. 61-3.

22 For such a view see, R. Pearsall, *Victorian*, p. 199.

23 For these three concerns see J. Reynolds, *Saltaire* (Bradford, 1976); R. Balgarnie, *Sir Titus Salt* (1878, reprinted Settle, 1970), which is essentially hagiography but contains much useful information; R. Bretton, 'Sir Edward Ackroyd', *Transactions of the Halifax Antiquarian Society* (1949); E. Sigsworth, *Black Dyke Mills* (Liverpool, 1958).

24 W. J. Galloway, *Musical England* (1910), p. 200.

25 For Foster, see J. Scott, thesis, *op. cit.*, p. 112; Marriner, Ms. history of Marriner's Band in R. V. Marriner and Co. records (box 117), Special Collection, Brotherton Library, Leeds; Fox, P. Young, *op. cit.*, p. 496.

26 *Brass and Band News* was published by Wright and Round's of Liverpool; *British Bandsman* initially by Richard Smith and Co. of Gloucester, and from 1898 by the concert promoter J. Henry Iles; *The Cornet* emanated from F. Richardson and Company of Sibsey, in Lincolnshire.

27 *Cornet* (October 1893).

28 *Ibid.* (February 1910).

29 Fletcher's career is dealt with in *British Bandsman* (14 June 1913), and the programme of *Labour and Love* in *ibid.* (6 September 1913).

30 E. Royle, *Victorian Infidels* (Manchester 1976), p. 233.

31 On song in the socialist movement see S. Yeo, 'A new life: the religion of socialism in Britain, 1873-1896', *History Workshop* 4 (1977), pp. 34-5. *Bradford Labour Echo* (18 and 25 May 1895), gives coverage to Labour Church concerts.

32 A handful of instrumental bodies did exist, the most notable being the

Milnsbridge Socialist Brass Band which gained considerable musical reputation in its native Colne Valley.

33 Montagu Blatchford (?–1910) was a brother of the more celebrated Robert. For details of his quite extensive involvement in the political and cultural life of Halifax, where he lived, see *Yorkshire Factory Times* (19 May 1910) and *Clarion* (22 April 1910). His articles promoting the value of music appeared in the *Clarion* (1, 15 and 29 September 1894).

34 *Clarion* (4 February 1910). Clarion Vocal Unions were founded eventually at Bradford, Dobcross, Elland, Halifax, Huddersfield, Keighley, Leeds, Morley and Slaithwaite.

35 *Clarion* (4 May 1906; 12 December 1895).

36 Boughton and Smythe's works are interesting, representing two of the tiny number of 'socialist' pieces produced by the late Victorian and Edwardian musical establishment. See *Musical Times* Supplement (May 1914), for coverage of these works. For a typical Clarion Concert programme, see *Yorkshire Daily Observer* (25 September 1904).

37 For late nineteenth and early twentieth century politics in the region, see E. P. Hennock, *Fit and Proper Persons* (1973), an exhaustive study of municipal politics in Leeds; Henry Pelling, *A Social Geography of British Elections, 1885–1910*, pp. 289–307 and *Popular Politics and Society in Late Victorian England* (1968), pp. 133–46; B. Barker, 'Anatomy of Reformism: The social and political ideas of the labour leadership in Yorkshire', *International Review of Social History* 18 (1973); E. P. Thompson, 'Homage to Tom Maguire', in J. Saville and A. Briggs (eds.), *Essays in Labour History, vol. 1*, pp. 276–316; K. Laybourn, 'Yorkshire trade unions and the great depression, 1873–96', University of Lancaster, Ph.D. thesis, 1972.

38 C. Pearce, *The Manningham Mills Strike*, University of Hull Occasional Papers (1975), provides an excellent analysis of this important strike.

39 J. Reynolds and K. Laybourn, 'The emergence of the I.L.P. in Bradford', *International Review of Social History* 20 (1975), p. 313.

40 *British Bandsman* (18 October 1913). For the article that caused the offence: *ibid.* (4 October 1913).

41 *Cornet* (July 1907).

42 *Yorkshire Orchestra* (8 January 1868).

43 *British Bandsman* (September 1891), for example, notes both Lindley and Liversedge bands playing at Primrose League functions. For examples of bands playing at Conservative Party activities, see *Brighouse Echo* (15 and 29 July and 19 August 1904).

44 J. Hesling White, *A Short History of Bramley Band* (Bramley, 1906), p. 7; *Brighouse Echo* (10 June 1904); Anon., *The Huddersfield Glee and Madrigal Society: a jubilee record, 1876–1926* (Huddersfield, 1926), p. 22.

45 *Yorkshire Factory Times* (2 and 23 June 1910).

46 E. Hick, Leeds Press Cuttings, vol. 8 (Leeds City Reference Library), p. 60; cuttings from *Pastime* (not dated but *c.* 1900) in Huddersfield Glee and Madrigal Society miscellaneous cuttings box, Kirklees Archives Department; S. Midgley, *My Seventy Years Musical Memories* (1934).

47 See article on Emley Band in *Huddersfield Weekly Examiner* (9 February 1957). By the early Edwardian period, a brass band soloist, if hired to play by a band, could earn £2 or £3 at a contest, thus doubling his weekly income. However, it should be noted that paid soloists numbered no more than a few hundred of the movement.

48 Foreign travel became fairly common in the Edwardian period. For example, Black Dyke Mills Band undertook a six-month tour of the United States and Canada in 1906; in the same year, the Leeds Philharmonic Choir visited Germany; in 1912 the Philharmonic visited Paris and in the May of that year, five choirs from the region joined another forty British choirs in the three-day International Music Tournament in Paris. Contest and concert engagements took bands and choirs all over the north of England.

49 S. Yeo, *Religion and Voluntary Organisations in Crisis* (1976), p. 273.

7 ALLAN REDFERN
Crewe: leisure in a railway town

Leisure in Crewe during the formative years between 1880 and 1914 had distinctive and sometimes paradoxical characteristics. In particular, worker-organised leisure remained a pervasive and integral part of community life, while outside commercial interests only had a limited impact on recreational developments in the town. Considering that Crewe was a one-company town, a seemingly unlikely context for autonomous worker activities, and that most recent studies of leisure during this period have described a process of rapid commercialisation, these characteristics demand specific explanations.

Recent developments in the historiography of leisure provide stimulating insights and a valuable analytical framework but, as the case of Crewe shows, additional local studies can add important new perspectives. Peter Bailey and Stephen Yeo[1] have made important contributions to our understanding of nineteenth and early twentieth-century leisure, but aspects of their treatment of such themes as patronage, class and commercialisation have less validity when applied to the context of Crewe. In contrast with their studies of Bolton and Reading, the place of work in Crewe had a central role in determining the nature of local leisure. As James Walvin has written, 'Beneath the common experience of industrialisation there lay a multitude of local, regional and trade differences, each of which could determine a different style of life for local people'.[2] In Crewe railway employment was the major local influence on social developments and this chapter inevitably focuses on this fundamental factor influencing leisure in the town.

Most people in the town were directly or indirectly dependent on the London North Western Railway Company, and the senior management of the company were able to exert considerable social influence both in their own right and as the principal representatives of company patronage or paternalism. On the face of it the leisure activities of railway workers would seem to have been particularly vulnerable to the influence of these men. In reality the social influence of the railway company was declining by the late 1880s, and even earlier several factors had limited company power. The town literally outgrew the paternalism which had prevailed during the two decades after the company[3] decision in 1840 to establish the industrial community. In 1841 the total population of the two rural townships which were eventually to become Crewe was 498, by 1881 24,385 and by the turn of the century over 42,000. In the early years large numbers of company employees had been transferred from workshops at Edge Hill and Wolverton, and many other workers came to Crewe from all parts of the British Isles. The railway directors recognised their responsibility for the social readjustment of their workforce. At the opening of the new workshops in December 1843 John Moss, chairman of the directors, stated: 'the men around him had, no doubt, by coming there, dissevered many ties of kindred and affection and deprived themselves of many of the enjoyments of more populous localities; but ... he and his brother directors were anxious to make them as comfortable as lay within their power'.[4] Thus early policy based on a mixture of principle and self interest resulted in the company initially providing a wide range of necessary facilities including housing, all main services, Anglican churches and schools and a public baths. With the exception of the Mechanics' Institution, established in 1843, and an allotment scheme introduced in 1850, the pre-1860 provisions did not relate directly to the secular spare-time activities of the workforce. In 1860 local government passed out of the hands of a small company Management Committee through the establishment of a local board, later replaced by the town council established in 1877. As a result of these developments and a simultaneous growth of liberal nonconformity, earlier paternalism became less pervasive and began to give way to an increasing company involvement in local politics. Senior management came closely to identify railway interests with the local Tory/Anglican group in the political struggles of the following decades. It is also noticeable that many of the recreational organisations patronised by the senior management from the late 1860s had a predominantly Tory/Anglican membership.

In the period up to 1880 there was a variety of such organisations. The policy of encouraging 'rational and improving' leisure activities was implicit in the patronage and benevolence shown, but at no time was the company and its senior management the sole agency for such social philosophy. Apart from the volunteer force which enjoyed very close connections with the railway company from its inception in 1863, every other form of 'respectable' recreational activity also developed in organisations outside company control. The Philharmonic Society, founded in 1867, enjoyed the patronage of senior railway officials and some of the surrounding gentry, but also had its often superior counterpart in the more popular choirs of the Nonconformist chapels. Both the Crewe (LNWR) Cricket Club (established in 1850) and the Crewe Alexandra Athletic Club (established in 1867) benefited from company support in spite of theoretical financial independence. Several of the founder members of these two clubs, and the volunteer force, were in due course to become senior railway officials and continued to be important supporters of these organisations. There were by 1880 several other sporting organisations, less dependent on direct company patronage, and these included at least ten cricket teams and four football clubs. Over half of these were based on churches or chapels. The Crewe Horticultural Society (founded by 1874) had the company chief mechanical engineer and company surgeon as president and vice-president, but was one of two organisations of this kind in the district.

By the 1880s the company had spent considerable sums on the construction or extension of social amenities and, with the exception of the Nonconformist buildings and the theatre, all major constructions by the late nineteenth century had been financed by the company. Between 1871 and 1880 the Mechanics' Institution was reconstructed and extended by the company (who kept finance and administration firmly in their hands). Until the turn of the century this building was a major social and educational centre. Although temperance reform was dominated by local Liberal Nonconformists, the company, though also owning three public houses in Crewe, made a major contribution to the cause in 1879 by constructing the extensive Euston Coffee Tavern adjacent to the Mechanics' Institution. The company also constructed a second public baths (which included a swimming pool) in 1866. By the late nineteenth century the company were less willing to spend money on public facilities, claiming that such financing was a municipal responsibility. For a Town Council accustomed to the benevolence shown by the company up to the 1880s this proved to be a difficult role to assume.

Recreational provision by 1880 was not limited to company benevolence or the patronage of its senior officials. Besides those Anglican churches built and patronised by the company, Nonconformist chapels had an important role in the respectable recreations of working people though the extent to which these facilities were used was limited. Further analysis of all organisations enjoying the patronage of élites reveals a quite narrow social composition. Nonconformity, particularly Primitive Methodism, allied with liberalism and temperance was relatively strong in Crewe but it is calculated that the proportion of adults who were members of Nonconformist churches never rose above seven per cent. Primitive Methodist membership was almost twice the national average but local membership in peak years was little more than one per cent of the population.[5] As in most communities the public house probably provided a more popular recreational centre than all other institutions combined. In 1881 the ratio of population to licences was 259 to one.[6] Since Crewe was a fairly new community most public houses were purpose-built and larger than elsewhere. These factors, combined with the existence of a strong local temperance movement (a characteristic associated by Brian Harrison with areas of heavy drinking),[7] suggest that drinking was clearly a major recreation in the town, and brings out the limited influence of local religious institutions and social élites before the 1880s.

A substantial increase in the number of people per pub and a decline in prosecutions for drunkenness from the early 1890s testify to a relative fall in the role of the public house.[8] Counter-attractions certainly played an important part in this. The primary concern of this chapter is to assess the source and nature of these developments during the period 1880-1914 and to examine the relative importance of patronage, the emergence of commercial entertainment and autonomous working-class activity.

Local patronage had distinctive characteristics and some of its limitations may explain parallel developments within the community. The surrounding gentry played a very limited role in the social life of the community and there was only a small local middle class. Inevitably, a large proportion of the latter were dependent in some way on the railway company and this may explain why the majority of those who were patrons of secular organisations were also Anglican and Conservative. Of those who were not senior railway employees many were publicans, several of whom were able to combine a traditional role as patron with an entrepreneurial approach to changing patterns in leisure. Local patronage differed from that provided by élites elsewhere. Most Crewe patrons were self-made men who, like the directors of the railway, based their social ideology primarily on economic expediency whilst subscribing to a concept of 'improvement' through supporting certain recreations. Patronage amongst the small Nonconformist and Liberal middle class was largely restricted to their own religious and political institutions. Thus patronage always had limitations, and for most secular organisations came mainly from a group identified in some way with the railway company.

The social influence of the company was exercised through a complex chain of command ranging from foremen and superintendents to the senior managerial staff working in Crewe. At the head of this hierarchy was the chief mechanical engineer who, as the principal representative of company interests and with a direct influence on the board of directors, was the most influential individual in the town. Three men held this position during the period but it was during the 'reign' of F. W. Webb, between 1872 and 1903, that the power of this office was at its height. Described just before his retirement as 'the King of Crewe'[9] Webb came to exercise control over the working lives of over 18,000 men – one third of the total LNWR workforce.[10] Over half these lived in Crewe, around 8,000 being employed at the locomotive works. Several recreational organisations were a direct result of Webb's influence and others received benefit from his support.

Collectively the organisations Webb supported spanned the range of recreations deemed respectable and improving by the middle-class reformers of the age, and he also saw them all as serving the broader interests of the company. Webb was president of several organisations, including Crewe Mechanics' Institution, Crewe Scientific Society, Crewe Horticultural Society, the Chess and Draughts Club, and the

LNWR Cricket Club. He played a central role in the history of the local volunteer force and the Crewe Alexandra Athletic Club. He also contributed to the temperance cause, in particular through his role in the establishment of the Euston Coffee Tavern. In a company structure which bred deference, his patronage of an organisation could be guaranteed to attract some of the workforce. His successors, G. Whale and C. J. Bowen Cooke, though less powerful men, continued many aspects of Webb's role in local patronage and encouraged additional recreations of their own. But a closer examination of many of the institutions promoted by senior management shows that the number of employees directly affected was relatively small and that many of these organisations were actually declining during this period.

This can be illustrated by reference to some of the groups fostered by Webb. Webb and his successors believed that their patronage would enhance the company's effectiveness and prestige. Support for the Mechanics' Institution rested largely on their need for skilled workers, but by the late nineteenth century this need was being increasingly met by State institutions. Patronage of sporting organisations was based in part on the belief that 'by encouraging the young people in athletic pursuits they assisted to make them healthy and in that way tended to make them better workmen'.[11] During this period all three chief mechanical engineers showed a particular interest in the volunteer force. Bowen Cooke's comments at their final parade in 1912 indicate some of the reasons. Expressing his 'deep regret at their disbandment' he spoke of his efforts via the War Office to prevent this happening and lamented the 'breaking of a bond of union between the company and their men and the company and the nation'.[12] Bowen Cooke had a particular enthusiasm for promoting inter-workshop ambulance competitions. George Whale's promotion of the Railway Temperance Union also stemmed from a desire to improve the efficiency and safety of workshops and departments. His role in this organisation began in 1886 when he was superintendent of the Running Department where sobriety was particularly important. When he became chief mechanical engineer the Union had a spectacular increase in numbers and by 1911 had 1,554 members and five branches. Even patronage of the Horticultural Society could be seen as contributing to railway interests. Speaking at an annual show of the society Webb endorsed the general aims of the group and also commented on ways in which the society influenced people to keep their gardens more tidily, with particular reference to the influence on signalmen's garden boxes.[13]

High subscription rates often put many organisations out of the reach of the majority of workers. By 1890 membership of the Mechanics' Institution was declining and only about 7.5 per cent of the population

were members. In spite of a reduction in the annual subscription from
10s. to 8s. in 1892 there was a continued decline in membership.[14] By
1907 there were only 261 full members compared with over two thousand
in 1890.[15] The Scientific Society, founded by Webb in 1884, was restricted to members of the Mechanics' Institution, and provides a good
example of how important the support of a powerful patron could be.
During the period when Webb was actively involved in the society it was
well supported by other senior employees and sectors of the workforce
but by the turn of the century Webb was a sick man and his presence at
meetings became increasingly rare. Support drifted away around the
same time and the organisation was wound up in 1902.[16]

Crewe Philharmonic Society and the Alexandra Athletic Club enjoyed
the support of senior railway employees and both had a limited social
composition because of the cost of membership. The cost of tickets for
most of the events of the former usually ranged from 1s. to 3s. and in
other ways their performances were an occasion for social display beyond
the means of manual workers: 'We used to have soloists from London
and we used to have parts of the Hallé Orchestra too. That was a great
night you know – all had cabs, long white dresses and long white gloves.'
This lady member described membership as: 'Folks like me! – well out
of the general office, teachers and that kind of thing. I think most of the
men worked on the railway but they were in the office.'[17] The Alexandra
Athletic Club was 'open to all who had been recommended to join the
society' but in 1898 it was forced to increase subscription charges to 7s.
and 10s., thus reducing yet further the potential for broadly-based
membership.[18] However this major amateur sporting organisation was
financially dependent on widespread support at its public events and by
the early 1890s debate within the club centred on the issue of professionalism. The football section of the club broke away from the parent
organisation in 1891 on this issue, as occurred at Reading Football Club
a few years later.[19] F. W. Webb's opposition to professionalism was
particularly virulent and at one point he threatened to refuse railway
employment to any man playing professional football.[20] Webb's successors proved less intractable and Bowen Cooke was president of Crewe
Alexandra Football Club and the professional athletics meetings it
organised. The athletics and cricket sections within the original club
continued to rely on gate money rather than private subscriptions but
despite its national reputation,[21] and some material support from the
LNWR, which accepted the introduction of a degree of professionalism,[22] the club was approaching extinction by 1914.

Each senior railway manager was answerable to the shareholders of
the company, and their primary role was to represent railway interests.[23]
By the late nineteenth century these interests were much more narrowly

defined. The company's gift of land and £10,000 for the construction of Queen's Park, which was opened in 1887, was the last major display of benevolence to the whole town. The formal opening in July was an impressive social event. Included in the ceremony were over six hundred members of the 2nd Cheshire Railway Engineer Volunteer Corps, all company employees living in Crewe, and nine bands from various regions of the LNWR including three from Crewe. In several respects the late 1880s represent a turning point in the company's relationship with the broader community. The political influence of the senior management, largely through the local Conservative party, was at its height, and Webb was re-elected as mayor in the year the new park was opened, but the direct political influence of the company was soon to be ended for ever. There is no doubt that intimidation of employees in addition to company benevolence helped win political power. The most startling examples of intimidation took place during the 1880s and included the dismissal of active Liberals from railway employment. By the late 1880s such actions culminated in what became known as the 'Intimidation Affair'. Following a local campaign by the Liberal *Crewe Chronicle* in 1885 and a letter in *The Times* from W. E. Gladstone, formal complaints reached the Railway Board and overt company interference in the political life of the workforce permanently subsided by the spring of 1890.[24]

From the 1890s onwards the company was increasingly cost-conscious about the provision of amenities for the town. The statement of Lord Stalbridge, chairman of the board of directors, regarding its attitude to contributions to education in Crewe typifies the Company policy by the late nineteenth century: 'What is done in Crewe is only done after most careful consideration as to whether it is cheaper for the shareholders ... the only consideration moving the directors being the economy which can be directed to the shareholders'.[25] The public baths constructed by the company in 1866 had by the late nineteenth century become totally inadequate to the needs of a population which had more than quadrupled. In spite of senior company officials patronising the Crewe Swimming Club, in 1899 the company refused requests from the Town Council for the enlargement of the baths adding that they 'thought the time had arrived when the Corporation should themselves provide the necessary bath accommodation'.[26] Support from senior management no longer assured an organisation financial support from the company. Provision of recreational facilities by the Town Council was notoriously sparse during this period and it was not until 1937 that the baths constructed by the company in 1866 were finally replaced.

The history of the Crewe Mechanics' Institution provides further evidence of the declining role of the company by the turn of the century. The company resisted State involvement in the affairs of the institute and at the same time failed to make adequate provision for the maintenance of high standards of teaching. The county-financed technical school took over many of the educational functions of the establishment. Some aspects of its decline were beyond the company's control. At one time it had been the major secular building for public entertainments but this function had declined by the late nineteenth century, largely owing to the building of the Lyceum Theatre which in 1887 replaced a small theatre built in 1881, and the construction of the Co-operative Hall in 1900. By 1913 the original function of the Institution was finally ended with the establishment in its stead of a licensed social club which drew its membership chiefly from among railway officials and well-to-do local business people.[27]

Some of the most thriving areas of locally-organised leisure, although benefiting from social and economic aspects of railway employment, were among the least dependent on direct company patronage. The fact that the community spawned by the company contained from the earliest years secular and religious groups capable of determining a social life independent of company paternalism was important. The majority of those workers involved were skilled and most were employed in one of a multitude of workshops or departments at the locomotive works. They came from diverse cultures and areas of the British Isles and the self-help, political and temperance traditions, and in particular the Nonconformity of many of these workers provided an important counterweight to the influence of the Tory/Anglican groups with whom the company closely identified its interests. However, even though the company became less willing to spend money, there continued to be a close relationship between social developments, local employment and the attitude of the railway company. Analysis should therefore seek to differentiate between developments in leisure which were a result of company policy and those which, though often relating to railway employment, were primarily under the control of working people.

Wage rates and the availability of free time were key factors in the development of mass leisure and in both respects considerable numbers of railway workers fared better than industrial workers elsewhere. Between 1880 and 1914 the basic wage of the lowest paid adult railway employees was below the Rowntree poverty line of 21*s.* 6*d.* and the scarcity of female employment meant that most families with young children were dependent on one wage. However the lowest wages were rarely below 18*s.* a week and a minimum wage of 20*s.* was established by 1911.[28] At the locomotive works a high proportion of employees received a basic wage of over 21*s.* Over 57 per cent of adults there had jobs with rates above 21*s.* and 42.5 per cent fell in the range 25*s.* to 35*s.* a week.[29] There were no significant increases during the period and by 1912 the preponderating and average rates in the locomotive department were 25s. 6d. and 29s. 7½d. respectively.[30] It is impossible to generalise about wages for, even within one of nearly fifty occupational groups at the works, the pay of individuals could vary by several shillings a week.[31]

Employees received a weekly half day, usually Saturday afternoon, from the late 1850s and annual holidays were established before 1880. From the beginning of the period a significant number of employees working in Crewe but employed outside the works received some holiday with pay and an increasing number of these men were included in this arrangement during the 1890s. By 1912 92.5 per cent of these workers were receiving six days' paid holiday after five years' service. [32] The six to eight hundred railway clerks in the town received two weeks' paid holiday throughout most of this period. An annual week's holiday was well established for wage earners at the works before 1880 although they did not receive paid holidays until 1938. There were also major travel concessions available to all employees and their families and these, coupled with other advantages of railway employment, enabled very significant numbers of them to enjoy the benefits of travel long before World War I.

Cheap and in some cases free travel was granted to employees before the 1880s and was already a factor explaining 'the usual deserted appearance of the town at holiday time'. Until successful agitation brought the granting of quarter fare travel in June 1890 the usual concession had been half-fare travel. Throughout the 1890s and the early twentieth century this privilege was slowly extended to the lines of other companies, largely through the work of the Employee's Interchange Privilege Ticket Movement. Supported by the company, this organisation negotiated and publicised concessions on the lines of other companies and on ferries operating across the English Channel and the Irish Sea. Obviously the extent to which advantage could be taken of cheap travel varied according to the trade cycle and the economic position of individual families, but it is clear that very large numbers were able to take advantage of these facilities and that some travelled very considerable distances.

All the evidence suggests that during the works holiday week large numbers visited seaside resorts throughout the country. It also seems that about fifty per cent of them took extended holidays rather than day trips by the turn of the century. By then, there were reports of large numbers travelling long distances during holiday week. In 1901, for instance, a thousand went to Liverpool, many *en route* for the Isle of Man, and there was 'a sprinkling at Aberystwyth, Barmouth and Bournemouth ... in Ireland and even on the Continent'.[33] In 1907 the *Crewe Chronicle* reported: 'A larger number than usual have gone longer distances. Ireland and Scotland and the Continent have claimed a share of patronage. Crewe will be nigh deserted this week, there has been a very large exodus of workmen and their families on holidays.'[34] Blackpool, though not the nearest, was the most popular seaside resort. Never less than two thousand and sometimes over three thousand tickets were sold for Blackpool in works week alone. Of the sixty-eight holiday advertisements for seaside accommodation in the *Crewe Guardian* in 1911 thirty-eight were from Blackpool. It is also apparent that many employed outside the works took their holidays at other times of the year and that quite a number of workpeople were travelling to their birthplace to visit relatives.

Following the introduction of quarter fares an unprecedented eleven thousand tickets were sold for the autumn holiday in 1891 and sales almost doubled within ten years. The works holiday was transferred from Whitsun to July in 1892 and by the early twentieth century up to twenty thousand privilege tickets were being sold in that week. The state of trade at the Works naturally affected purchases and a pre-1914 peak of twenty thousand sales in July 1901 occurred during a period of particular prosperity.[35] The years 1908 and 1909 also saw good trade and overtime at the works, and it was reported that record sums of money were being spent.[36] The introduction of a free pass for the summer holidays of 1914 led to 'A great exodus from the town of nearly 10,000 artisans with their wives and families leaving their homes for holiday resorts'.[37] It seems likely that Crewe railway families were more experienced holiday travellers than workers in most non-railway towns.[38]

Activities involving travel were often individualistic or family-based but as with most recreations they were also promoted by railway workers' organisations. Trips were arranged by friendly societies and trade unions and also by groups of workers in particular departments. Holiday saving clubs were also established by some of these groups by the turn of the century. Outings reinforced group identity and these were also used to raise funds for other purposes. Workers' organisations were important as bases for leisure activity which in turn owed much of its strength to the economic position of many railway workers. This, coupled with the structure of railway employment, gave the place of work a distinctive role in the leisure activities of the community.

Skilled workers had well-established trade organisations by 1880, and from the mid-1880s there were phases of rapid expansion in unionism among nearly all sectors of railway workers. The Amalgamated Society of Engineers remained the largest union in Crewe and increased from three to six branches during the period. Locally new mass unions grew rapidly between 1888 and 1894, and by 1913 amalgamation led to the formation of the National Union of Railwaymen which had five branches by 1914. Each union had social as well as economic functions and many of them organised a variety of recreational activities. The Amalgamated Society of Railway Servants was particularly active and by the turn of the century was organising large-scale social events. Their annual charity tea parties could attract over eight hundred people and were considered at one point to be 'one of the most if not the most popular gatherings of this kind in the town'.[39] This union also held concerts and dances and came to exploit the commercial potential of modern entertainments like animated picture shows.[40]

Friendly societies, normally more attractive to skilled workers, were particularly strong in Crewe probably because of the high proportion of skilled local railwaymen.[41] The social activities they organised often involved wives and children and on some occasions attracted thousands of people within the wider community. The scale of some of their activities made them among the pioneers of mass leisure activities before 1880. The leading societies had organised an annual gala since 1866 which by 1875 was capable of attracting over ten thousand people. Events that year included bicycle and athletic sports and other entertainments including trapeze and gymnastic artists, Punch and Judy, two military bands and a firework display.[42] Although the organisation of such events eventually passed into the hands of other groups, such as workers at the steam sheds and carriage works, friendly societies still actively contributed to charitable events at the turn of the century.

Friendly societies and trade unions helped nurture self help and mutual assistance traditions and these were further stimulated by the social needs of working people in the town. This ethos ultimately found its most distinctive expression in the workshop or department-based activities of railway workers where the most dynamic, persistent and broadly-based active participation occurred. Such activities fell into three broad categories. There were general social events like dinners, dances, smoking concerts and outings; activities such as those based on bands, choirs and dancing troupes; and sport. Often particular groups also became involved in other activities. The Carriage Works Band, for instance, organised seaside trips, a large fête in aid of local charity and numerous socials, dances and dinners. The importance of the place of work for local leisure is shown by the fact that the band's party and ball in May 1896 was held in a recently-opened portion of the carriage works.[43] The most widespread activities, however, were connected with sport, particularly football and fishing, but the carnival dancing troupes also involved hundreds of workers from the workshops and departments. Annual dinners were an established institution for thousands of workers by the late 1890s.

Competitiveness, fund raising and team-work characterised many of the large scale activities. The Hospital Cup Competition involved up to thirty-eight workshop and department teams, and cup final day could attract over six thousand spectators.[44] Many of these teams were also members of the local football association and some were involved in the county organisation. In the 1912–13 season twenty-seven of the thirty-nine teams in the Crewe and District Football Association were based on railway shops or departments. The Station Employees Football Club and the Permanent Way Football Club were two of the five Crewe clubs in the Cheshire Football Association during that season. Membership of these teams also involved social activities like dances and dinners. Works-based dancing troupes, as well as hundreds of individual railway workers played the major role in the Crewe Fête, which was a fund-raising event crucial to the financing of the local hospital. During some years in the decade and a half before 1914 it attracted over thirty thousand spectators. In 1911 nineteen workshop troupes besides many other workers competed at the event.[45] Contemporary reports leave no doubt that railway workers were vital to the success of the fête. Between 1906 and 1911 it raised a total of £3,150 for the cottage hospital, and between 1895 and 1914 the football competition had raised £1,555.[46] It is significant that these sources of income were far more important to the hospital than élite patronage. In 1912, not a particularly good year for the fête or the football competition, the two events raised £460 and £40 respectively towards the total income of £1,124 19s. 4d for the hospital that year. Governors' subscriptions that year amounted to £155 18s.[47]

Leisure activities based on place of work not only played an important economic role in the broader community but also could foster a community of interest and a common culture among workers of widely different status. Some workers were united by trade and union membership but it is also true that many workers were part of organisations which stemmed from a sense of common identity through working in a particular workshop or department. For example the permanent way, carriage works, erecting shops, station and transit sheds employed men of different status who nevertheless enjoyed some of their leisure time together. Some workers were 'labour aristocrats' who may also have enjoyed the more exclusive social activities of their trade organisations but they also seem to have identified themselves with a particular department. Boilermakers, for instance, were part of a working unit which also contained unskilled workers. Patternmakers, fitters and riveters similarly worked in shops alongside unskilled workers. While the patternmakers' annual picnic was a fairly exclusive event those men might also take part in the wider recreational activities of their particular workshop. Inter-departmental competition between football, cricket and dancing teams brought a wide range of workers together. Thus clerks in the general office came into contact with teams of manual workers of varying status. In some respects the interaction between works-based recreational groups may also have helped to blur the lines of class in the town.

From the early 1890s employees at the railway station began to organise a variety of social and sporting activities. In 1892 they organised their annual dinner and these continued throughout the period. They do not appear to have been exclusive to the best-paid workers, but an annual picnic, started in 1907 for station clerks and officials, suggests that certain events catered for specific groups. Station employees were involved in football and dancing competitions organised outside their department but they also organised events and competitions. The Station Employees' Cycling and Athletic Club was established by 1895 and by 1902 this club had started to organise its own athletics festival. This event attracted workers throughout the LNWR system and by 1908 had been extended to French railway employees.[48] Besides this event the club had regular local matches against the Goods Department Athletic Club. The Station Football Club was established by the turn of the century and was an early member of the Crewe Wednesday Football League, established in 1907.

Workers at the steam sheds similarly organised their own recreational activities. By the mid-1870s the Steam Shed Gala was an established event in which the Steam Shed Band played an active part. Several cricket teams comprising shed workers existed by 1875. There were keen cricket and football rivalries between the North and South sheds throughout the period. The 'combined' Steam Shed Cricket Club also had fixtures against sheds in other towns besides having local matches. Football was a well-established recreation ten years before the founding of the Hospital Cup Competition. Shed workers were closely involved in Crewe Fête from its inception, and a tradition of annual outings organised by employees was well under way by 1900.

Permanent Way workers also participated in a diverse range of activities, and their sporting organisations provide useful insights into the role they, rather than employers, had in establishing particular activities. One member remembered the founding of the Permanent Way Hockey Club and recalled that the establishment of the club was 'nothing to do with the railway, nothing at all, we were on our own, it was run separately'.[49] Speaking at a Permanent Way Cricket Club dinner two of its founders, B. W. Lomas and B. A. Edmunds made the point. They spoke of the founding meeting taking place in the latter's house in 1887 and of a membership of forty by the end of the first season.[50] The report in the *Crewe Chronicle* of the opening of the club's pavilion in July 1891 referred to 'it being built entirely by the members themselves'.[51] The company owned the land but the club members paid a rent and financed their activities. Such overheads necessitated membership subscriptions as well as fund-raising and it seems likely that the poorer workers would have been unable to afford to belong to organisations of this sort.

It appears that many of the recreational activities based on railwaymen's place of work took place at two levels. Worker-organised activities were usually more exclusive when they were either linked to a specific trade or when the activity involved capital outlay and heavy annual overheads. In the case of the larger or trade-based organisations significant numbers of workers would have effectively been excluded from active participation. The widest participation seems to have occurred in the context of the smaller departments or workshops whose football teams and dancing troupes and more individualistic activities like fishing involved large numbers of workers.[52] Similarly seasonal events like galas, fêtes, outings and dinners attracted wide participation. These recreations did not involve heavy annual subscriptions and often aimed at attracting large numbers in order to raise money for charity. In some respects the more broadly-based worker activities were self-supporting commercial ventures and while enjoying various forms of encouragement and help from the company, their real strength lay in the support they received from the community.

Without doubt the most flourishing worker-organised leisure activities took place amongst railway company employees. Although groups of workers at other places of employment organised recreational activities, they felt disadvantaged in comparison with the average railwayman. Most post-office workers, Co-operative Society employees and shop assistants worked on Saturday afternoon, and although Wednesday sports were organised by such workers from the 1890s these activities were on a fairly small scale. Activities lacked facilities and sufficiently large numbers of participants in comparison with those of railway workers. In particular their recreations lacked the sharp competitive edge that the structure of railway employment gave to many activities, as well as the advantages stemming from cheap rail travel.

When the full context of worker-organised activities is considered it becomes apparent that many of them were exclusively the product neither of employer patronage nor of their own autonomous actions. Very often the two were inter-related, usually to the benefit of workers, employers and indeed the whole community. The nature of a particular place of work could be a crucial factor determining what form of leisure was possible. Tracing the original source of initiative for a particular recreation can often obscure the actual course of its development. Working people came to adopt, adapt and even dominate activities previously promoted by social élites. Furthermore many of the skilled workers who came to Crewe already possessed ideas of respectability and self-help valued by middle-class reformers. Also, employers responded to initiatives taken by workers, particularly when they involved fund raising. Charitable work, particularly that serving the needs of the hospital, played an important role in moulding developments and also assured popular support.

The tradition of worker-organised entertainment aimed at fund-raising for local purposes was developing some time before 1880. This increasingly important feature of popular leisure is not apparent in Yeo's study of Reading, as a response to the problems facing many voluntary organisations by the late nineteenth century. Purposeful community action within the framework of railway employment also seems to have been an agent for social harmony. The growth and persistence of such recreational activity may have been a factor limiting the ability of outside entrepreneurs to penetrate the community. There was a commercial theatre, though it is significant that it was rebuilt along smaller lines after a fire in 1910, and by 1914 there were four small cinemas in the district, though only one of these was purpose-built. Several organisations suffered from competition from cinemas and professional sport, but it is also significant that the Crewe Alexandra Football Club had to struggle to survive. Organisations worst hit were those like the Alexandra Athletic Club which rested on a narrow socio-economic base, made no contribution to charities and yet needed to attract spectators. At a time when local leisure and active participation seems to have been declining in towns like Reading, dancing troupes and sporting competitions organised by workers were able to attract the active support of hundreds of people and managed to raise thousands of pounds for local charity. It could be argued that by the turn of the century in Crewe there was a relative decline in patronage and religion and that the most significant local response to community needs came essentially from working-class institutions and their exploitation of the commercial potential of leisure.

Other factors also explain the limited role of commercial entertainment. Relatively high wages and the availability of cheap or free travel made other centres of commercial entertainment, besides seaside resorts, accessible to significant numbers of people. Several elderly residents of Crewe recall that along with many others they travelled to Manchester (particularly Belle Vue), Chester and Liverpool for shopping and entertainment. This reduced yet further the commercial potential of a fairly small urban community. Thus the consequences of railway employment helped nurture and maintain localised activities and at the same time enhanced workers' opportunities to enjoy commercialised recreation outside the town.

NOTES

1 See in particular: P. Bailey, *Leisure and Class in Victorian England* (1978), and S. Yeo, *Religion and Voluntary Organisations in Crisis* (1976).

2 J. Walvin, *The People's Game* (1975), p. 51.

3 At that point the Grand Junction Railway Company which through further amalgamation became the London and North-Western Railway Company in 1846.

4 Quoted in W. H. Chaloner, *The Social and Economic development of Crewe* (Manchester, 1950), p. 48.

5 I am particularly indebted to P. Ollerhead, 'Protestant Nonconformity in Crewe', M.A. thesis, University of Keele, 1975 for these statistics. He shows that in 1881 the national membership population ratio for Primitive Methodism was 0.58 per cent whilst in Crewe it was just over 1 per cent (pp. 152–3).

6 *Crewe Guardian*, 27 August 1881.

7 B. Harrison, 'Pubs' in H. J. Dyos and M. Wolff, *The Victorian City*, 2 vols. (1973), p. 162.

8 In 1892 there was a peak of 93 licences but by 1913, in spite of a 12,000 increase in population, the number of licences had dropped to 77. By 1911 the ratio of population to licences was 519. Prosecutions for drunkenness declined from 256 in 1895 to 193 in 1906. 'A continued decline in drunkenness' was reported at the licensing session in 1912. *Crewe and District Directory*, 1913, pp. 23–34; *Crewe Guardian*, 3 March 1911; *Crewe Chronicle*, 9 February 1907; *Eardley's Almanac*, 1913 for 6 December 1912.

9 *Crewe Chronicle*, 23 August 1902.

10 *Crewe Chronicle*, 9 June 1906.

11 Report of speech by Dr J. Atkinson, Chief Surgeon LNWR, on the role of F. W. Webb in encouraging sport, *Crewe Chronicle*, 21 May 1895.

12 *Crewe Guardian*, 28 March 1912.

13 Report of speech given at 7th Annual Show, *Crewe Chronicle*, 7 August 1880.

14 *Annual Report of Crewe Mechanics' Institution*, 45 (1890) 47 (1892), Crewe Reference Library.

15 J. E. Williams, *The Crewe Mechanics' Institution, 1843–1913*, M.Ed. thesis, University of Manchester, 1969, p. 209.

16 *Op. cit.*, p. 276.

17 Interview with Mrs S. 1.78, pp. 32–3. This is one of twenty interviews conducted in 1978 and 1979 – transcripts are available at Crewe and Alsager College of Higher Education and Crewe Reference Library.

18 Report of AGM 1898 when it was claimed that in spite of the 2s and 3s increase, rates were 'still half those of lesser clubs', *Crewe Chronicle*, 21 May 1898.

19 See Yeo, *op. cit.*, pp. 187–96.

20 *Crewe Chronicle*, 28 March 1891.

21 The Crewe Athletics Festival enjoyed a national reputation during this period and the grounds were good enough for the AAA to hold the National Championships there in 1888.

22 Diehards like T. M. Abrahams eventually accepted the need for a cricket professional and reluctantly credited the club's improved performance to his

employment; *Crewe Chronicle*, 29 September 1906, 13 April 1909.

23 Only F. W. Webb gave substantial sums to local organisations on his own account. During the latter years of his life and in his Will he gave over £40,000 towards the establishment of various welfare institutions. However this money made little contribution to the financing of institutions once they were built.

24 For further details, see, Chaloner, *op. cit.*, pp. 150–66 and 300–10.

25 *Crewe Chronicle*, 17 November 1894.

26 Market, Cemetery and Water Committee minutes, Crewe Town Council, quoted in Chaloner, *op. cit.*, p. 54.

27 See Williams, *op. cit.*, *passim* and Chaloner, *op. cit.*, pp. 233–48.

28 Proposed scale of rates, 1 November 1911, *Locomotive Circulars*, NPR 1/4, Cheshire Record Office.

29 These figures are based on the *Register of Crewe Works Staff*, RAIL 410 1968/1969, Public Record Office. These also show that of the employees under the age of twenty-one years 58% were apprentices and 42% boy labourers.

30 The preponderating and average rates of wages of adult staff in each department, *Census 1912: giving information as to the rates of wages and hours of labour and other conditions of service, January 1912*, NPR/1/2/8, Cheshire Record Office.

31 *Ibid.*

32 Chaloner, *op. cit.*, p. 7.

33 *Crewe Chronicle*, 6 July 1901.

34 *Crewe Chronicle*, 6 July 1907.

35 *Crewe Chronicle*, 6 July 1901.

36 *Crewe Chronicle*, 4 July 1908, 10 July 1909.

37 *Crewe Guardian*, 30 June 1914.

38 There is evidence that workers in cotton towns and in Sheffield had extensive experience of holiday travel by this time; see J. K. Walton, 'The demand for working class seaside holidays in Victorian England', *Economic History Review* xxxiv (May 1981), pp. 249–65.

39 *Crewe Guardian*, 21 April 1900.

40 *Crewe Chronicle*, 19 March 1910.

41 By 1913 several societies had ceased to function but there were still thirty-nine branches, lodges and courts listed in the *Crewe and District Directory*, 1913. Twenty-five of these were members of the Crewe and District Association of Friendly Societies in 1908, and represented a total of seven thousand members; *Eardley's Almanac*, 1909 for 29 August 1908.

42 *Crewe Chronicle*, 3 July 1875, 10 July 1875.

43 *Eardley's Almanac*, 1897 for 16 August 1896.

44 From the turn of the century there were never fewer than thirty teams entered. The peak season was 1909–10 but there were still thirty-six teams entered in the season before World War I broke out. Final day usually involved a parade around the town and performances by local bands and dancing troupes. There were usually around three thousand spectators in the years before 1914 but twice that number attended in the early twentieth century. See report of final day, *Crewe Chronicle*, 27 April 1901.

45 *Crewe Guardian*, 21 July 1911.

46 Report of the Fête Committee AGM, *Eardley's Almanac*, 1912, for 20

November 1911; report of AGM of Cheshire Football Association, *Crewe Guardian*, 16 May 1914.

47 Annual Report of Cottage Hospital Committee, in *Crewe Guardian*, 20 February 1914.

48 *Eardley's Almanac*, 1909 for 8 August 1908.

49 Interview with Mr G, 1.78 (see note 17 above).

50 Report *Crewe Guardian*, 5 December 1911.

51 *Crewe Chronicle*, 1 August 1891.

52 For example the 5th Annual Fishing Match organised by the fitting shop attracted between five and six hundred competitors in 1908; *Eardley's Almanac*, 1909 for 29 August 1908.

8 RICHARD ROBERTS
The Corporation as impresario entertainment in Victoria

I

The subject chosen by Sir Henry Fowler M.P. for his presidential address to the Royal Statistical Society on 15 May 1900 was the topical question of 'Municipal Finance and Municipal Enterprise'.[1] He identified a series of stages in the evolution of the functions of local government over the preceding century. His framework offers a context to the growth of the provision of leisure amenities by public authorities in towns.

In its infancy, he said, urban local government was concerned with public order and public health. First came 'the relief of the poor, the protection of public peace by means of the police, the construction and maintenance of roads and streets and the lighting of the same'. Gradually the scope of public provision extended to encompass 'works necessary for the preservation of the public health, such as drainage, scavenging, and sewering, asylums for lunatics, and hospitals for the isolation of infectious diseases, and the establishment of public baths, and the other steps necessary to prevent the spread of such diseases, and the improvement of the dwellings of the working classes'.[2]

The provision of services and amenities for the improvement of the quality of the lives of citizens was identified by Fowler as a second stage in the development of local government. The 'improving' activities of local authorities included 'provision for the intellectual wants of the community in the shape of education, and free libraries', and for its recreational requirements by 'the establishment of art galleries and the acquisition of parks and open spaces'.[3]

A third phase, identified by Fowler as commencing in the 1870s, saw the development of local government undertakings 'embracing new areas of commercial and industrial activity'.[4] A broadening view of the responsibilities of local government for the welfare of the community led many authorities to assume control over local supplies of water, gas, electricity and urban transport. The establishment of municipal utility enterprises, a development known as municipal trading, took the functions of local authorities, in Fowler's view, 'beyond what may be called the primary objects for which local taxation is raised'.

A fierce controversy raged at the turn of the century around the question of municipal trading. Fowler's paper was a contribution to this debate. Trading enterprises were so called because individual customers were charged for the supply of services received, a financial basis which more closely resembled the conduct of private business than familiar local authority services such as roadworks or police. Indeed, most municipal undertakings were former private utility companies and the wave of municipal takeovers of private enterprises in the 1890s and early 1900s aroused demands for a definition of the legitimate limit of public owner-ship. The argument was fanned by the unparalleled number of applica-tions by local authorities in local acts for 'novel powers' to undertake hitherto untried forms of municipal trading in industries that were not natural monopolies, which thus raised the spectre of local government conducting trading undertakings in competition with private business. Many of these proposals for 'novel powers' came from resort towns which sought consent for the establishment of municipal entertainments enterprises.

The activities of British local government authorities are constrained by the long-established legal doctrine of *ultra vires* which makes it illegal for a corporation to do anything unless it is specifically empowered to do so by Parliament.[5] In matters other than public health the general statutes governing local authority powers in the nineteenth century were mostly permissive not mandatory measures. In some cases a general power was given though often a local authority had deliberately to adopt a power subject to confirmation by Parliament in each case. Powers to provide for recreation in general acts were usually of this adoptive type. The earliest, which concerned pleasure grounds and places of public recreation, were included in the Towns Improvement Clauses Act, 1847, and the Public Health Act, 1848. The Museums Act, 1845, and the Public Libraries Act, 1855, allowed the acquisition of powers for these purposes. The Baths and Washhouses Act, 1878, empowered local autho-rities to build and run swimming baths and an amending act of 1899 permitted them to close the premises on occasion and for music and dancing to take place 'subject to a licence being obtained under the Disorderly Houses Act, 1751'. The Public Health Acts Amendment Act, 1907, was 'the first piece of general legislation of real substance in this field'.[6] It enabled local authorities to employ a band to perform in a public park, to provide a pavilion to be used for entertainments, for which admission charges could be made, to maintain refreshment rooms in parks and to set aside portions of parks to be used for organised games from which the public was excluded for the duration of the game.

The clauses of the Public Health Acts Amendment Act, 1907, were an attempt to codify in a general statute the powers which had been applied for, time after time, over the preceding decade in local bills. The presentation to Parliament of a local bill was the means of achieving powers to undertake a particular purpose when there was no pertinent clause in a general statute. It was an uncertain procedure since the Local Government Board and parliamentary committees had to be con-vinced of the special local need for a 'novel power'. The initiatives for extending the functions of local government to the provision of municipal entertainments and recreation facilities came from the local authorities themselves. 'In other words', states the standard legal manual on the subject of the Law of Municipal and Public Entertainments, 'there was no direction from the central government that local authorities must undertake entertainment, but acquiescence, often only grudgingly given, by Parliament'.[7]

Resort towns led the field in the presentation of local bills to Parliament seeking consent for powers to conduct entertainments, notably the employment of bands for public concerts and the provision of municipal concert halls. Powers granted to resorts, pleading pressing local circumstances, anticipated the Public Health Acts Amendment Act, 1907, by many years. Blackpool, for instance, achieved powers in 1879 to use rated revenues to provide a band; Cheltenham, in 1889, to provide 'exhibitions, lectures, concerts, and entertainments'; Bournemouth, in 1892, and Harrogate, in 1893, to provide a pavilion and a band. The motives of the local authorities of resorts for the provision of entertainments differed, however, from those of the other towns which started to seek similar powers. In most towns the actions had the familiar improving welfare objective which had led them to provide municipal parks. In resorts the motive was commercial to boost the holiday industry. The conspicuous eagerness of the local authorities of resorts for municipal entertainments arose, 'with a view to providing additional inducements to holiday-makers to leave their money behind them'.[8]

II

Resort towns faced special commercial problems. Their local economies were usually composed of a large number of small-scale enterprises almost entirely devoted to satisfying the demands of visitors or retired residents. The concentration upon these service activities made local prosperity deeply dependent upon the town continuing to find favour with the public as a leisure resort. The highly seasonal nature of demand for holiday services presented tradesmen with cash-flow problems and caused workmen to be laid off in slack times. In some resorts, notably Blackpool, initiatives were taken to extend the length of the season, though in most the fluctuations were simply accepted as the way of the industry. Whims of fashion and the development of new attractions by rival resorts presented further threats to local livelihoods. If potential patrons went crowding to another place, for whatever reason, the result was a sorry season for the local economy. Competition for visitors between resorts grew ever more intense in the late nineteenth century and early twentieth century as local businessmen strove harder and harder to promote the popularity of their resort and ensure the prosperity of their enterprise.

What could be done to make a resort more attractive? Contemporaries advocated three types of measure: investment, control and advertisement. Investment in an infra-structure of recreational amenities, such as parks, or places of entertainment, such as piers or pavilions, extended the range of attractions offered by a resort. A reputation for salubriousness, based on a health record free from epidemics, was an important asset for a Victorian resort. Careful control over building standards, sewering and water supply was dictated by commercial as well as public health considerations. A town's standing as a pleasant and respectable resort was safeguarded by regulation of the business practices of tradesmen and the behaviour of the public. Advertisment could be employed to keep the name of a resort before the public and to build up an image.

The commercial challenge which confronted resorts was best met by a co-ordinated response. In some resorts there were private interests of sufficient size and resources to take the lead.[9] Landowners and railway companies sometimes shouldered the burden. In many resorts, however, it was left to the local authority to take initiatives to promote the prosperity of the local economy on behalf of every shopkeeper, hotelier and builder.

Bournemouth is an example of a resort in which the local authority played an active part in support of the local economy. Public assistance included by-laws designed to preserve the town's good name and contributions to publicity and promotional activity. Municipal investment in recreational amenities and expenditure upon entertainments, made the local authority the resort's foremost showman, 'the Barnum of Bournemouth'. By the outbreak of World War I it owned several venues for public entertainments – the two piers, upon which bands regularly played, the large concert hall called the Winter Gardens – while the town hall was often used for concerts and lectures. Recreational amenities included 620 acres of parks and gardens, thirty-three bowling greens, twenty tennis courts, ten cricket pitches, six football pitches, three croquet lawns, two golf courses, overcliff and undercliff carriage drives, electric cliff lifts, beach, beach huts, refreshment kiosk and municipal deck chair service, libraries, and a museum. Furthermore, the town employed a municipal symphony orchestra and municipal band. Bournemouth's municipal recreation amenities and diversions went beyond the public provision found in other towns and most rival resorts.

Bournemouth was one of the most successful resorts and fastest growing towns in the late nineteenth century. In the fifty years from 1861 to 1911 the settlement was transformed from a village of under two thousand inhabitants to a county borough with a population of almost eighty thousand. The most important factors behind its success were the natural charms of its location, the close control over development exercised by the half-dozen leading leasehold estates and the economic initiatives of the local authority. But why was it that Bournemouth's local authority was inclined to take such an active interest in the local economy?

Local circumstances at Bournemouth prompted a particularly vigorous collective response to the economic problems common to resorts. First, its clientèle was especially fickle and footloose. Thanks principally to the exclusive estate development policies pursued by the resort's ground landlords, Bournemouth enjoyed the patronage of prosperous and patrician visitors. It became the local authority's self-appointed purpose to sustain the attraction of Bournemouth to this 'high-class' clientèle in the face of mounting competition from rival British resorts and especially from the Continent. It was essential to ensure that suitably seemly amenities and diversions were available. The neglect of landowners to provide important amenities, such as carriage drives, and the failure of private enterprise to establish appropriate entertainments threatened to allow the resort's advantage to slip away by default. Bournemouth's local authority took steps to ensure that this did not happen.

The second local factor was the commercial orientation of the local authority. From the outset Bournemouth's local authority regarded its economic function as at least as important as its policing and welfare functions. The economic inertia of landowners and the London and South Western Railway Company persuaded local tradesmen to look to the local authority for initiatives which they believed to be in the best interests of the local community. Bournemouth's local authority served as the instrument of the resort's tradesmen. The absence, prior to 1916, of a chamber of commerce in a town boasting so many small businessmen is perhaps surprising. But so long as the council chamber served as an alternative forum it was simply not needed.

III

Two major departures may be identified in the establishment of the municipal leisure amenities in Bournemouth. The first was the construction of the pier in the late 1850s. The second was the acquisition of the Winter Garden and the formation of the orchestra in the early 1890s. Both were occasioned by the absence in the resort of amenities for which the business community considered there to be a pressing need. The establishment of these municipal enterprises led to further initiatives in later years and caused the local authority to become even more closely involved in the local economy.

From the outset Bournemouth's local government authority was conceived as an instrument for the promotion of the resort's economy. Local government in Bournemouth began with a body formed primarily for the purpose of erecting a pier. The lack of a landing stage became a cause for concern in the mid 1850s.[10] It was believed that a pier, serving both as a point of disembarkation for the passengers of coastal steamers and as a pleasure promenade, would add to the amenities of the resort and attract visitors and new residents. A scheme of the Gervis Estate, the most extensively developed estate, for the construction of a pier in 1847 had come to nothing. Since neither landowners nor entrepreneurs were interested in pursuing the project residents and tradesmen took action on their own behalf.

In 1855 a jetty was erected, paid for by public subscription. Although the steamers now had a place to dock, this expedient was no more than a stopgap before the building of a proper pier. A pier, however, was a substantial undertaking which could be financed and managed only by an appropriately permanent body. Local enthusiasm, and the proven local willingness to subscribe for the construction of a pier, might have sustained the successful promotion of a pier company by taking up shares issued in sufficiently small denominations to allow widespread participation in the undertaking, 'so that every tradesman and lodging-house keeper might have an interest in it'.[11] This was the form of community enterprise that was to be employed for the launching of the local steamship company in 1881, the Boscombe Pier Company in 1885, and by the promoters of various temperance hotels and coffee-houses. In 1856, however, limited liability was perhaps rather too recent an innovation to be familiar to the tradesmen of a tiny settlement like Bournemouth. Instead it was decided to form a local government authority, which would raise subscriptions in the form of rates, to construct and to run the pier.

Bournemouth's first pier, a wooden structure 1,000 feet long, opened in September 1861. Construction in wood proved to be a false economy and in the mid-1870s, after many costly repairs, it was decided to rebuild in iron. The new pier, which cost £22,833, a sum which almost doubled the town's outstanding debt, was opened with fitting pomp by the Lord Mayor of London in August 1880. A further £80,000 was spent on capital improvement works up to 1914.

The substantial public investment in the new pier led Bournemouth's local authority to take over its running. It was hoped that close control by a permanent sub-committee of the Improvement Commission, the Pier Committee, would yield a higher revenue than the practice of seeking tenders for the pier tolls hitherto employed.[12]

The Pier Committee was the first trading committee of the Bournemouth Improvement Commission – a committee responsible not only for expenditures but for the management of a commercial undertaking. The Pier Committee soon realised that to maximise ratepayers' returns on their investment required entrepreneurial initiative. Steps were taken to generate business for the pier and for Bournemouth. The Committee arranged visits to the resort with excursion operators, co-ordinated the activities of the organisers of special events, such as fêtes and regattas, and itself provided diversions for visitors including free band music. The Pier Committee served as the instrument for securing municipal control over the front. It employed beach inspectors to enforce the bathing and vending by-laws, took over beach catering and the hire of beach huts and deck-chairs and initiated the building of the electric cliff lifts.

These extensions of local authority involvement in the local economy might never have happened had the Commissioners sold the pier to the Bournemouth Promenade Pier Company, a company formed in 1875 to build a pier at Bournemouth. The 'private adventurers', a syndicate of local and London businessmen, held negotiations with the Council during 1875, 1876 and 1877, but the parties were unable to agree on terms. Local opinion was generally hostile to the proposed sale. The strength of feeling emerged at the public inquiry of the Local Government Board's inspector in February 1878 into the council's application to borrow to build the new pier. A widespread fear was voiced that a pier run along profit-maximising lines by a private company would turn the town into 'a sort of tea and shrimp resort'. The inspector concluded 'that in his opinion a pier in the hands of the Commissioners would be much better than one in the hands of a company, whose object might be to make it attractive, probably in a way which the residents of Bournemouth would not approve'.[13]

The trading balance of the Bournemouth Pier usually showed a small surplus of receipts over working costs, though some subsidy from the rates was often required to meet interest payments on capital. Few ratepayers objected to these subsidies. The case for the municipal ownership, and if necessary subvention, of a vital amenity was almost universally accepted.

The argument was reiterated by spokesmen for Boscombe, Bournemouth's eastern quarter, in 1902 when Boscombe pier, the resort's second pier, was threatened with closure.[14] This 'great addition to the social amenities of Boscombe' had never been a profitable undertaking for its shareholders, local tradesmen, builders, landlords and residents, though its contribution to the success of Boscombe as a holiday resort may have indirectly compensated those with interests in real estate or the holiday trade.[15] In 1902 it became apparent that expensive repairs were required which the company could neither afford nor justify owing to its persistent trading deficits. Bournemouth council purchased the pier in 1903 in the full knowledge that it was unlikely ever to be a profitable undertaking.[16] Despite the provision of a twenty-man band to play during the summer season and other enterprising entertainments, the Boscombe pier required more than £1,000 per annum subsidy from the General Fund during the decade following its reopening under municipal control in 1904. Yet again there was little criticism of the decision to rescue the pier or of the subventions. Such attractions and amenities were too important to be left to the mercy of the market. Mate and Riddle, the resort's official centennial historians of 1910, expressed the general attitude towards the pier and the subsidies. 'It is not a profit-producing concern', they wrote, 'but the deficits which so far have had to be met, year by year, are more than compensated for by other advantages conferred upon the ratepayers.'[17]

Takings from visitors to Bournemouth Pier rose fivefold between 1881 and 1914, from £2,000 to £10,000. In part this increase resulted from the growth of the town and the general expansion of summer visitors in the final decades of the nineteenth century. It also reflected the enterprise of the Pier Committee and its success at promoting the pier, endeavouring to make it the focus of festivities for the resort's summer holidaymakers. The heavy expenditure upon improvements to the landing stage in 1909, for example, was an investment to foster pleasure steamer traffic.

Music was a pleasure which Victorian holidaymakers expected to enjoy at the seaside,[18] and the Committee strove to meet this demand.[19] In 1885 regular band performances commenced on the pier in summer evenings. By 1888 the price of admission to the pier included a serenade by one of the town's two bands every night of the week save Sunday from July to September. It was considered preferable for the pier to meet the cost of the band, £18 18s per week, than to permit the vulgarity of a collection. In 1896 the Committee initiated daily morning, afternoon and evening variety entertainments in addition to the several band performances during the summer months. Catering further to the growing excursion trade the Committee organised special programmes of entertainments on the Bank Holidays at Easter and Whitsun from 1904 and finally, despite protests from the resort's vociferous sabbatarians, Sunday band concerts on the pier began in the summer of 1913. By then the municipal music, which had begun as no more than an enticement to walk the pier, had become one of the resort's principal attractions in its own right.

IV

In the final decades of the nineteenth century Bournemouth became a resort with two distinct groups of visitors at different times of the year.[20] In summer came a growing number of middle-class holidaymakers who took a house or rooms or stayed at one of the growing number of private hotels and boarding houses, *en famille*, for a week or two. At weekends and Bank Holidays they were joined by an ever-increasing influx of excursionists. In winter arrived the traditional clientèle of invalids and wealthy rentiers who planned to pass the frosty months in Bournemouth's dry and mild climate.

During the 1850s, 1860s, 1870s and 1880s the winter visitors generated little effective demand for the services of commercial entertainments. Their diversions were restorative and private. By day they enjoyed a promenade in the Invalids' Walk in the Central Pleasure Gardens, Bournemouth's Bath-chair Rotten Row, a carriage drive to Corfe Castle or the New Forest, or a stroll along the beach and cliffs. The Bournemouth Club, founded in 1871, was the resort of the town's leading tradesmen and physicians and of many gentleman visitors though it offered neither food nor games, other than billiards, and served only as a place for 'reading the newspapers and studying notices anent spittoons and cigar-ends'.[21]

Evenings were passed at decorous and domestic activities, over dinner, at whist or mah-jong, or around the piano for a private recital. Balls for visitors were organised with the sponsorship of the local gentry though comments in the local press suggest that attendance was often disappointing. The social habits and institutions of Bournemouth did not impress an emissary of 'society' who visited the town in 1878 and returned a caustic and supercilious report to the *Whitehall Review* which caused great local offence:

> The dissipations of Bournemouth are mostly confined to dinner parties, five-o'clock teas, and prayer meetings. At Christmas there are sundry private dances and one or two public balls, the latter being held in the Town Hall, which is really a finely-proportioned building, and suited to such delights. On one point Bournemouth is united, and that is in a love for music. The highest form of amusement is a concert by the Amateur Musical or Philharmonic Society, when the friends and relatives of the performers gather together in force, and vigorously applaud a love song from one of the clergy, or a cantata executed by a bevy of dames and damsels with better intentions than voices ... Bournemouth is the worst place in the world to bring daughters to. There are very few young men and there is no attraction to bring others. Yet is Society in and about Bournemouth decidedly above the average; but those who form it seem more or less stricken with apathy ... and ... there is no place in Bournemouth where people congregate to meet and be met by friends.[22]

The leisure habits of Bournemouth's winter visitors frustrated the enterprise of private promoters of entertainments. Although the absence of a suitable 'rendezvous', noted above, was an increasingly acutely felt want during the 1870s and 1880s, the private schemes to provide such a place failed. In 1877 a Winter Garden opened in the centre of the town as a venue for concerts and exhibitions but it was soon evident that demand for commercially-provided diversions had been overestimated and the company went into liquidation the following year.[23] The company was a local speculation, although the list of those who subscribed the £12,000 for the erection of the hall included several London solicitors and 2,355 of the £1 shares were taken by the London contractors responsible for construction, Fletcher Lowndes and Company. A rescue attempt was made by a local consortium led by Christopher Crabbe Creeke, surveyor to the large Dean Estate and the Improvement Commission, and Joseph Cutler, a prominent local developer and businessman, who registered the Bournemouth Winter Garden and Aquarium Company in May 1878 to acquire the property.[24] Shortage of funds frustrated the bid. The structure was taken over by nurseryman John White from the trustees of the company in May 1883. White revived the concerts but again they proved unprofitable.[25] The Winter Garden was turned over to his plants until 1893 when it reverted to its original function under the management of Bournemouth Corporation.

For twenty years the Belle Vue Assembly Rooms, built in the early 1850s, were Bournemouth's principal venue for social events and entertainments and were the first meeting place of the Improvement Commission. They were superseded in 1875 by the new Town Hall which accommodated not only the Improvement Commission but also 'first class companies' of players.[26] The formation of the Bournemouth Theatre and Opera House Company in 1881 led to the construction of the first purpose-built theatre in the resort:[27] it was not a financial success. In 1887 the Improvement Commission moved in and for five years it served as the town hall. It became a theatre once again in 1892 and prospered thereafter as the Bournemouth Theatre Royal and Opera House.

The successful reopening of the Winter Garden and the Theatre Royal in the early 1890s was testimony both to the changing social habits of Bournemouth's valetudinarian visitors and to the fortification of their ranks by a growing number of retired permanent residents. It also reflected a deliberate effort on the part of local businessmen and the local authority to enhance the resort's attractions. During the 1880s tradesmen, hoteliers, builders and estate agents became increasingly concerned that Bournemouth was falling behind in the highly competitive market for holidaymakers and new residents on account of a lack of suitable attractions. The dissatisfied verdicts of contemporary visitors suggest that their misgivings were not unfounded. Robert Louis Stevenson, a convalescent in the resort for three years, 1884-7, likened his sojourn to the life of a weevil in a biscuit.[28] Harry Furness, who visited the resort in 1891, described it as 'this most decorous and dull of watering places', and complained of 'the extraordinary absence of any provision for promoting the gaiety of nations'. 'Of course,' he added, 'it must be remembered that the place exists chiefly for the invalids'.[29]

Advocates of improvement demanded a building which would provide a social focus, a worthy meeting place for 'high-class' visitors after the example of a Continental casino, and they looked to the local authority to build it. A pavilion came first in the programme of necessary additions to the resort's attractions presented to each member of the Commission in 1887 by Horace Dobell of the Mont Dore Hotel. His proposals, he explained, 'formed from long and careful observation, enquiry and consideration . . . constitute the desiderata for putting Bournemouth in its proper position as the leading fashionable South Coast health resort for the wealthier classes'.[30] He argued that the pavilion was Bournemouth's most urgently needed amenity for 'without this it does not matter what else is done, it will not continue to prosper'.

Proposals for the construction of a pavilion on the pier were heard many times during the 1880s, and in March 1883 the Commission even passed a resolution to proceed.[31] Action, however, waited upon local politics. During the 1880s the spokesmen for the resort's retired residents, the 'Resident Ratepayer' representatives, were able to muster sufficient support to block the more costly projects of the tradesmen commissioners, known collectively in the 1890s as the 'Progressives'. The achievement of municipal borough administrative status for the town in 1890, after two strongly contested and unsuccessful bids in 1884 and 1886, was not only an an expression of political support for the programme of the Progressives, it shifted the balance of power decisively in their favour by the introduction of the broader borough franchise and the abolition of the plural voting privileges of house owners which had usually been exercised in support of Resident Ratepayer representatives. Having secured their hold over Bournemouth's local government the Progressives moved to put their plans to enhance Bournemouth's attractions into effect.[32]

The provision of municipal music in a municipal concert hall, the Winter Garden, was the outcome of their initiatives. The acquisition of the Winter Garden, upon which a lease was taken in May 1892, was a compromise choice, which commended itself on grounds of economy, between rival proposals to build a pavilion on the pier or in the pleasure grounds. It proved to be a damp and draughty building with high maintenance costs, and many councillors, not to mention the orchestra, were soon dissatisfied. The proponents of a proper Continental-style casino continued to agitate for it during the 1890s and 1900s. Unfortunately the scheme aroused the hostility not only of those ratepayers who opposed all municipal expenditure at all times, the 'do-nothing party', but also the town's powerful temperance lobby which objected to a municipal licensed premises which they regarded as civic encouragement of an immoral pastime. The hostility of 'do-nothings' and teetotallers, and the continuing disagreements as to the site, blocked the scheme until 1908 when the Council at last resolved to proceed with the acquisition of a site in the pleasure gardens. Further challenges and the outbreak of war delayed the completion of the Bournemouth Pavilion until 1929.

The Bournemouth Improvement Act of 1892 sanctioned the expenditure of £20,000 upon a pavilion and the cost of placing bandstands in the Central Pleasure Gardens and empowered the Council to spend a $\frac{1}{2}d$ rate for the maintenance of a town band. During the 1880s bands had been recruited by the Pier Committee on a season-by-season basis to play on the pier. Proposals for the formation of a municipal band were first seriously discussed in 1891, and in 1893 Dan Godfrey Junior was engaged as Musical Adviser to the Corporation charged with providing and directing a band of thirty players in the summer season.[33] It was a fortunate choice. Indefatigable in the exercise of his duties, he also had a keen business sense and an entrepreneurial flair which placed him nearer the tradition of Beau Nash than to that of simple masters of music. In 1897, upon the retirement of the Winter Gardens business manager, Godfrey assumed the role, thereby taking full control of both orchestra and concert hall.[34]

The establishment of a municipal orchestra was an unprecedented departure in municipal enterprise. The credit belongs jointly to Godfrey for his drive and foresight and to the Winter Garden and Band Committee of the Council which supported him. He recruited sufficient 'double-handed' players for the twenty-five-member military band of 1893–4 to provide a small string section to play in the Winter Garden while the rest of the band performed upon the pier.[35] The municipal orchestra proper emerged following the acceptance of Godfrey's proposal for afternoon symphony concerts in November 1894. Expansion of the musical establishment proceeded during the 1890s and by 1903 the winter strength was forty players, rising to forty-eight in summer when there were additional band duties to be undertaken on the piers and in the parks. A separate military-style brass band, of twenty players, was recruited in 1904 to play during the summer at Boscombe. In 1912 the orchestra was relieved of all band duties by the establishment of an independent band for the summer season.

Band duties had long been a tiresome obligation and hindrance to Godrey's ambition, 'to establish for Bournemouth a reputation for high class music not enjoyed by any other town in the kingdom'.[36] He was successful in his bid to turn the Bournemouth Winter Garden into a concert hall with an international reputation by his sponsorship of contemporary British composers. Yet he realised that the majority of his audiences preferred to hear overtures and vocalists and his programmes included leavenings of these items which ensured the continued popularity of the Winter Garden concerts among visitors and residents.

Bournemouth's municipal bands and orchestra established the local authority as the resort's leading impresario. Municipal policy was to provide 'higher entertainment' which would bolster the town's reputation as a respectable and up-market resort where affluent visitors could mingle with their own kind and find diversions which fitted their refinement.[37] The Council well understood that the attention which music correspondents paid to the orchestra and the esteemed standing of its programmes carried the resort's name abroad more effectively than any puff. The author of the pamphlet issued in 1911 to celebrate twenty-one years of municipal music in Bournemouth concluded that 'music has long since proved to be one of the most effective commercial assets to the town, and in regard solely as a means of advertisement, it stands without a rival'.[38]

V

By the late nineteenth century the provision of recreational amenities for the enjoyment of the local population, in the form of parks, sports grounds, art galleries or libraries by local authorities was commonplace. Fowler explained that many councils acted 'upon the principle of the co-operation of the many to secure for the advantage of all those opportunities for the healthy and elevating enjoyment of life which were previously confined to a limited section of the inhabitants who were able to procure them at their own cost'.[39] In Bournemouth too the provision of outdoor recreational amenities was achieved co-operatively through the municipality. The motive of Bournemouth's local authority, however, was fundamentally commercial. The recreational benefits enjoyed by the local population were additional to the over-riding purpose of providing an infrastructure of attractions to lure visitors to the resort.

The earliest development at Bournemouth was along the valley of the Bourne. Houses were built on the hillsides overlooking the stream while low-lying land either side of the stream bed was set aside by the landowners as a garden with a promenade soon known as the Invalids' Walk. In the early 1870s, after a decade and a half of negotiations, the Improvement Commission took leases on the Lower Pleasure Garden from the Lord of the Manor and on fields further up the valley. The twenty-nine acres of the Lower and Upper Central Pleasure Gardens were laid out and henceforth maintained, at substantial cost, by the local authority.

Eulogistic descriptions of the delights of the Central Pleasure Gardens took pride of place in the descriptions of Bournemouth's attractions published in the visitors' guidebooks of the 1870s and 1880s, outshining even the rapturous sketches of the municipal cemetery and its splendid avenue of *Araucaria Imbricata,* or monkey-puzzle trees.

In the decade from the early 1890s to the mid-1900s the local authority acquired further parks and recreation grounds which transformed the opportunities for athletic and outdoor recreation in the resort. The title to several large tracts which had been placed in the care of the Lord of the Manor in trust for local inhabitants upon the enclosure of the heathland in 1802 was acquired by the local authority in these years. The land constituted the basis of Meyrick Park, 118 acres, King's Park, 58 acres, and Queen's Park, 173 acres. Leases were taken from local landowners by the corporation on Dean Park, 14 acres, Boscombe Gardens, 9 acres, Boscombe Cliff Gardens, 6 acres, Knyveton Gardens, 4 acres, Winton Recreation Ground, 14 acres, Argyll Gardens, 2 acres, and the three chines, gullies issuing on to the sea, 36 acres. The Council's initiatives for the acquisition of these lands for laying out as parks led to the rupture of the hitherto harmonious relations between landowners and local government in Bournemouth. Councillors accused landowners who did not respond positively to its suggestions for turning open spaces into parks tended by the Corporation of neglecting their duties to the resort. Local landowners resented the interference in their affairs and were offended by the abuse to which they were subjected. Good relations resumed in the mid-1900s after the local authority had achieved its aims and taken control of most of the areas that it coveted.[40]

The parks programme of the 1890s and 1900s complemented the opening of the municipal Winter Garden, the formation of the orchestra and the purchase of Boscombe Pier. They were all measures intended to assist the local economy by the Progressives, the tradesmen's party, who dominated the Council after 1890. Behind the moves lay concern for the competitive standing of Bournemouth as a resort. In the early 1900s that section of Bournemouth's tradesmen which catered to the most affluent visitors suffered a trade depression and an attack of acute anxiety for the future. As an act of patriotic self-denial Britain's upper class forsook Continental spas and resorts for the duration of the Boer War. Bournemouth, in particular, benefited from their patronage. The withdrawal of their spending power upon the resumption of vacationing abroad provoked a sense of crisis which led to the dispatch of a delegation of councillors in 1903 to tour rival resorts, both British and Continental, to prepare a report upon the state of the opposition and to suggest measures which might be taken to keep abreast. The committee's report confirmed that local worries were well founded:

On every hand we learned that the towns visited had gone into this, that, or the other expenditure, because they had felt that ever-growing competition was threatening their business, and they were determined not to fail for want of an effort to succeed. Whether they were right or not to enter on ambitious schemes is a question we need hardly discuss for we have the fact that they have done so, and that Bournemouth is now feeling, or must soon feel, the effects of their enterprise, unless we in like manner realise the needs of the situation and enter upon a policy of enterprise.[41]

It presented a five-point programme to enhance the resort's attractions:

[a] course of action embracing – (1) An undercliff drive ... (2) A pavilion ... (3) An entire reconsideration of the policy of issuing licences or permits for the vending of wares or the provision of entertainments. (4) The obtaining control as early as practicable by the town of the bathing from the beach. (5) The provision of bands of music in the open air without the objectionable accompaniment of collecting boxes, to fill which visitors are importuned to their annoyance.[42]

These proposals, all of which had been heard before, were followed up during the subsequent decade. The plan's first point, the construction of a carriage drive at the foot of the cliff had long been a cherished objective of the Progressives. They urged that 'the greater the attractions we offer the wealthy, the more they will patronise our town instead of Brighton, Hastings etc., and more especially the Riviera'.[43] The large capital cost of the works, however, had frightened other ratepayers who feared that a large rates rise would result. Negotiations between the Meyrick Estate, the owner of the cliffs and foreshore, and the local authority regarding the construction of the drive and associated cliff protection works, made little headway during the 1890s. In December 1897 Sir George Meyrick entered into a 'provisional agreement' with a private developer, Archibald Beckett of Boscombe, for the construction of a drive plus hotels and shops on the front. 'A remarkable change of opinion soon manifested itself', wrote the resort's centennial chroniclers in 1910.

Many of the most strenuous opponents saw that an undercliff drive – for weal or woe – was bound to come, and the scheme foreshadowed by Mr Beckett included so many objectionable features that they themselves memorialised the Council to reopen negotiations with Sir George, submitting that 'the control of any Under Cliff Drive should be entirely in the hands of the Town Authority', and respectfully asking them to take such steps as in their best judgement might 'seem most fitting to protect the best interests of the town in this matter'.[44]

All shades of local opinion feared that commercialisation of the front would vulgarise the town and attract trippers who would drive middle-class holidaymakers and 'high-class' visitors into the arms of still seemly rival resorts. Sir George Meyrick bowed to the force of local feeling and agreed to grant the Council a 999-year lease on the cliffs and beach in 1902 on condition that an expeditious start be made to the work. In the event the works were not completed until 1914.

It was the same concern for the resort's tranquillity and reputation, and the fear of its desertion by the affluent with all that it implied for local tradesmen, builders and property owners, which led Bournemouth's local authority to build a municipal tramway in the early 1900s. An application by the British Electric Traction Company to Parliament for powers to build a tramway in Bournemouth in 1899 appeared to stand a good chance of being granted unless the local authority chose to act itself. The Council had already fought off a couple of attempts to build tramways in Bournemouth and councillors were of virtually unanimous opinion, 'that it was not desirable to construct or to allow others to construct tramways within the borough', because they would be detrimental to its standing as an exclusive resort.[45] Since it appeared, however, that a tramway was inevitable then all agreed that it was preferable that it should be conducted by the local authority, which might minimise the nuisance, rather than by outside interests who 'come to Bournemouth as speculators, pure and simple, seeking a chance to make money, and having no other interest in the place'.[46] The local authority submitted a successful counter-proposal for a municipal system which it was obliged to build and operate. Construction began in 1902. The tramway soon became the most substantial of the corporation's trading enterprises. By 1914 the system, which employed 450 men and carried fourteen million passengers each year, extended over thirty miles of track and had cost in excess of £400,000.

VI

The expansion of the municipal provision of facilities for recreation and leisure in the late nineteenth century, a development common to many British towns, has been attributed by Meller to two motives.[47] First, a growing concern for the welfare of citizens, particularly for their health and education. Second, a widespread waxing of civic pride which led to rivalry between towns to boast the most ample amenities and the most splendid municipal monuments. In the case of Bournemouth another motive has been suggested – support for the business community and the local economy.

Other considerations, such as those identified by Meller, were not entirely absent from the minds of Bournemouth's councillors but they were subordinate to the commercial motive. Intense municipal pride was manifested in the frequent civic ceremonials and led to episodes such as the controversy in the 1890s as to the correct form of address to the Mayor. Having sought the counsel of half-a-dozen venerable corporations it was regretfully concluded that there was no precedent, after all, for 'Right Worshipful' and that 'Worshipful' would have to do.[48] The presentation to the town of the residence and art collection of one of the leading citizens, Merton Russell Cotes, as a municipal museum and art gallery in 1907 echoed similar gestures for the intellectual enrichment of the community by civically concerned rich men of other towns. Yet in Bournemouth even the ceremonies and art gallery had a commercial dimension. The Russell Cotes benefaction was hailed as an addition to the resort's attractions while the organisation of civic ceremonies on the slightest pretext was a deliberate device for attracting attention to the resort. Concern for public health, as already mentioned, was not unconnected to concern for the salubrity of the local economy. The priorities of the resort's rulers and ratepayers were demonstrated by local reaction to the 1902 Education Act. Common hostility to the measure united Progressives and 'do-nothings'. The latters' objection to the increase in municipal expenditure caused by its mandatory provisions were only to be expected. The opposition of local tradesmen, the same staunch supporters of the pavilion, parks, orchestra, piers and undercliff drive, was provoked because it became more difficult to find money for further commercial projects.

Bournemouth and the other resorts were a special case. The actions of their local politicians were prompted by the peculiar economic problems described above. Their ambitions to assist their local economies led them to seek powers to provide leisure services and facilities beyond those contemplated by the councillors of non-resort towns. The resorts were heavily represented in the list of applications for 'novel powers' appended to the report of the Joint Select Committee on Municipal Trading of 1900.[49] Because they could make a convincing case of local necessity, albeit in exceptional circumstances, they were able to push forward the frontier of municipal ownership into fields of enterprise hitherto the exclusive preserve of private business. Although the novel measures they sought were usually for small-scale recreational projects, they found themselves caught up in the debate about the legitimate limits to the municipal and private spheres of enterprise and among the vanguard of the municipal movement.

The local authorities of the resorts earned the plaudits of the radical advocates of the wholesale extension of municipal responsibilities around the turn of the century. The pages of the *Municipal Journal*, a mouthpiece of the municipal movement, were full of praise for the enterprise of the local authorities of the resorts. Of Southend, for example, it was stated that 'its very life-blood is municipal trading. It owes its wonderful vitality to the foresight of the local authority'.[50] Likewise in Blackpool another correspondent discovered that 'at the turn of every street you meet with municipal enterprise'.[51] Brighton, too, 'owed its preeminence as a watering-place to the numerous public improvements and public works which have been carried on by the municipal authorities'.[52] And Bournemouth's '"going ahead" is due to the enterprise and judgement of the corporation', concluded a correspondent in 1906.[53]

The correspondents of the *Municipal Journal* expressed not only their approval of the actions of the local authorities of resorts but also some surprise at the support they received from local tradesmen for measures which led to rates rises. 'It is not often that tradesmen can be induced to see things in this light,' wrote one after a visit to Blackpool in 1905, 'as a rule they form themselves into destructive ratepayers' associations and oppose everything for the mere joy of opposition'.[54] The origin of the exceptional enlightenment of the tradesmen of the resorts was a transparent self-interest. It had little to do with the radical vision of the broad social responsibilities of local government and less to do with municipal socialism. To the local tradesmen of Bournemouth their local authority was unrecognisable as the instrument of a collectivist tendency which threatened the very institution of private property as alleged by the more extreme critics of municipal trading.[55] The initiatives of Bournemouth's local authority were parochial responses to local conditions. As such they were typical of the actions of the vast majority of local authorities in the period up to 1914.

NOTES

1 Sir H. H. Fowler, 'Municipal finance and municipal enterprise', *Royal Statistical Society Journal* LXIII (1900), pp. 383–407.

2 *Ibid.* p. 386.

3 *Ibid.* p. 386.

4 *Ibid.* p. 394.

5 W. A. Robson, *The Development of Local Government* (1931), p. 195.

6 F. D. Littlewood, *The Law of Municipal and Public Entertainments* (1951), p. 8.

7 *Ibid.* p. 5.

8 S. K. Ruck, *Municipal Entertainment and the Arts in Greater London* (1965), p. 22.

9 See, for example, J. K. Walton, 'Railways and resort development in Victorian England: the case of Silloth', *Northern History* XV (1979), pp. 191–209, R. Gurnham, 'The creation of Skegness as a resort town by the ninth Earl of Scarbrough', *Lincolnshire History and Archaeology* 7 (1972).

10 Bournemouth Town Hall [BTH], 'Minutes of a Committee Established to Obtain an Act of Parliament of 1856'.

11 J. Cutler, *Life, Letters and Speeches* (1890), p. 30.

12 BTH Pier Committee, 23 April 1877.

13 *Bournemouth Visitors' Directory*, 2 February 1878.

14 BTH Pier Committee, 10 January 1902.

15 C. H. Mate and C. Riddle, *Bournemouth 1810–1910* (Bournemouth 1910), p. 154. Public Record Office [PRO], BT/31 381/23895. Boscombe Pier Company, Limited.

16 BTH Pier Committee, 25 April 1902; 15 December 1903.

17 Mate and Riddle *op. cit.*, p. 155.

18 E. D. Mackerness, *A Social History of English Music* (1964), pp. 197, 207.

19 The source for this paragraph is the minutes of the Pier Committee, BTH.

20 See R. Roberts, 'Landowners, local government and the development of Bournemouth', in D. Cannadine (ed), *Patricians, Power and Politics in Nineteenth Century Towns* (Leicester 1982).

21 'Provincial Society', *Whitehall Review* (1878), p. 205.

22 *Ibid.* p. 205.

23 PRO, BT/31 1910/7789. Bournemouth Winter Garden Company, Limited.

24 PRO, BT/31 2431/12308. Bournemouth Winter Garden and Aquarium Company, Limited.

25 W. Mate, 'Bournemouth in 1884', *Mate's Bournemouth Business Directory* (1885), p. 6.

26 PRO, BT/31 1802/6898. Bournemouth Town Hall and Public Buildings Company, Ltd.

27 PRO, BT/31 2743|14883. Bournemouth Theatre and Opera House Company, Limited.

28 D. S. Young, *The Story of Bournemouth* (1957), p. 217.

29 H. Furniss, 'An English watering place', *Good Words* (1890), p. 120.

30 H. Dobell, *Notes on Bournemouth and Its Wants in 1887* (Bournemouth 1887), p. 4.

31 J. Cutler *Life, Letters and Speeches* (1890), p. 43.

32 'Charter Supplement', *Bournemouth Observer*, 30 August 1890.

33 BTH, Bournemouth Council, 28 May 1891.

34 BTH, Pier, Winter Garden and Band Committee, 17 February 1903, 'Report on the Duties of the Musical Director'.

35 The source for this paragraph is the minutes of the Winter Garden and Band Committee, BTH.

36 BTH Pier, Winter Garden and Band Committee, 17 February 1903, 'Report on the Duties of the Musical Director'.

37 *Ibid.*

38 Bournemouth Corporation, *Twenty One Years of Municipal Music, 1893–1911* (Bournemouth 1911), p. 23.

39 Fowler, *op. cit.*, p. 386.

40 See R. Roberts, *op. cit.*

41 BTH, Report of the Under Cliff Drive Deputation (1903), p. 54.

42 *Ibid.*

43 *Bournemouth Visitors' Directory*, 14 September 1901.

44 Mate and Riddle, *op. cit.*, p. 169.

45 BTH, Bournemouth Council Minutes, 15 December 1897.

46 *Bournemouth Guardian*, 26 February 1898. Town Clerk's evidence to inquiry of Light Railway Commissioners.

47 H. E. Meller, *Leisure and the Changing City, 1870–1914* (London 1976), pp. 96–7.

48 M. R. Russell Cotes, *Home and Abroad* (1921), vol. II, p. 82.

49 Other Miscellaneous Proposals in Private Bills Promoted by Local Authorities, Appendix VI, evidence, Joint Select Committee on Municipal Trading. British Parliamentary Papers (1900), vol VII, pp. 511–13.

50 'The progress of Southend', *Municipal Journal*, 13 October 1905.

51 'The secret of Blackpool', *Municipal Journal*, 4 August 1905.

52 'London-by-the-sea', *London*, 6 June 1895.

53 'The parks of Bournemouth', *Municipal Journal*, 5 October 1906.

54 'The secret of Blackpool', *Municipal Journal*, 4 August 1905.

55 Report on the deliberations of the Westbourne Literary and Debating Society, 1 March 1901, 'Municipal trading: its scope and limitations', *Bournemouth Visitors' Directory*, 2 March 1901.

9 JOHN K. WALTON
Municipal government in Blackpool

I

In the late nineteenth and early twentieth century English municipal government was at the zenith of its vitality and power. With relatively few constraints imposed from the centre, the substantial business and professional men who dominated council proceedings in most large towns were able to act upon an unarticulated but pervasive civic ideology which legitimated, and even prescribed, a steady extension of municipal activity which went far beyond a basic concern for public order, 'services to property' and public health. Corporations became involved in municipal trading and welfare measures, and as local authorities tentatively accepted a role as civilisers and educators, civic concern extended with growing conviction into the dispensing of polite culture and 'rational recreations' to the masses. This activity rested firmly on initiatives taken in mid-Victorian times and earlier; but only now did a favourable economic and political climate encourage a full flowering of municipal enterprise.[1]

The expanding responsibilities of the larger corporations gave them an increasingly pervasive influence on most aspects of urban economy and society, especially as they became responsible for the supply, price and quality of essential commodities and services. Already in the 1850s and 1860s municipal gas and water were becoming commonplace, municipal docks were vital to many seaport economies, effective drainage and sewering improvements were beginning, and street improvements were beginning to spread beyond the central business and residential districts. These commitments were greatly increased and widely generalised during the last quarter of the nineteenth century, and the 1890s saw a new burst of municipal involvement in tramways and electricity supply, with here and there a few tentative moves towards municipal housing. The larger boroughs also retained important public order functions, with their own police forces responsible to a Corporation Watch Committee, and often with their own borough bench of magistrates recruited largely from the same sources as the local council itself. By the turn of the century most large urban authorities were important employers of labour in their own right. They could call on the skills and expertise of a growing body of professional specialists, and they could draw on impressive and expanding financial resources, as their own rateable values and borrowing powers rose, and the flow of exchequer grants grew stronger. In 1902 their influence was increased still further, as they took over the educational duties of the School Boards. All these powers, resources and responsibilities gave the larger urban authorities a deep and far-reaching influence on local economic structure as well as on the quality of life, and ensured a growing eagerness among late Victorian industrialists and other leading citizens to share in their prestige and participate actively in their deliberations.[2]

Leisure and entertainment were not exempt from the rising tide of municipal intervention. The public order functions of borough councils had long enabled them to regulate, control and even prohibit entertainments in public places (especially streets and markets) or those connected with the drink trade (and subsequently music and dancing). Existing powers here were increased in the early 1870s by new national legislation on public house licensing, and by an act of 1871 which made the abolition of fairs administratively much easier, providing a procedure which was often initiated by municipal authorities.[3] Subsequently, towns increasingly sought special by-law powers from Parliament and the Local Government Board for the regulation of stalls, shows and processions, and for more effective control of the large music halls and other manifestations of an increasingly capital-intensive entertainment industry, which were proliferating rapidly and spreading even into the smaller towns by the 1890s.[4] Many such initiatives were controversial, and attempts to suppress (or revive) wakes and fairs, to abolish singing-saloons, and to suppress (or promote) race meetings, brought the municipal regulation of leisure into the forefront of local political conflict, which usually polarised around Liberal Nonconformist interventionists on the one hand, and the drink interest on the other.[5]

Alongside this generally restrictive activity, municipal governments were also making positive contributions to cultural and recreational amenities, as growing financial support was given to parks, libraries, museums, art galleries, recreation grounds and swimming baths. These 'rational', 'improving' recreations, aimed at expanding the range of intellectual and athletic pleasures for the masses, were generally outside the realms of commercial entertainment, although circulating library stocks were not entirely composed of three-volume romantic novels, and suburban pleasure gardens offered flowers, fresh air and participant sports as well as dancing and fireworks. But these commercialised pleasures did not come cheaply, and the efforts of voluntary organisations remained even further out of reach of the mainstream working-class public. The literary and scientific clubs and societies raised high financial and social barriers, while most Mechanics' Institutes soon became the preserves of the lower middle class, and mutual improvement societies were all too often starved of resources. Municipal intervention for the provision of free and accessible opportunities for fresh air, healthy exercise and the appreciation of the arts was very limited almost everywhere until the late nineteenth century, because of the high capital cost of sites and buildings, the pressing claims of rival objects of expenditure, and the prevailing mid-Victorian ethos of strict economy among ratepayers and councillors alike. Urban parks multiplied steadily from the 1830s and 1840s, but until the last quarter of the nineteenth century initial costs had to be met by gifts and public subscriptions. The same applied to public libraries, which were widely seen as instruments for public order and class collaboration. Legislation in 1850 and 1855 which allowed local authorities to levy a penny library rate was almost unworkable without substantial private assistance. Only in the 1880s and 1890s did the private philanthropists who identified a duty to spread 'liberal culture' and social harmony began to give way to, or to work through, municipal bodies whose accepted sphere of activity was widening rapidly as resources increased, expectations broadened and the calibre of councillors and aldermen improved. Even then, the municipalisation of culture was far from complete, for gifts from landowners (often with an eye to the value of their adjoining building land) remained important to park provision, and expansion of the public library system in the early twentieth century depended heavily on the Carnegie Trust. Voluntary organisations remained vitally important, especially in music, though they increasingly used municipal premises. The municipal role in mainstream working-class leisure, of course, remained very limited when compared with the commercial sector; but the public libraries were very heavily used, and in general the achievements of the late nineteenth century were considerable. Imposing new buildings housed central libraries, art galleries and museums in the larger towns, sometimes with more attention to civic pride and architectural effect than to function or contents; and branch libraries, parks and recreation grounds proliferated in the suburbs and working-class districts. By the early twentieth century the principle of municipal involvement in recreational and cultural life had become firmly established; and although facilities provided with the perceived needs of the working classes in mind were often enjoyed disproportionately by their 'betters', local government in many towns had taken on an indispensable, if not predominant, role in these spheres.[6]

II

The relationship between leisure and local government was particularly important in seaside resorts, for here a town's prosperity in a highly competitive world was strongly influenced by its recreational amenities and public order machinery. Except where natural attractions were sufficient in themselves, entertainments had to be provided to suit the tastes of the best-paying or most-desired class of holidaymaker; and the regulation of streets and beach had similarly to be tailored to match the preferences of the chosen visiting public, although the needs of prosperous residents had also to be considered in many resorts.

Where entertainment provision by private enterprise was perceived to be inadequate, seaside local authorities in the late nineteenth and early twentieth century were increasingly willing and able to step in and make up the deficiency. Sometimes, as at Southend, Great Yarmouth and Brighton, they bought up ailing private concerns; sometimes, as at Margate and Torquay, they promoted new schemes of their own, in spite of persistent doubts in Parliament and at the Local Government Board about the propriety of such use of the ratepayers' money.[7] Occasionally, municipal entertainment was intended to please (and provide shelter for) lower-class visitors whose contribution to the local economy was important but unattractive to private entrepreneurs and investors. More usually, intervention was in the interests of the 'better classes', with a view to providing classical concerts or secluded promenades in protected surroundings over an extended season. Bournemouth provides perhaps the best and most thoroughgoing example of this kind of municipal activity, but it had plenty of emulators elsewhere, especially along the south coast.[8]

Unlike the great industrial and commercial centres, seaside resort municipalities invested in recreational and cultural provisions for commercial rather than philanthropic motives, and for the delectation of comfortably-off visitors rather than the moral and intellectual improvement of the local working class. The eager provision of parks and heavy investment in promenades generally had similar motives, although the need to find room for swelling throngs of working-class visitors was a powerful, even over-riding motive for promenade widening and extension in resorts like Blackpool and Southend. The usual balance of priorities, however, was far removed from ideals of 'social citizenship' or a 'civic gospel'. Bridlington's Local Board went to the expense of a parliamentary hearing in 1889 to confirm its right to charge a steep threepenny admission fee to an enclosed section of its promenade, because: 'It is of the greatest importance to the town that the better class of visitors should have a secluded place where they can go away from the rough excursionists who come there in swarms during the season; and this is the only place where the better class of visitors can resort and get quiet.' The House of Commons committee which considered this submission had its doubts about the legitimacy of this arrangement; as Mr Kenrick remarked, 'I do not like public gardens or public parks in which you have to pay for anything'. But Mr Hardcastle's point of view, that the true interest of the ratepayers lay not so much in their own access to the promenade as in getting people to spend money there, eventually carried the day.[9]

Similar justifications could be made for municipal expenditure on advertising a town's attractions, and even on tramway extensions, although the arguments rang hollow in the ears of those ratepayers who did not have a financial interest in the holiday industry, especially if increased visitor numbers threatened the amenities of residential areas.[10] Wherever resorts attracted a socially mixed clientèle, with conflicting ideas about the ideal way to spend a holiday, further divisions came to the fore; for disputes over the preferred 'social tone' of a resort were likely to involve a split in the holiday industry itself, between (very broadly) 'better-class' and 'working-class' interests, as well as exacerbating the almost universal division between the holiday trades and the residential and other interests.

Public order, public morality and the regulation of amusements were thus particularly sensitive issues at the seaside. Where a resort's interests were clearly bound up with the decorous, upper-middle-class family trade, a consensus in favour of strict controls on behaviour was relatively easy to achieve, and a range of restrictive by-laws could be enforced with appropriate strictness, especially where ground landlords, Corporation, magistrates and police force were capable of acting in concert. Eastbourne, with its late Victorian and Edwardian campaigns against hawkers, beach entertainers and barking dogs, is an unusually clear-cut example.[11] At the other end of the scale, however, even the most plebeian resorts could not afford to offend their self-consciously 'respectable' visitors of all classes, and all had residential interests to consider. The ideal balance between the restraint necessary to retain 'better-class' and 'respectable' custom, and the permissiveness needed to create a free-and-easy atmosphere for the numerous visitors (usually working-class) who enjoyed stalls, showmen and alcoholic indulgence, was very difficult to achieve, especially as the latter group became increasingly important to many resort economies. Morecambe, New Brighton and Weston-super-Mare were prominent among the resorts which faced problems of this kind in the late nineteenth and early twentieth century, as boisterous excursionists competed with 'better-class' families to enjoy the beach, promenade and central streets, and entertainment companies adjusted their programmes and attractions to cater for an increasingly lucrative mass market.[12]

The growing powers of municipal government gave it a pivotal position in the determination of a resort's fortunes, both in the provision of services to the holiday industry, and in the development of policies regarding public order and social regulation which could strongly influence the evolution of a resort's character and 'social tone'. Despite its importance, however, seaside local government has been little studied by historians of holiday towns and the holiday industry.[13] Case-studies of the relationship between local government and resort development have long been needed, and what follows is a complementary study to

Richard Roberts' work on Bournemouth, analysing the relationship between the Corporation and the entertainment industry in the contrasting but equally successful resort of Blackpool.[14]

III

During the last quarter of the nineteenth century, Blackpool easily outdistanced its competitors to become Britain's most successful and highly-specialised working-class holiday resort. This was partly due to its proximity to the Lancashire textile towns, among whose tightly-packed working-class communities the annual seaside holiday first became a mass experience.[15] It also owed much to the pioneering role of Blackpool's leading entertainment companies in catering explicitly for a working-class market. This began in the early 1870s with the South Jetty (the present Central Pier) and the Raikes Hall pleasure gardens, and culminated in a burst of heavy and uniquely successful investment in the pleasure palaces of the 1890s, when the Winter Gardens of 1878 completed its journey down-market and was joined by the Tower and Alhambra as well over half a million pounds were poured into the entertainment industry. Pre-dating this, and running through into the twentieth century, was an even more important theme. Blackpool had long been attractive to working-class visitors because of its easy-going homeliness, its lack of pretensions and petty restrictions on public enjoyment. This found expression in the unassuming houses and ill-planned streets of a town of small estates and lowest-common-denominator development; the ready tolerance of open-air amusements and boisterous enjoyment; and not least in the ample supply of public houses. These attributes had much to do with the lack of a dominant landowner with aspirations to high-class development; but they owed even more to the policies of local government, and to the legal constraints within which it operated.[16]

Despite a spectacular working-class invasion in the later nineteenth century, Blackpool kept a significant share of middle-class patronage, as quieter outposts of relative gentility survived on either side of the town centre. Corporation policy at the turn of the century helped to safeguard the amenities of North Shore, a haven for propertied widows and spinsters, commuting businessmen and the 'better-class' holidaymaker, and in Edwardian times municipal advertising, which had been devoted to extending the catchment area for working-class visitors, was widened in scope to find room for a policy of season extension aimed at a more affluent clientèle.[17]

In Blackpool, as in other resorts where a working-class holiday economy was grafted uneasily on to an established 'better-class' season in the last quarter of the nineteenth century, local government had to walk a tightrope, balancing the claims and needs of conflicting interest-groups within the holiday industry as well as beyond it. Before we examine municipal policies more closely as they affected, and were affected by, the holiday industry in this highly-specialised town, we need to know how those interest-groups were represented on the town's governing body, and how they affected its deliberations.

IV

The social composition of Blackpool's most important mid-Victorian local government body, the Local Board of Health, changed rapidly in the mid-1860s as the promenade scheme which began a Blackpool tradition of active, interventionist local government got under way. Parsimonious farmers, small landowners and petty tradesmen of limited ambition and ability gave way to professionals, retired residents from inland, and prospering shopkeepers with a growing stake in the 'better-class' holiday industry, as tens of thousands of pounds were poured into piers, theatres and assembly rooms by private investors.[18] When the town was incorporated in 1876, a similar pattern of representation persisted at first on the borough council, although the personnel changed as the result of a thoroughgoing (but short-lived) introduction of national political labels into local elections, which produced a Conservative landslide and brought several untried men into the council chamber. Of the twenty-seven councillors elected in April and November 1876, six were 'gentlemen' (five of whom are known to have retired from business inland), four were doctors, and sixteen were tradesmen of various kinds, most of whom were connected with the holiday or building industries. Over the next twenty years, a period of rapid and accelerating growth and successful specialisation in the working-class market, the influence of the holiday interest on the Council increased steadily at the expense of the professionals and retired businessmen. More than a quarter of new entrants during these crucial formative years depended directly on the holiday industry for their living. On top of this, over twenty per cent were in the building trades, and nearly thirty per cent were retailers and tradesmen of other kinds. Moreover, the tradesmen stayed on the council longer than the other groups: the average length of service for those first elected between 1877 and 1897 was seventeen years for the holiday industry, sixteen for the building trades and fourteen for other tradesmen, against only nine for the other groups. Only after 1898, when the council was doubled in numbers after a campaign against alleged corruption and undue influence by an inner circle of leading local businessmen, did the pattern begin to change. Between 1899 and 1913 recruits came increasingly from the shopkeepers and the lower reaches of the holiday industry, and professionals and the retired now accounted for over twenty per cent of new entrants, while the holiday and building trades each fell to about one-sixth of the total. Table 9.1 provides fuller documentation of these trends.[19] The social composition of Blackpool's borough council was distinctive, indeed remarkable, throughout the years between 1876 and 1914, and especially between 1876 and 1898. The absolute dominance of businessmen, whether employers or self-employed, was a general norm (although the complete absence of working-class representatives was becoming very unusual by 1914); but the dominant role played by the holiday industry and the building trades

Table 9.1: Occupations of new entrants to Blackpool borough council, 1876–1913, number and (%)

	Overall	1876	1877–96	1898	1899–1913
Gentlemen of no known Blackpool occupation	7 (4.5)	1 (3.7)	4 (6.9)	1 (4.3)	1 (2.2)
Retired from inland	15 (9.8)	5 (18.5)	4 (6.9)	1 (4.3)	4 (8.7)
Professional	14 (9.1)	4 (14.8)	3 (5.2)	2 (8.7)	5 (10.9)
Holiday industry	32 (20.8)	4 (14.8)	15 (25.9)	6 (26.1)	7 (15.2)
Building industry	33 (21.5)	6 (22.2)	12 (20.7)	7 (30.4)	8 (17.4)
Retailers and other tradesmen	49 (31.7)	6 (22.2)	17 (29.3)	6 (26.1)	21 (45.6)
Agriculture	4 (2.6)	1 (3.7)	3 (5.2)	– –	– –

may well have been unique even at the seaside. At Morecambe, superficially a very similar resort, only a handful of Local Board members and councillors had strong interests in the holiday industry, whether accommodation or entertainment, and at Eastbourne, less surprisingly, a similar situation prevailed.[20] The strength of Blackpool's building lobby was matched at Eastbourne and Torquay, reflecting the disproportionate importance of building to resort economies; but Morecambe and Ilfracombe showed lower levels of representation, running consistently at about ten per cent of all councillors, and few inland towns could claim higher proportions. At Birmingham, Leeds and Wolverhampton, for example, the building industry as such was almost unrepresented in municipal government, although many councillors must have speculated in property.[21]

If we look more closely at the economic interests of Blackpool councillors, we find that the influence of the holiday and building industries was much stronger than at first appears. Thirty of the 154 councillors elected between 1876 and 1913 held fifty-two directorships in local entertainment companies during this period. Eleven sat on the Winter Gardens board, seven on that of the Raikes Hall pleasure gardens, and five on that of the Tower. If we adjust the overall figures in the light of this, thirty-two per cent of councillors were active in the holiday industry, and the figure rises to thirty-six per cent if we include sea-front hotels. Moreover, more than half the councillors are known to have been shareholders in local entertainment companies at some point during this period. Similarly, more than half the councillors were engaged commercially in property development or land speculation, some on a very large scale.[22]

When we look beyond occupational labels (some of which are necessarily arbitrary) at wider business interests, the drink trade also emerges as a major influence on municipal government in Blackpool. There were never more than four hoteliers on a twenty-four-strong council before 1898, and they owed their position mainly to their role in the holiday industry. On this basis, the drink interest was stronger in Blackpool than in the major cities, but weaker than in smaller service centres like Newcastle under Lyme and Exeter, where licensing matters bulked large in local politics. When we include owners of licensed property, former publicans, off-licence holders and directors of hotel companies in an extended drink interest, however, we find that it embraced more than two-fifths of the council in 1876 and more than a quarter of the new entrants over the next twenty years. When friends and camp-followers are taken into account, the drink interest begins to rival the building lobby in the range and scope of its potential influence.

These inter-related vested interests were particularly strong between 1876 and 1898, and it is no coincidence that these years saw Blackpool's wholehearted acceptance of the working-class holiday industry. Subsequently, the rise of a powerful and well-organised Tradesmen's Association brought the shopkeeping and small business interests to the fore, while the professional presence also increased as the town's economy grew more complex and a residential element became more prominent. But the distribution of seats was biased increasingly in favour of the central business wards, and the retired residents and commuters who congregated in the new houses at either end of the town still had few voices in the council chamber. Indeed, throughout this period the professional and residential element carried much less weight than in Eastbourne, Ilfracombe or even Morecambe.

The holiday and building interests dominated the council numerically, and this was bound to affect the overall strategy and tone of municipal policy. Each of these overlapping groups, however, contained a cross-section of its industry, ranging from lodging-house keepers, small property owners and self-employed craftsmen to the promoters and directors of the leading entertainment companies and the heads of the very large building firms which were emerging at the turn of the century. These internal divisions sometimes found expression in conflicts over particular issues, as the big business interests were sometimes too ambitious in their planning to carry with them the owners of marginal family firms, who looked askance at the possible impact of large rate increases on their overheads. In practice, however, such disputes were rare, and the leading local businessmen tended to get their way in important matters, as the entertainment company directors, in alliance with some of the most successful property speculators, came to exercise effective control over most aspects of council policy during the late nineteenth century.

The Corporation was strongly influenced at important stages in Blackpool's development by two powerful cliques, each firmly grounded in economic interests, but cemented and extended by friendship and kinship ties. The first such group, known as 'the Ring', was effective for several years after incorporation in 1876. It centred on W. H. Cocker, the town's leading citizen and most important property-owner, a physician and a Conservative, and the Liberal Congregationalist grocer Henry Fisher. It was based on the network of companies founded to service and promote the 'better-class' holiday industry in the 1860s and 1870s. Cocker was the owner of the Aquarium and a director of the Sea Water Company, Assembly Rooms, Prince of Wales Theatre, South Jetty and Winter Gardens. Fisher was a director of three of these companies, and he was also involved in the Raikes Hall pleasure gardens and the short-lived Borough Bazaar, which brought him new associates on the council. At least ten allies either held interlocking directorships or shared common interests in property development, reinforced by conviviality in the form, it was alleged, of after-hours drinking. The 'Ring's' most ambitious projects for street improvements and extensions were defeated by an alliance of suspicious smaller ratepayers, but its period of ascendancy did much to establish and confirm a philosophy of active and innovatory municipal involvement in the local economy.

As the influence of the first 'Ring' faded in the mid-1880s, its successor began to coalesce, reaching the height of its power during the working-class holiday boom of the 1890s. At the centre was John Bickerstaffe of the Wellington Hotel, who began his municipal career in 1880 as a spokesman for the boatmen and the drink interest, but subsequently extended his activities to the central Pier and its steamboat company, becoming a local hero in the early 1890s when he rescued the infant Tower Company from the destructive financial machinations of a London syndicate. Bickerstaffe's brother Tom joined him on the council in 1891, and common interests in the drink trade, the steamers and the

Tower brought them several allies among the other new councillors of the early 1890s, especially the publicans John and Fred Nickson and R. B. Mather, and the theatre proprietor Thomas Sergenson. The property syndicates which flourished in Blackpool at this time brought them into contact with land and building speculators on the council, and the Bickerstaffe circle soon had a stranglehold on local affairs. Again, economic ties were cemented by conviviality, as members of the group went on excursions together and exchanged elaborate practical jokes. It was under these auspices that the Corporation displayed its firmest commitment to the working-class holiday industry.

The Bickerstaffe group over-reached itself at the height of the local building boom in 1896–7, when its members were active in several syndicates which tried to sell land to the Corporation at inflated prices. As before, this provoked a reaction among the smaller ratepayers, and as a result the council was doubled in numbers in 1898, diluting the clique's influence. But its leaders had strong personalities and economic muscle, and opponents felt that they still exercised disproportionate influence as long-serving aldermen and committee chairmen in Edwardian times.

The members of these influential groups had several important characteristics in common, over and above their entertainment interests. The central figures were almost all members of well-established local yeoman families, and they entered the council while still building up their businesses. Under the circumstances it was not surprising that private and municipal concerns sometimes intersected. Just as significant was the prevailing lack of religious commitment beyond (usually) a nominal Anglicanism. Calls for restraints on excursionist behaviour on religious and moral grounds were thus unlikely to make much headway unless financial interests were also threatened. In this respect Blackpool's civic élite stands in sharp contrast with nearby Southport's militantly interventionist nonconformists. In Blackpool, indeed, the ruling groups recruited from Liberals as well as Tories, as the first election of 1876 was forgotten and national party labels became increasingly irrelevant to council proceedings, though they sometimes added spice to election campaigns. Nor did competition between the entertainment companies usually spill over into council decision-making, except at the turn of the century when the Tower Company looked askance at the beach showmen and the new Pleasure Beach amusement park at the southern edge of the town.[23] The companies generally saw their roles as complementary rather than competitive, helping to increase Blackpool's attractiveness to a swelling flood of visitors who would sample a variety of delights on arrival; and there were many overlapping directorships and large shareholdings to link the major enterprises at a personal level. The entertainment industry was almost always able to present a united front in the council chamber, and to exercise a disproportionate influence on policy even when specific cliques were not in the ascendant.

Blackpool thus had no difficulty in attracting its captains of industry into the council chamber, where these generally self-made men revelled in the insults and personal exchanges, and projected to their constituents a materialist and philistine but practical and effective vision of the functions of municipal government. Their ideas were best expressed by a business analogy: Blackpool as limited company, run by an enterprising board of directors for the benefit of the shareholders, in competition with rival enterprises. Success required a high standard of services to visitors, and the Corporation's role was to assist the entertainment industry by providing those services cheaply and attractively, while placing the minimum of constraints on the town's continuing growth, which would give opportunities for upward social mobility to all.

There was no effective challenge to this businessmen's ideal of municipal government, so different from Birmingham's civic gospel or Bristol's version of 'social citizenship'.[24] The established urban patriciates, who brought high-minded motives to municipal action in some of the great cities, were conspicuously absent in Blackpool, and serious-minded nonconformity on the model of Birmingham or even Southport was negligible as an influence on the council.[25] Systematic advocates of municipal economy also made little headway, for Blackpool's rapidly rising rateable value and profitable utilities enabled improvements to be undertaken without spectacular rate increases. Only between 1895 and 1903, when rates rose from a twenty-year pattern of fluctuation between 3s 7d and 4s 6d in the pound to reach an Edwardian plateau of between 5s 0d and 5s 6d, was there a sustained agitation against high expenditure; and this movement was also fuelled by Nonconformist ire at alleged moral laxity, by anger at the under-representation of lodging-house keepers and other small ratepayers, and above all by a strong whiff of corruption, especially from the land syndicates.[26] Caution had also been the watchword in the early 1880s, after confidence had been undermined by the bad season of 1879. But a high tolerance of expenditure prevailed throughout, always provided that it could be shown to benefit the holiday industry; for this touchstone of utility remained valid throughout the period in this highly-specialised resort. The periodic ratepayers' reactions against expenditure, which were the norm in most towns, were ineffective in Blackpool after the successful completion of the first Promenade in 1870.[27] Projects were sometimes shelved for a time when the rising municipal debt began to look overwhelming, but the consensus in favour of expansion through heavy investment and a minimum of social controls gathered momentum, to be regularly expressed at municipal elections which were remarkable for frequent contests and high turnouts.[28]

V

We have offered, in passing, a broad outline of Corporation attitudes and priorities; but we need to know more about their embodiment in specific policies and actions. In what ways, and with what results, did Blackpool Corporation intervene in the provision of amenities, and in the regulation of entertainment and behaviour?

The Corporation's greatest success story, and its most significant contribution to Blackpool's economy, was the Promenade. The Local Board scheme of 1865–70, which eventually cost £60,000 but proved a resounding success, remained adequate (if increasingly overcrowded) until the 1890s, when the sheer pressure of visitor numbers made widening almost unavoidable. Meanwhile £60,000 was spent on refurbishing and improving the Land, Building and Hotel Company's promenade and sea defences at North Shore, despite opposition from the competing 'better-class' area at South Shore. The need to take over the Land Company's crumbling cliffs temporarily outweighed the pressure to widen the existing promenade, but powers were obtained for a seaward widening of 100 feet in 1899, and six years later the work was completed at a cost of £350,000. Sectional interests, in both cases, were overridden by a massive vote of confidence from the town as a whole. As the *Blackpool Gazette* remarked, 'We can well afford to sink a third of a million in perfecting our sea-front. It is our principal market-place, and must ever be our greatest attraction.'[29]

In such resorts as Eastbourne and Bexhill, promenades and sea defences could be provided by large landowners as part of a general programme of urban estate development.[30] Elsewhere, speculative developers and estate companies performed a similar role on parts of the coastline, as at Bridlington or Southend.[31] Blackpool was less fortunate, and had to rescue its own Land Company when it proved incapable of coping with persistent erosion. Over most of the town's shoreline, the fragmentation of property ownership soon made it obvious that local authority finance and control would be the only basis for providing and maintaining a safe and attractive sea-front. Blackpool's municipal authorities had learned this lesson early, and the spectacularly successful promenade improvements at the turn of the century, readily endorsed by the ratepayers, represented a far greater allocation of resources for this purpose than any of Blackpool's rivals provided at this time. In grandeur of conception, in quality of execution, and in acceptability to the inhabitants at large, Blackpool's promenade improvements were unique.[32]

All sectors of the holiday industry could agree on the need for promenade improvements. Advertising, which was the Corporation's second major direct contribution to the visiting season, was more controversial, but here again Blackpool's local authority intervened on a unique scale, although the policies of its Advertising Committee underwent significant changes of emphasis over time.[33]

Like several other resorts, Blackpool had ventured tentatively into advertising in the 1850s, but the *ad hoc* committee which distributed framed views to railway waiting-rooms was crippled by a low level of subscription income. Similar problems restricted the activities of Trade Councils (organisations of local shopkeepers) in 1869 and 1875, and in 1879 the Corporation stepped in. It had already helped to finance a series of fêtes, aimed at extending a season which was already becoming uncomfortably crammed into July and August, and at attracting additional 'better-class' visitors outside the excursionist season. The fêtes were funded by the entertainment companies, with substantial assistance from the Corporation's gasworks profits, supported in the council chamber by a 'better-class' interest centred on the Cocker circle and assisted by professionals and retired businessmen. The same group was probably responsible for the inclusion in the 1879 Improvement Act of power to levy a twopenny rate for advertising and the payment of a town band. Unexpectedly, and to their subsequent regret, the watchdogs of Parliament and the Local Government Board allowed the proposed clause to stand; but they refused to allow it to act as a precedent for other local authorities who sought similar powers. A few limited concessions were made elsewhere, but Blackpool's twopenny rate was a unique privilege until beyond the First World War.

The advertising rate provided an income which could expand in step with Blackpool's growth and needs, without the publicity and potential controversy attendant on an annual request for a specific sum. In 1879 £500 was available, and a rising rateable value brought the total up to nearly £2000 in 1895, £3600 in 1901, and well over £4000 by 1914. Additional sums were sometimes available from the gas and electricity profits, or by allocating a mayoral salary to cover the cost of special fêtes and other attractions. Attempts to cut the advertising budget were rare, and always unsuccessful; but the uses to which the money was put were sometimes controversial.

The first municipal Advertising Committee, formed in February 1880, consisted of a plumber, a publican, a chemist, a baths proprietor, an architect and a cab proprietor. Between them, they held at least six directorships of local hotel and entertainment companies, but only the solitary Raikes Hall representative was directly identified with the working-class season. Initial policy, indeed, was to continue existing support for fêtes in pursuit of a longer season, and to produce an illustrated guide for distribution to railway waiting rooms, hotels, reading rooms,

Mechanics' Institutes, Free Libraries and newspaper editors in Lancashire, Yorkshire, the Midlands and London. The chosen outlets for this well-produced publication, ten thousand copies of which appeared in 1881, suggested a continuing commitment to extending the catchment area for middle-class visitors, and for that working-class élite which used Mechanics' Institutes and Free Libraries.

Already, however, the emphasis was changing, as W. H. Cocker and the publican John Nickson gave added weight to the entertainment interest on the committee. In 1881 Blackpool took up the relatively new medium of the picture poster, and twenty thousand were distributed at railway stations throughout Lancashire, the West Riding of Yorkshire, the Birmingham area and the Black Country. For the next two decades the poster dominated Blackpool's advertising budget, and its range was steadily extended into the East Midlands, the London area, Wales and the south coast. This was classless advertising with a particular (but not exclusive) appeal to the potential excursionist and short-stay visitor, and it soon eclipsed the original season extension policy. The fêtes fizzled out in 1882, and newspaper advertising faded into the background, as the influence of the popular entertainment interest became increasingly powerful on the Advertising Committee. By 1890 five of the ten members were directors or large shareholders in companies providing entertainment for the mass market, while another was a restaurateur on South Beach, the future Golden Mile. Six years later the Tower Company interest, represented by the Bickerstaffe and Nickson brothers, could expect support for further expansion of the poster campaign from the baths and theatre proprietor W. H. Broadhead and two town centre restaurateurs.

Season extension and the 'better-class' market were never abandoned altogether, and fêtes were revived in 1887-9, while support for the cultivation of a winter season and a re-planning of the unsightly town centre area was always expressed by an articulate minority who also favoured advertising in high-class periodicals like the *Contemporary Review* and *Nineteenth Century*. The doubling of council numbers in 1898 brought a majority of shopkeepers and lodging-house keepers on to the Advertising Committee just as a spectacular rise in the proceeds of a twopenny rate made it possible to pursue season extension and newspaper advertising without abandoning the town's poster sites to eager competitors. Systematic season extension campaigns, aimed mainly at the 'better-class' market, began in 1901, with fêtes, a regular Musical Festival and a brief excursion into motor racing on the promenade, followed by a successful Aviation Meeting. By 1907 the autumn season had become sufficiently established for the railways to extend their summer service through October, and in 1912 the Corporation ensured the long-term success of their efforts by inaugurating the autumn Illuminations. The conference trade was booming by this time, and Christmas visitors and winter weekenders were also much in evidence. Even in 1912, however, the picture poster, despite increasingly vociferous critics, continued to account for over forty per cent of Blackpool's advertising expenditure, in contrast with Douglas and the North Wales resorts, which concentrated on newspaper advertising to woo a very similar clientèle.

Municipal advertising clearly did wonders for Blackpool, although it is hard to pin down its precise influence, especially as railways and entertainment companies had growing advertising budgets of their own. The Advertising Committee was able to present a rounded picture of the town's attractions, and the first Advertising Manager, Charles Noden, had a flair for imaginative stunts which themselves generated further publicity. The development of large-scale excursion traffic from the Midlands and more distant areas followed so closely after the introduction of advertising campaigns, coupled with cheap rail fares, that a cause-and-effect relationship seems certain. The autumn season, too, was orchestrated by the Advertising Committee, and the eventual success of the Illuminations depended on the expertise and flexibility of another pioneering Corporation department, the electricity works. Blackpool used its unique advertising rate to good purpose, and the sheer scale of its resources stood in sharp contrast to the limited impact made by rivals who depended on the uncertain bounty of public subscriptions and mayoral salaries. As in the case of the Promenade, an innovative Corporation with the promotion of the holiday industry in mind was backed consistently by a consensus of the ratepayers, enabling local government to make a unique contribution to resort prosperity.

Where the interests of the holiday industry were less clear-cut, this unity of purpose (occasionally fragile even in the case of advertising) was not so apparent. Entertainment itself posed no problems, for private enterprise offered such abundance that there was no need for the Corporation to become involved in enterprises of its own, apart from occasional special attractions. This spared Blackpool the controversies over municipal entertainment which occurred in towns with a large residential interest, or where the Corporation's activities competed with private enterprise.[34] The Corporation's attitude to public health, however, showed a sliding scale of concern, which declined sharply as the immediate benefits to the holiday industry as vested interest became less visible. In general, of course, a good public health record was an essential element in the stock in trade even of a working-class resort, and Blackpool's local authority stepped up its campaigns against nuisances and possible sources of epidemic disease during the 1880s and 1890s. Drains, sewers, street cleaning, yards and milk supplies all came in for careful attention, as did the notification of infectious diseases. But this concern was not strong enough to push the Corporation into treating its sewage, in the face of high costs and the perceived threat of a sewage farm to residential amenity. Solid sewage deposits on the beach brought swift action, especially when reported in the inland press; but improvements stopped short at extending the outfall pipes, and even the most rudimentary screening apparatus was not introduced until 1909.[35] Even more telling was the Corporation's unwillingness to provide public baths for its poorer citizens; as the Medical Officer of Health observed in 1898, 'A great deal is heard of this subject in the October of every year, but after the November elections the subject is allowed to drop ...'.[36] Most glaring of all was the persistent and systematic failure of the Building Plans Committee, dominated as it was by the powerful builders' lobby, to enforce the building by-laws, especially with regard to air space within rooms and at the backs of houses which were regularly overcrowded by working-class visitors in the summer. This was a genuine health hazard, and it was perpetuated by the combined strength of the holiday and building lobbies, with their obsession with freeing land for new development as rapidly and cheaply as possible.[37]

A similar sliding scale of commitment can be seen in attitudes to public parks and libraries. Park proposals fell victim to the same arguments as public baths and wash-houses: the promenade, foreshore and (in the latter case) private sea-water baths were said to meet the needs of residents as well as visitors. Regular offers of free or cheap sites for parks came from landowners from 1890 onwards, but most were associated with plans for housing development, and contained expensive conditions involving access roads and drainage. Many were on the fringes of the town, and difficult of access for most residents and visitors. Blackpool's elongate urban shape ensured that each specific proposal aroused opposition from the large proportion of the ratepayers who thought themselves too far away to benefit, and this geographical sectionalism was reinforced by appeals for economy or for a higher priority for promenade spending, and in some cases by accusations of profiteering and corrupt practices. Even in 1908, when demand was indicated by the four thousand visitors to the cemetery every Sunday afternoon during the season, a proposal to convert part of the disused Raikes Hall pleasure gardens into a public park foundered on these objections. Nothing of significance was achieved before World War I. Blackpool could only have acquired a park if the perceived needs of the holiday industry had been sufficient, as in the case of the promenade, to override sectional jealousies and suspicions. The recreational needs of the locals were hardly considered, and the entertainment industry may have been unwilling to see visitors diverted away from the central pleasure palaces. The lack of a large local landowner with an interest in encouraging 'better-class' amenities was a further obstacle. Even so, the absence of public parks contrasted starkly with the lavish arrangements in many other resorts, and even with provision for the local working classes in manufacturing towns of comparable size.[38]

On the other hand Blackpool's adoption of the Free Library Act, at a unanimous town's meeting in 1879, came very early, especially in relation to the town's size. But the circumstances are revealing, and so is the subsequent course of events. Initial support for the library owed much to the expectation that it would be an attraction for 'better-class' visitors, and its opening in 1880 at an early-season fête, presided over by the Earl of Derby, reflected that view. In the early years this expectation was borne out, with library use reaching a peak in July, August and September; and modest expansion was undertaken, with branches at South Shore and even working-class Marton. Soon, however, the pattern began to change, and twenty years later local users predominated, with a mid-winter peak. Not surprisingly, the main library remained in unsuitable premises, and proposals for increased expenditure met fierce opposition. A £15,000 Carnegie donation for a new central building was almost spurned in 1908 when councillors could not agree on a site, and the Company-house Keepers' Association objected violently to paying for the land out of the rates. Councillors urged that 'We have to live first,' and described libraries as 'machines to grind away the public money'. Eventually a site was agreed, and paid for out of the gas profits; but it was touch and go, and the adjoining Art Gallery owed its existence entirely to a private donation. Many other resorts similarly put the holiday industry first and neglected public libraries, but the saga contrasts sharply with developments in the great industrial cities, and again highlights the narrow commercial ethos which dominated Blackpool's municipal activity.[39]

The Corporation's investment in servicing the holiday industry did bring tangible benefits to ratepayers in other ways. Blackpool was able to develop a dense and profitable tramway network because the joy-rides of summer visitors more than covered the losses incurred for the rest of the year.[40] The desire to provide a novelty for the visitors led to the inauguration of electric lighting along the promenade as early as 1879, with subsequent rapid expansion from the early 1890s in the supply of domestic current as well as public lighting.[41] The gasworks also benefited from high levels of summer demand, and by the 1890s it provided remarkably cheap gas, with various concessions to consumers, at a profit which sometimes amounted to ten per cent of the borough's income from rates.[42]

As the examples in the fields of recreation, culture and public health suggest, however, the characteristic ratepayer identification with municipal economy was close to the surface even in Blackpool. It was sufficient to outweigh civic pride and administrative convenience by delaying the construction of a purpose-built town hall and seriously limiting its size, and it also ensured that the original market of 1844 remained on its cramped, insanitary central site until 1893.[43] Where the holiday industry was not a direct beneficiary of municipal action, economy remained the ruling passion.

VI

Advocates of the strict regulation of open-air entertainment in the streets and on the beach, and of the imposition of a narrow Evangelical code of conduct on the public behaviour of visitors, also remained noisily in evidence, in Blackpool as in more socially aspiring resorts. But their influence was always limited, and declined sharply towards the turn of the century, as the 'better classes' in the town became increasingly tolerant of excursionist behaviour, and as working-class visitors became more acceptable to their 'betters' in dress and demeanour.[44]

In the absence of ground landlords who were willing to impose and enforce restrictive covenants against public houses and excursionist attractions such as stalls and fairgrounds, Blackpool depended heavily on a growing armoury of local authority by-laws to supplement the common law. An early influx of excursionists around mid-century had been controlled in this way by the Local Board; but the 1870s saw a much more numerous working-class presence which posed problems of order and regulation on an altogether novel scale. The trippers enjoyed noise, bustle, fairgrounds, street music and stalls, and a host of hawkers and showmen followed in their wake, obstructing the streets and beach and annoying the more fastidious visitors. Regulation was made more difficult by the refusal of the county police to enforce the Blackpool by-laws, which left the control of noise, obstruction and touting to 'a nuisance inspector and a couple of carriage inspectors'. Incorporation in 1876 was partly a response to this problem, and it gave the new Watch Committee a limited summary jurisdiction over by-law offences referred by the inspectors. In 1887 practical advantages outweighed fears of expense and undue influence, and a borough police force was established, directly accountable to the Watch Committee. By this time by-law offences were increasingly being tried by Blackpool magistrates, and in 1899 the town acquired a separate Borough Bench.

The popular entertainment interest generally kept a low profile. The Cocker circle was well-represented on the Watch Committee in the early years, and at one point three of the nine members were publicans; but by 1885 these elements had practically disappeared, as shopkeepers, builders and independent gentlemen dominated proceedings. Apart from a brief and closely-scrutinised spell of strong influence by the Bickerstaffe clique in the mid-1890s, this pattern persisted.[45] The Watch Committee never became the vehicle of an interest-group, although militant Non-conformists thought otherwise at the turn of the century, when an agitation against the drink interest was sustained successfully. Most Watch Committee members favoured quite strict controls on most aspects of open-air entertainment and crowd behaviour, and in this they had the support of two powerful and long-serving officials, Town Clerk Thomas Loftos and Chief Constable J. C. Derham. Moreover, the new Borough Bench interpreted its licensing duties with strictness and zeal at the turn of the century, although showmen and street traders were treated leniently when they came before the magistrates, and the full rigour of the law was reserved for cheapjack auctioneers and others whose businesses involved an element of fraud.[46]

The Corporation was particularly keen to minimise annoyance to visitors and residents from noise, obstruction and assertive touting for custom in the streets and on the beach, although the urge to prohibit and suppress was inhibited by legal difficulties, by the numbers involved, and increasingly by the need to take account of excursionist tastes and preferences. It should be stressed that the Corporation's wish to govern with a firm hand was often frustrated by legal loopholes and by the unwillingness of central government, in the form of Parliament and the Local Government Board, to grant the extended by-law powers against stalls and hawkers which the Town Clerk strongly felt to be needed. Even so, the number of hawkers was kept down by a local licensing quota system from the early 1880s, although many unlicensed men were prepared to tolerate the occasional small fine. The outward spread of forecourt stalls from the central entertainment area was halted by new powers obtained in 1901, although central government's concern to safeguard existing property rights made it impossible to banish them from their existing strongholds. Legislation against touting was steadily extended to cover eating-houses and entertainment as well as accommodation, but convictions were hard to secure, and magistrates were lenient towards small ratepayers with no other means of advertisement. 'Nigger minstrels' and street musicians were regularly prosecuted for obstruction, and in 1879 the Corporation obtained additional powers against them; but in all these cases the Corporation inspectorate, and later the borough police, were too hard-pressed to do more than keep the problems within bounds. Moreover, as the power to intervene increased, so did the economic importance of those visitors for whom noisy outdoor fairground-style entertainments were positive attractions. This was especially apparent in the case of the fairground which grew up on the foreshore at South Beach from the early 1870s. Complaints from the 'better-class' interest came early and often, but the Corporation, though sympathetic, was unable to respond. Endless disputes over the ownership and control of the beach below high-water mark delayed the introduction of a full system of licensing and regulation until the mid-1890s, and even then there were enforcement problems. By this time the fairground contained over three hundred stallholders and showmen, and an attempt in 1897 to suppress it altogether, engineered by the entertainment companies (resentful of competition) and the 'better-class' and residential lobbies, was frustrated by an outraged response from the newspapers of Lancashire and Yorkshire, which drew attention to the fairground's contribution to the town's popularity. In the end the Corporation retreated, allowing the fairground to continue on a smaller scale, shorn of its most obnoxious features (though palmists and other proscribed groups merely moved across to the South Beach promenade). A few years later, a similar campaign against the Pleasure Beach amusement park near the southern tram terminus likewise ended in compromise.[47]

The Corporation was much less restrictive in its attitude to the behaviour of the visitors themselves. The *Blackpool Gazette* spoke for the town as a whole in 1887: 'The inhabitants of Blackpool are not the moral preceptors of their visitors, and have no right to dictate morality to them, the duty of the Corporation being merely to protect the best and largest number of visitors from discomfiture by having their moral instincts shocked.'[48] This meant that Corporation policy would have to change in step with the changing behavioural norms of the mainstream visiting public; and it did so to such effect that Edwardian Blackpool probably imposed fewer petty restrictions on visitor behaviour than any other major British resort.

Sexual taboos died hardest. Bathing regulations were thoroughly enforced, and in 1884 the foreshore inspector was provided with a telescope to ease the apprehension of offenders at low tide.[49] Blackpool was not among the pioneers of mixed bathing. Mutoscopes (or 'What-the-butler-saw' machines) showing scantily-clad ladies were impounded in 1899, and determined attempts at comic postcard censorship followed in Edwardian times. Brothels were not tolerated, and in 1900 the new Borough Bench closed the public-house singing-saloons, which were seen as a threat to the morals of young visitors.

Drink posed fewer problems. The number of convictions for drunkenness stagnated as visitor numbers and resident population increased rapidly, and this probably says something about police and public tolerance as well as improved standards of behaviour. Public houses were not allowed to multiply, but they remained numerous in the central entertainment area, and the lack of specific intervention bears out contemporary suggestions that Blackpool was an excellent advertisement for the value of counter-attractions as an antidote to drunkenness.[50]

Most distinctive of all was the Corporation's attitude to Sunday observance. Blackpool progressed steadily towards an unfettered Sunday from the 1860s onwards, as Local Board by-laws fell into disuse. Attempts in the 1870s to tighten up controls, to appease the Nonconformist (and Evangelical Anglican) conscience and the 'better-class' visitor, came to nothing as entertainment companies began to open on Sundays and the Winter Gardens pioneered Sunday concerts in the town. During the 1880s it became apparent that most 'better-class' visitors were eager to patronise Sunday cabs, concerts and steamers, and in 1887 the failure of prosecutions for Sunday trading led the new Chief Constable to abandon any attempt at enforcing the Sunday observance laws, as local magistrates refused to convict. In 1896 the Corporation itself joined the Sabbath-breakers, having long tolerated them, when a Sunday tram service was inaugurated. In most of these respects Blackpool was years ahead of its rivals, and Nonconformist wrath spent itself in vain. The weakness of organised religious influences on the Corporation and magistracy enabled Blackpool to put commercial considerations before religious taboos, uncovering and exploiting a widespread demand for Sunday entertainment long before the other large resorts were willing or able to come to terms with it.

VII

This case-study shows the importance of municipal government to the late Victorian and Edwardian development of Britain's largest and most successful working-class resort. In the absence of a dominant landowner, the Corporation was probably the single most important internal influence on Blackpool's character and social tone. But the remarkable extent of municipal activity in the town was rooted in the need to service the holiday and entertainment industries which bulked so large in the local economy; and where this basic need faded, a familiar impulse to cheeseparing asserted itself, as befitted a town numerically dominated by the insecure small businessmen who formed the backbone of ratepayers' defence movements inland.

Blackpool's record in providing municipal services and amenities was distinctive in three conspicuous ways. The scale and range of municipal activity, and the tolerance of high levels of expenditure on holiday-industry-related projects, stand out even by comparison with other major resorts. Within this framework, however, Blackpool's good fortune in the vitality of its entertainment companies absolved the Corporation from the need to invest directly in this field, except in connection with advertising; and this freed it from responsibilities which often imposed heavy expenditure elsewhere.[51] Thirdly, the strength of the entertainment companies inverted the usual relationship between leisure provision and local government at the seaside: for a crucial transitional period in the late nineteenth century, Blackpool's entertainment companies effectively controlled its municipal government in several important respects, whereas elsewhere local authorities were beginning to control most aspects of organised entertainment by the early twentieth century, as private enterprise faltered in the face of seasonal and fluctuating demand.

Blackpool was also unique in its permissive attitude to many (though not all) aspects of visitor behaviour, though the free and easy atmosphere which made it so attractive to excursionists was due as much to policing and legal problems, and to the sheer numbers involved, as to Corporation policy. Away from the crowds, indeed, the quiet residential character of North Shore was carefully defended by the Corporation.[52] But the unique and pioneering laxity of official attitudes to Sunday observance brings out the flexibility of a highly commercially-minded and undogmatic local authority in responding to real but unarticulated changes in popular tastes and attitudes.

Blackpool owed its municipal successes to the adoption of a business ethic in the council chamber. The high-minded ideological approach to municipal expansion, which was displayed so prominently in Birmingham and Bristol, was conspicuous by its absence here. It is too early to say whether Bristol's social citizenship, Birmingham's civic gospel or Blackpool's philistine pragmatism was closest to the national norm; and this case-study has been more useful to the understanding of how holiday resorts worked, than to the elucidation of wider problems of municipal history. Before the important questions about the relationships between economy, society and municipal government can be taken much further, indeed, we need several more case-studies which will bring together the social composition, political attitudes, policies and impact of local authorities, in the manner of Professor Hennock.[53] Meanwhile, the message of this chapter to students of Victorian and leisure towns is clear, and reinforces that of Richard Roberts. The mid-Victorian period was the age of the landowner, as much as the age of the railway, at the seaside;[54] but the most significant internal influence on the rapid large-scale resort growth of the late nineteenth and early twentieth century was the growing power and scope of the local authority.

NOTES

1 E. P. Hennock, *Fit and Proper Persons* (1973); H. E. Meller, *Leisure and the changing city* (1976); D. Fraser, *Power and authority in the Victorian city* (Oxford, 1979), especially pp. 170–3; G. W. Jones, *Borough politics* (1969), p. 26.

2 Hennock, *Fit and Proper Persons*; Fraser, *Power and authority*; M. E. Falkus, 'The development of municipal trading in the nineteenth century', *Business History* 19 (1977), pp. 134–61. See also M. J. Daunton, *Coal Metropolis: Cardiff 1870–1914* (Leicester, 1977), pp. 149–77.

3 P. Bailey, *Leisure and Class in Victorian England* (1978); B. Harrison, *Drink and the Victorians* (1971), especially pp. 262–347; H. Cunningham, 'The metropolitan fairs: a case study in the social control of leisure', in A. P. Donajgrodzki (ed.), *Social Control in Nineteenth-Century Britain* (1977), especially p. 173; R. D. Storch, 'The problem of working-class leisure', in Donajgrodzki, *Social Control;* Storch, 'The policeman as domestic missionary', *Journal of Social History* 9 (1976), pp. 481–509; F. Bealey, 'Municipal politics in Newcastle-under-Lyme 1872–1914', *North Staffordshire Journal of Field Studies* 5 (1965), pp. 64–71.

4 D. Russell, 'The popular musical societies of the Yorkshire textile district 1850–1914', D.Phil. thesis, Univ. of York, 1979, pp. 165–73. Requests for tighter by-law powers can be investigated through the minutes of select committees on local Improvement Bills in the House of Lords Record Office, and (with great difficulty) in the unwieldy MH.12 series at the Public Record Office.

5 Cunningham, 'Metropolitan fairs'; R. D. Storch (ed.), *Popular Culture in Nineteenth-century Britain: Persistence and Change* (1982); J. K. Walton, 'The demand for working-class seaside holidays in Victorian England', *Economic History Review*, 2nd series, 34 (1981), p. 261; W. R. Cockcroft, 'The Liverpool police force 1836–1902', in S. P. Bell (ed.), *Victorian Lancashire* (Newton Abbot, 1974), pp. 150–68; Sir William Nott-Bower, *Fifty-two Years a Policeman* (1926), pp. 133–46; A. Redford, *The History of Local Government in Manchester*, vol. III (1940), pp. 3–27.

6 See especially Meller, *Leisure and the Changing City*, pp. 65–71, 96–116.

7 This theme will be fully documented in chapter 6 of my book on the English seaside holiday town, 1750–1914, now in progress.

8 See Richard Roberts, 'The Corporation as impresario', above.

9 House of Lords Record Office, Select Committee on the Bridlington Local Board Bill, 1889, pp. 7–8, 67–9, and *passim*.

10 For examples see D. Cannadine, *Lords and Landlords: the Aristocracy and the Towns 1774–1967* (Leicester, 1980), pp. 373–5.

11 *Ibid.*, pp. 354–8, 375–6.

12 J. Grass, 'Morecambe, the people's pleasure', M.A. dissertation, Univ. of Lancaster, 1972, pp. 38–46; M. J. Winstanley, 'Conflicting responses to New Brighton's role as a popular seaside resort, 1896–1914', M.A. dissertation, Univ. of Lancaster, 1973, especially pp. 29–40; B. J. H. Brown, 'A survey of the development of the leisure industries of the Bristol region, with special reference to the history of the seaside resorts', Ph.D. thesis, Univ. of Bath, 1971, pp. 185, 194–6.

13 Conspicuous exceptions include Cannadine, Winstanley, Roberts and

F. B. May, 'The development of Ilfracombe as a resort in the nineteenth century', M.A. thesis, Univ. of Wales, 1978.

14 For a fuller development of some of the themes examined here, see J. K. Walton, 'The social development of Blackpool 1788-1914', Ph.D. thesis, Univ. of Lancaster, 1974, especially chapters 4, 8 and 9.

15 Walton, 'Working-class seaside holidays', pp. 253-8.

16 A more extended treatment can be found in J. K. Walton, *The Blackpool landlady: a Social History* (Manchester, 1978), especially chapter 2.

17 Walton, *Landlady*, chapter 7; thesis, chapters 1 and 7; 'Residential amenity, respectable morality and the rise of the entertainment industry: the case of Blackpool 1860-1914', *Literature and History* 1 (1975), pp. 62-78.

18 Walton, *Landlady*, pp. 24-5. The following section is based on Walton, thesis, chapter 9 and appendix, where full documentation can be found.

19 Walton, thesis, pp. 466-7. The 'holiday industry' category was made up as follows: 9 hoteliers, 5 lodging-house keepers, 4 restaurateurs, 3 theatre proprietors/managers, 2 photographers, and one each of the following: pier manager, baths proprietor, boatman, steamboat company manager, park manager, phrenologist, waxworks proprietor, amusement park proprietor, charabanc proprietor.

20 K. R. Wilson, 'Social leaders and public figures in the rise of Morecambe', M.A. dissertation, Univ. of Lancaster, 1972, pp. 35-60; Cannadine, *Lords and Landlords*, pp. 308-9, 356-7.

21 Hennock, *Fit and Proper Persons*, pp. 49-50; Jones, *Borough Politics*, p. 106; R. Newton, *Victorian Exeter* (Leicester, 1968), pp. 325-41; Bealey, 'Municipal politics', p. 66; Wilson, 'Social leaders', p. 48; Cannadine, *Lords and Landlords*, pp. 309, 356; May, 'Ilfracombe', p. 211; and for an earlier period G. S. Duncan, 'Church and society in early Victorian Torquay', M.A. thesis, Univ. of Exeter, 1972, pp. 39, 393.

22 This paragraph is based on biographical evidence drawn from obituaries, supplemented by shareholders' registers, rate-books and newspaper reports.

23 *Blackpool Gazette* (*B.G.*), 9 March 1906, 7 May 1907, 5 July 1907.

24 Hennock, *Fit and Proper Persons*, pp. 61-176; Meller, *Leisure and the Changing City*, chapter 4 and *passim*.

25 Walton, thesis, table 9.8 and pp. 478-80.

26 For the rates see Walton, thesis, pp. 180, 214-5.

27 Hennock, *Fit and Proper Persons*, *passim*. For a sceptical view based on the experience of Cardiff, see Daunton, *Coal Metropolis*, pp. 163-7.

28 Walton, thesis, p. 449.

29 *B.G.*, 13 August 1897.

30 Cannadine, *Lords and Landlords*, p. 273; L. J. Bartley, *The Story of Bexhill* (Bexhill, 1971), p. 130.

31 Victoria County History, *Yorkshire: East Riding*, vol. II (1974), pp. 37-9; J. W. Burrows, *Southend and District* (1909, repr. Wakefield, 1970), pp. 225-6.

32 See above, note 7.

33 E. S. Turner, *The Shocking history of Advertising* (1952) is still the best introduction to the subject. For what follows, see Walton, thesis, chapter 7, which provides documentation. For the advantages and limitations of the poster advertising on which Blackpool came to rely, see T. R. Nevett, 'The develop-

ment of commercial advertising in Britain 1800-1914', Ph.D. thesis, Univ. of London, 1980, pp. 244-5.

34 See above, notes 7 and 8.

35 Town Hall, Blackpool, minutes of Highway Committee, 2 June 1881, 20 October 1885; Annual Reports of Medical Officer of Health, Blackpool; *Manchester Guardian*, 23 September 1878; *B.G.*, 4 May 1883, 13 November 1885.

36 Medical Officer of Health, 1898 Report, p. 43.

37 Walton, thesis, chapter 1; *Landlady*, chapter 3.

38 *B.G.*, 3 October 1890, 24 October, 1890, 5 March 1897, 9 August 1901, 30 August 1901, 20 September 1901, 10 January 1908 to 22 June 1909, 29 September 1911; Lancashire Record Office DDCl/1325 Box 8.

39 Town Hall, Library Committee, Annual Reports and 10 August 1880, 21 July 1903, 12 May 1908; *B.G.*, 7 November 1879, 18-25 June 1880, 27 April 1906 to 5 June 1908, 27 October 1911.

40 *B.G.*, 29 April 1910.

41 Walton, thesis, p. 198, based on council minutes; *pace* W. E. Swale, *Forerunners of the North-Western Electricity Board* (Manchester, 1963), p. 7.

42 H. Monks, 'Some notes on the municipal gas undertaking', typescript in Blackpool Central Library. Mr Monks kindly provided access to minutes and other documents in his custody at Blackpool Town Hall, and I am very grateful for his assistance.

43 *B.G.*, 9 January to 13 November 1891, 24 November 1893.

44 For what follows, see the fuller treatment in Walton, thesis, chapter 8.

45 Town Hall, minutes of Watch Committee.

46 For the Borough Bench, *B.G.*, 8 April 1898, 1 September 1899, 6 October 1899, 31 August 1900.

47 Walton, 'Residential amenity'.

48 *B.G.*, 9 September 1887.

49 *B.G.*, 7 March 1884.

50 *B.G.*, 26 April 1898.

51 As at Brighton, Margate and Bournemouth. See above, notes 7 and 8.

52 Walton, 'Residential amenity'.

53 Hennock, *Fit and Proper Persons*.

54 Cannadine, *Lords and Landlords*, especially chapter 26; H. J. Perkin, *The Age of the Railway* (1970), chapter 8, and 'The "social tone" of Victorian seaside resorts in the North-West', *Northern History* 11 (1976 for 1975), pp. 181-94.

lwardian Ilfracombe

From the time it first found favour as a bathing place towards the end of the eighteenth century, Ilfracombe remained the principal resort on the north Devon coast. At its peak before 1914, when it drew hundreds of thousands of visitors annually, it was being described as 'a social, large-hearted, modern democratic, romantic, laughter-loving spot'.[2] But to view its development simply as a Bristol Channel tripper resort would be seriously misleading. In many ways it typified the growth of the select watering places dotted along the coasts of Devon and Cornwall, now the most popular holiday area in Britain. And, after two centuries of transition from a traditional economy based mainly on agriculture, fishing, woollen textiles and coastal trade, tourism has become its most important asset.

The immediate origins of the Devon resorts lay in the eighteenth-century leisure revolution, stimulated by many of the same factors as the transformation of the manufacturing cities. The fashion for taking the cure at the inland spas is relatively well documented, as are the eighteenth-century prescriptions of Drs Floyer, Russell and others for sea-water drinking and bathing. Their first use in medical practice in Devon seems to have been in the 1720s and 1730s at Exmouth. But the real growth of the county's seaside resorts began in the second half of the century when the wider social range from which the 'company' at Bath and newer spas like Clifton was increasingly being drawn led many to forsake them for less accessible bathing places on the remoter coasts of the south-west. Compared with Bath, Devon's eighteenth-century resorts were small indeed; their very rusticity was part of their attraction.[3]

Ilfracombe became the only sizeable resort on the north Devon coast. By 1788 it was reported to be 'remarkably full of genteel company ... from most parts of the country', attracted by 'the convenience of the bathing machines and the great attention of the townspeople to accommodate them'.[4] Its situation, described as 'a beautiful natural basin sheltered by craggy heights that are overspread with foliage', with the 'magnificent sweep of the Bristol channel with the Welsh coast beyond' also captured the romantic imagination and, following the closure of the Continent during the war against France, played its part in the rediscovery of the beauties of English scenery. Indeed the writings of Coleridge, Shelley and Southey among others gained the whole stretch of coast between Ilfracombe and Lynmouth celebrity as 'the English Switzerland', while the therapeutic benefits of its 'bracing' climate in contrast to the 'relaxing' atmosphere of the south Devon coast found increasing medical favour.[5]

For a small settlement like Ilfracombe facing ominous signs of economic decay, this discovery provided a rare opportunity for new growth. In 1841 it appeared, along with 'Tor Bay', Exmouth, Sidmouth and

Teignmouth on Dr Granville's influential map of the twenty-six 'principal sea-bathing places of England'. Ten years later, despite severe economic setbacks, the national census also included it and Torquay among eleven watering places and four spas with faster growth rates than the industrial centres with which they were compared.[6] From then on – the bulk of the period covered here – it remained much closer to the mean size of the other Devon resorts. In this respect it serves as a more representative indicator of the dynamics of resort growth than its illustrious south Devon rival, Torquay, which, after a late start, outstripped all its neighbours so quickly that it should perhaps be compared more with spectacular success stories like Bournemouth or Brighton. Indeed

Table 10.1: Population and housing, Ilfracombe parish 1801–1911 (source: Census Reports)

	Population	*% change*	*Houses*	*% change*
1801	1838			
1811	1934	5.2	447	
1821	2622	35.6	531	18.8
1831	3201	22.1	681	28.2
1841	3679	14.9	795	16.7
1851	3677	−0.1	852	7.2
1861	3851	4.7	857	0.6
1871	4721	22.6	1042	21.6
1881	6255	32.5	1242	19.2
1891	7692	23.0	1738	39.9
1901	8557	11.2	2142	23.2
1911	8935	4.4	2236	4.4

the more popular holiday centres produced some of the fastest urban growth rates of the period, whereas many small watering places, developing from pre-existing settlements, experienced much less upheaval with more gradual adjustment to their new economic role. Nevertheless Ilfracombe, like other Devon resorts, had constantly to compete with Torquay's jealously guarded reputation as the 'Queen of south-western watering places,' setting the standard for all to follow; and rivalry between the two proved a formative influence on the town's development.

From the outset this was hampered by its isolation from the more heavily populated south of the county and the transport network that grew up to serve it. Its unique location at the mouth of the Bristol Channel tended to dominate the growth of the resort, as of the maritime community before it, providing an otherwise insignificant coastal settlement strategic importance as a harbour of refuge until the decline of sail and of Bristol as the nation's principal west coast port. It also constituted a major attraction for visitors. Paradoxically, however, Ilfracombe's ability to capitalise on its natural assets was for long circumscribed by its very geographical location. Recent research, focusing on the north-west of England, has suggested that internal factors were primarily responsible for the growth patterns and social tone of individual holiday towns.[7] In the isolated south-west, though detailed comparative studies are still needed, the interplay of internal and external forces is less clear cut. Even crucial internal features like the pattern of landownership have in Devon to be seen in the light of serious topographical constraints which made the linear coastal expansion, so marked elsewhere, virtually impossible. For many small settlements like Ilfracombe outside influences such as the provision of adequate transport often appeared to loom larger. Its distance from Bristol and beyond and the catchment area it wished to cultivate heavily influenced the social composition and expectations of its visitor population.

Clearly this was initially restricted to the small aristocratic and upper-middle-class élite with the time and means to travel to such a remote spot, whether as tourists to enjoy the beautiful surroundings or as valetudinarians. Royal patronage greatly enhanced the healthy reputation of resorts like Weymouth and Sidmouth, but, despite the brief visit of the future Queen Adelaide as Duchess of Clarence in 1827 and even shorter stays by the Prince of Wales later in the century, Ilfracombe's isolation, while guaranteeing its fashionable status, made this a less important factor.[8] Yet as the wages and living standards of workers in the south Wales mineral industries slowly began to rise, boatloads of roistering 'Welshies' posed a potential threat to its social tone, in some ways providing a foretaste of its later dual market situation.

Containing this influx became a perennial concern, but full commitment to the town's holiday industry emerged only gradually. By the early nineteenth century the outstanding features of the local economy were its seasonality and the consequent extent of multiple occupations. Fishing, coastal trade, boat building and repair, supplemented by occasional smuggling or wrecking, and servicing the agricultural hinterland frequently provided local families with joint if precarious sources of income, instilling a tradition which was to ease adjustment to equally seasonal employment in the holiday trades. Yet, despite the rapid decline in vessels registered at Ilfracombe after 1815, the loss of its status as a customs port in 1839 and widespread distress, forcing many families to emigrate in the 1840s, numerous attempts were made to revive the port's flagging fortunes before it was finally recognised that the town's future lay in catering for visitors.[9] At mid-century the picture presented by the occupational census is still essentially that of a small coastal servicing centre, with relatively few shown in the holiday trades. But measurement of these is bedevilled by the extent of dual employment and consequent under-recording, the co-existence of new and traditional occupations emerging more clearly from other sources which suggest, in particular, a heavy reliance on providing accommodation, with over two hundred lodging-house keepers, mainly female, in the town.[10]

The impact of increasing numbers of fashionable visitors is also revealed by the town's physical growth and changing pattern of local government. In 1811 Ilfracombe was little more than a village with under two thousand inhabitants, most housing clustering around the harbour or straggling inland along the main street to the parish church. By mid-century its appearance had altered markedly, with the number of buildings rising by nearly two thirds between 1821 and 1851 as property owners endeavoured to meet the demand for new accommodation. In the absence of an effective local authority only they and builders could exert any control over resort development and consequently did much to set its tone. But fears that the town would spread like Torquay over the surrounding countryside, destroying the scenic splendour that visitors had come to enjoy, also proved a powerful constraint.

Whenever property distribution remained unfragmented and capital was available estate control made possible grand building schemes like those of the Palks and Careys at Torquay. At Ilfracombe, however, large-scale planning was limited both by topography and fragmented landownership, the extent of which emerges from the 1840 tithe survey: fifty-four of those properties within the area built up by 1914 were under one acre; twenty-five were between one and five, seven over ten acres, and only one – the Torrs – over a hundred. The larger holdings, owned by local gentlemen or farmers, were still under pasture; the majority were odd plots scattered over the town, permitting only piecemeal development.[11] The largest proportion, including the harbour, boatyard, the scenic Capstone, Compass and Lantern Hills and over a hundred houses was owned by the Lord of the Manor, Sir Bourchier Palk Wrey. He can hardly have been unaware of the potential of much of his property. Indeed after retiring to the town he enlarged the harbour and pier and became a notable supporter of projects like the Ilfracombe Railway. But his overall attitude remained one of benevolent but passive paternalism, unlike his close relatives the Palks who did much to develop Torquay.[12] As summer residents only in the first half of the nineteenth century the Wreys were less prominent in local affairs than several inter-related landed families, notably the Lees and Vyes, magistrates, bankers and gentlemen farmers. With other wealthy residents, some retired from distinguished military or public service careers, like Admirals Bowen and Down or Sir James Meek, these constituted the town's social and political leadership, increasingly bolstered by a number of professionals and businessmen who aspired to similar status. Collectively they also provided the emergent resort with its entrepreneurial élite, sometimes developing their properties themselves; but more commonly selling individual plots to local builders with covenants and ground rent charges restricting use and appearance.

Early resort construction followed the lines established by the maritime settlement, often filling in spaces between existing properties and setting the principal direction of development until the 1860s. In 1800 the Reverend R. Warner noted 'a number of good houses chiefly for the accommodation of visitors range alongside [this] harbour', though seventeen years later Fanny Burney's removal from quayside apartments kept by a Captain's widow because of the stench at low tide presaged the trend towards more salubrious accommodation in elevated locations on the steep slopes above the town where the atmosphere was more refined in every sense.[13] With the advent of regular steamboat services in the Bristol Channel from the early 1820s and a new turnpike road from Barnstaple in 1829, the pace of growth quickened and the erection of elegant terraced residences and villas for wealthy patrons confirmed the resort's high social tone so assiduously cultivated throughout the century.

By 1828 Thomas Cornish commented on the number of 'new buildings . . . in such a state of forwardness which will prove not only profitable to the owners but commensurate with the rise and opulence of the town'.[14] With the opening by the Sea Bathing Company in 1836, of baths and tunnels to segregated ladies' and gentlemen's bathing beaches at the previously inaccessible Crewkhorne Cove, sites nearer the sea were also considered 'well-calculated' for development.[15] The bath-house itself became a popular social centre, soon flanked by detached villas and luxurious *cottages ornés*, attracting famous visitors like Charles Kingsley and Dr Pusey for long stays. Unfortunately in the absence of detailed records it is impossible to measure the overall capitalisation of building, though the press impressionistically reported up to £150,000 being invested in the town in the second quarter of the century, mostly from local sources.[16] The pace slackened in the late 1840s, but Ilfracombe's new buildings ensured its status among the first rank of watering places, signifying the slow reorientation of the local economy which also impelled a more systematic approach to town improvement.

Early on this was largely left to private enterprise. Street lighting by gas, for example, was established in 1837, soon after Torquay, by a Company comprising many of the same 'spirited band' of local entrepreneurs who promoted the Sea Bathing Company the previous year. But relations between private initiative, the existing authorities and public opinion were often strained to breaking point, as in the early 1840s when an 'anti-improvement and non-accommodation clique of ratepayers' contested a new contract to supply Ilfracombe with gas and the town was plunged into darkness, the first of many similar occasions.[17] Faced with such difficulties businessmen like publisher John Banfield, father of Ilfracombe's press and promoter of its earliest guides, and professionals such as surgeons Thomas Stabb and John Jones, who backed most of the town's early self-improvement schemes, began to press for greater local government powers. The necessity for this was most clearly demonstrated in the crucial areas of highway administration and especially public health, where traditional parish administration in the form of vestry overseers and waywardens and manorial officers like the Port Reeve proved inadequate to meet the needs of an emerging health resort anxious to avoid the squalor and congestion of inland towns.

With most sewage emptying into the harbour and its badly surfaced streets providing the main method of refuse disposal, a thorough overhaul of Ilfracombe's internal transport network became imperative for it to remain attractive to fashionable visitors. Spurred on by improvements at several south Devon resorts, uncertainty over responsibility for street repairs, and complaints that the 'badness' of the roads, especially between Barnstaple and Ilfracombe, deterred potential visitors, the Barnstaple Turnpike Trust gained powers in 1827 to maintain and improve roads through and to the town. Though not recognised at the time, the body of trustees which was constituted as an *ad hoc* 'Town Improvement Committee' to implement the legislation became in effect the town's chief authority for a number of years.[18] But its failure to recoup its initial outlay prevented essential sanitary works. It was also blamed as one cause of severe economic distress after further powers in 1841 permitted the collection of additional half tolls. With the collapse of the herring fishery and local agriculture the numbers forced to leave the district increased rapidly. Relief works like the Capstone Parade – Ilfracombe's major promenade – were commenced in the winter of 1842–3 and within five years the extension of the south Devon railway to Torquay threatened the Ilfracombe's holiday industry.[19]

The trustees' strict interpretation of their role helped crystallise the central conflict in Ilfracombe's local government between those for and against town improvement. In many ways the twin dilemmas of Ilfracombe's administrative and economic weaknesses were aspects of the same problem. The holiday industry provided the only alternative and so the future lay with a local authority strong enough to secure its development as a resort. Predictably matters came to a head over public health. The town escaped the cholera epidemic of 1831–2, but, confronted with mounting complaints of its lack of sanitary facilities and a second major epidemic in the late 1840s, the need for strong central government assistance rapidly overtook its half-hearted campaign for an Improvement Act like Torquay's. Potentially crippling losses if the season collapsed gave added impetus to humanitarian concern. A 'labour fund' had already been established in 1849, prompted by Charles Kingsley, who was recuperating in Ilfracombe from one of his periodic breakdowns, and it was his plea to the town to tighten its 'sanitary slackness' which set in train a movement leading to the adoption of the Public Health Act of 1848 and establishment of a Local Board of Health.[20] The exposure of its insanitary conditions, ironically, produced a municipal authority with enough teeth to ensure its future as a health resort.

Taking as its motto *Potens Salubritate* the Local Board steadily if unspectacularly fostered the development of the watering place until superseded by the Urban District Council in 1894. Chiefly inspired by the need to compete with its rivals in the attraction of visitors, the Board's success clearly depended on its leaders' ability to kindle a spirit of improvement. Indeed its early chairmen, Drs Stabb and Jones, had considerable success in mobilising the town's sometimes narrow-minded shopocracy, though, as elsewhere, their efforts were often hindered by angry ratepayers' associations proclaiming themselves to be bastions of individual freedom against encroaching centralism, and voicing the fears of those with no vested interests in the holiday industry.

In tackling the immediate problems that had brought it into existence the new body was not so hard pressed as the larger resorts experiencing a mass influx of visitors each summer. On the other hand it commanded far fewer resources. Rapid results were expected but progress was often sluggish. By-laws governing many aspects of life at the resort were issued and the town's drainage improved by the building of a new sewage works by 1853. But a much needed reservoir was completed, after many delays, only in 1866.[21] Despite the resolve of the Local Board economic recovery was also extremely slow, and the town remained in the doldrums for much of the 1850s. The parish population continued to stagnate and local unemployment remained high, with many still leaving the district. Relief works like the cutting of Sandy Lane in 1854 provided only a temporary respite and few proved willing to sink capital into the resort until it gained improved access. But this was largely in the hands of outside agents. From the 1820s the Bristol Channel steamboat services had brought an increasing flow of visitors during the summer season. But, though movement of passengers certainly became both speedier and easier as a result of intense company competition, even bringing the first Welsh working-class excursionists in the 1840s, the boats were ultimately run in the interests of their owners rather than the resort, and they proved unwilling to provide what Ilfracombe needed above all to balance its economy, an adequate service out of season.[22]

Additional provision in the form of a railway thus became crucial. In spite of improved coach services, the overland journey remained daunting and already several efforts had been made to promote lines to north Devon; one from the south of the county was proposed in 1836 and the first scheme to Ilfracombe in 1844. Its potential was fully demonstrated by the extension of Brunel's broad gauge line to Bristol and beyond from 1841 which initially greatly benefited Ilfracombe. Journey times from London tumbled and coach and boat services quickly adjusted to cater for the upsurge in demand from passengers previously unwilling to travel such distances. But after 1844, when Exeter was reached, and especially 1848 with the opening of the South Devon Railway's branch to Torquay, the conditions of competition between north and south coast resorts were dramatically reversed.[23] Subsequently, as the mid-Victorian boom began to affect leisure patterns, the development of the Devon watering places without railway access was dominated by the drive to get back on terms with their rivals by the successful promotion of branch lines.

For Ilfracombe, however, this proved a lengthy and tortuous process. Despite further schemes during the railway mania of 1845–7, the North Devon Railway only reached Barnstaple, eleven miles short of Ilfracombe, in August 1854.[24] This proved a psychological turning point, the immediate influx of visitors travelling on to the resort and crowding it until October providing a much-needed stimulus to growth and raising hopes of a rapid extension to the town. Over the next twenty years the growth of the resort has to be seen in the context of the fluctuating fortunes of the various attempts to promote such a branch. To a large extent these determined the timing and extent of resort development in the third quarter of the nineteenth century.

Hopes of emulating Torquay's success as a winter resort proved short-lived. Two schemes in the mid-1850s foundered and despite an increase in summer visitors Ilfracombe remained handicapped by poor rail, coach and boat services after the summer season, making it very difficult to complete the journey from London in one day. Indeed, even in summer, before the opening of an alternative standard gauge route from London to Exeter avoiding Bristol in 1860, steam packets provided the easiest route to Ilfracombe from most parts of the country. The broad gauge companies had until then shown little interest in north Devon, concentrating on the more lucrative south–coast traffic. But when the South Western Railway Company gained powers to convert the north Devon line to mixed gauge and operate trains over it from Waterloo, a new era of passenger transport eventually encompassing Ilfracombe seemed at hand.

The private wranglings of the railway companies in the 1860s repeated many of the worst features of local railway promotion in the late 1840s, and delayed completion for many years.[25] It is possible to argue that without such aggressive territorialism the companies would never have undertaken to assist such local projects as the Ilfracombe Railway. But the failure of schemes aimed at sole or joint ownership and operation repeatedly dampened hopes of competing with the resort's rivals on a more equitable basis. The defeat of the 1863 Ilfracombe Railway bill produced street riots, and local opinion divided over which company to support and which of two routes to adopt, especially after revival of an earlier broad gauge scheme for a line to north Devon from Taunton avoiding the usual detour via Exeter.

Construction of the South-Western-backed Barnstaple and Ilfracombe Railway finally began in 1871, and the line opened, after further delays, at the height of the 1874 season, reducing the journey time from London to seven hours eighteen minutes. Broad gauge interests in the town were maintained by fast coach services from the newly opened Devon and Somerset Railway terminus, completing the journey in little more time, and eleven years later the broad gauge companies gained running powers to Ilfracombe over the mixed gauge from a new junction at Barnstaple.[26]

The immediate impact of the railway after so many years proved both momentous and anticlimactic. The boost to Ilfracombe's holiday trade was considerable, but the standard of service to north Devon left much to be desired. Pooling agreements effectively ended company competition for long periods, and even when through running from the North and Midlands became common with the end of the broad gauge, the service never matched that to the south Devon coast, nor seriously threatened the steamboat traffic. Indeed the latter capitalised to some extent on its limitations, benefiting particularly from the construction of a much enlarged pier after 1870 to accommodate the bigger boats coming into service in association with new dock facilities at Bristol and later Avonmouth and Portishead. The effect of the railway was consequently more limited than it might have been ten or twenty years earlier. None the less it was a vital development, raising expectations, helping to lift the town out of its mid-century depression, improving its accessibility and redirecting the resort's whole pattern of growth.

In 1861 the entire parish population was still under four thousand, while Torquay's meanwhile exceeded ten thousand. A decade later the total was still only 4,721, and the Census of that year clearly revealed the constraints that Ilfracombe's isolation had placed on its development. Maritime employment had fallen by ten per cent since mid-century and, although alternatives such as conducting sea excursions for visitors had emerged, the numbers recorded in the primary holiday trades remained

small.[27] But while the overall change in Ilfracombe's occupational structure had been marginal, the expanding business and construction sectors
indicated its potential for more rapid growth.

Already in the 1860s a 21.6 per cent increase in the number of houses
had done much to compensate for previous stagnation, and the town had
begun once again to enjoy a modest prosperity. Much of the impetus for
this originated outside the resort in anticipation of the railway, and
investment was on a grander scale than hitherto. In 1860, with the
shortage of superior accommodation becoming acute, the formation of
the Ilfracombe Joint Stock Land and Investment Company, for example,
set in motion the trend towards estate development on the town's
widening perimeter that characterised its physical growth for the rest of
the century.[28] The Torrs Park Company, as it became known, also
initiated a new line of building towards the site of the future railway
terminus leading in turn to the development of a new route to the
harbour, Wilder Road, which became the resort's second main thorough-
fare and esplanade. Significantly, numbers of wealthy retired families
started to take up permanent residence in its imposing villas, inaugurating a trend of great future importance and by the 1870s gaining
Ilfracombe increasing recognition as a desirable location at all times of
the year. With the town's wider promotion as a winter health resort,
other similar developments also made their appearance. But the summer
season remained the first priority and increased demand for high-class
accommodation for prosperous long-stay visitors led to the establishment
of the largest single undertaking at the resort, the Ilfracombe Hotel.

Despite brief royal patronage, neither of Ilfracombe's principal hotels
had been able to match those of its south-coast rivals. The scale of the
new two hundred-bedroom projected hotel, set in six acres of prime
beach frontage and undertaken in anticipation of the railway, was thus
a considerable gamble. Initially it received little local support, with most
capital coming from elsewhere in the country and from London. But
from its opening in 1867 it came to symbolise the town's revival, its
finances even being regarded as an index of the resort's prosperity. By
1870 it was reported to be overflowing, with dozens of additional guests
having to be bedded out each night.[29] Its famous patrons included the
future Kaiser Wilhelm in 1878 and in 1884 the Vanderbilts, first in a
succession of American plutocrats. Indeed the Hotel seems always to
have had a special appeal to fashionable and titled visitors from overseas,
but also became interested in developing holidays at special rates on
inclusive terms to meet increasing competition from less formal private
hotels catering for respectable middle-class families.[30]

With transport improvements imminent, the successful activities of
the Hotel and Land Companies, and the proliferation of lodging houses,

villas, apartments and rooms available at rates from 5*s* to over £10 per week, Ilfracombe was becoming a recognisably modern holiday resort. Growth accelerated from the late 1870s as the boarding house principle became more popular. But the decrease in the length of time stayed was constantly bemoaned, as far fewer now spent the one to three months which had been usual in the first half of the century, though this was more than compensated for by increased numbers. Measurement of visitor population is notoriously difficult, press reports tending to exaggerate and arrival lists to underestimate the numbers involved. Clearly, however, contemporary estimates in the 1880s of six to ten thousand staying visitors at the height of the season are quite feasible, and continued growth even brought reports by the mid-1890s of twenty-five to thirty thousand present at peak times.[31]

Such increases inevitably produced great changes in the nature of holiday making at Ilfracombe. While the 'company' remained small enough for a close circle of personal contacts to be maintained, the régime, like that at most watering places, still essentially resembled that of the eighteenth-century spa. Visitors to early-nineteenth-century Ilfracombe could be counted in hundreds. From the first, high-ranking professional and military families were well represented, and increasingly the rich and fashionable were joined by the prosperous middle classes, anxious to emulate such social superiors. Eminent early visitors included south Wales ironmasters like the Marquess of Bute, Lord Uxbridge and the Homfrays, the Bristol banking family of Coutts and tobacco manufacturers Wills.[32] A bracing climate, secluded bathing and magnificent scenery in a select location were the main attractions. To these were added the usual fashionable diversions. Assembly Rooms, with facilities for the seasonal round of soirées and balls, were provided from the 1830s; fêtes, regattas, concerts, flower shows and similar charitable activities completed the social calendar.

The aesthetic allure of the north Devon coast and the desire to see holidays 'well-used' also accorded well with the rising popularity of the whole area among the middle-class Victorian reading public. By mid-century its scenic splendours were well known and interest in its natural history soon became a craze. In particular the works of Philip Gosse and G. H. Lewes, whose *Sea-Side Studies* was published after a visit to Ilfracombe with George Eliot in 1856, brought flocks of town-dwellers eager to investigate and classify the flora and fauna of every rock pool. Local lanes were similarly scoured for flowers to pick and press and, after publication of *Ferny Combes* by Charlotte Chanter, daughter of the vicar, in the same year, the resort became a popular centre for collecting ferns.[33]

In subsequent decades, as more and more lower-middle-class families arrived, this pattern of activities required little modification. As one journalist in the early 1870s, having noted its popularity as a honeymoon centre, observed,

> The world of Ilfracombe fashion is a slightly miscellaneous one. First and foremost comes the Bristolian contingent ... then there is always a large floating population of tourists ... They have no time to lose ... so they race around the place, headed probably by a demented ecclesiastic, staff in one hand, guide-book in the other. ... Then we have a truly formidable array of elderly spinster ladies ... They swarm prolifically over rocks and hills, distribute tracts to the thoughtless, talk scandal and call it charity.[34]

Even the thousands of excursionists arriving from the late 1880s were primarily drawn by the same simple attractions as the fashionable company half a century earlier. Ilfracombe's geographical catchment area had always been broad-based, with London, Bristol, the inland spas and southern counties predominant. But the introduction of Campbells' and other fast pleasure steamer services during the decade opened the whole area to day trippers drawn from the most affluent sections of the Midlands and northern working class. Already the frequently drunken exploits of the 'Merry Cymri' had produced an ambivalent response at the resort, lowering its tone but bringing much-needed revenue in poor seasons. By the end of the century, however, Ilfracombe could afford to be more selective in its intake. The floating beershops from Swansea and elsewhere were banned and it successfully avoided what the District Council Chairman called 'the ordinary tripper element', adding that the town was 'too far away for them to stay very long' and that 'usually we get a very nice lot of people by boat'.[35] Indeed the town retained its solid middle-class base and was still sufficiently fashionable to attract European royalty and wealthy Americans at the end of the century. But the gradual democratisation of leisure was irreversible. The typical excursion fare from Bristol at the turn of the century, at 5s saloon or 3s on deck, generated a still larger tripper boom in the 1900s, the numbers passing through the harbour turnstiles rising from 96,000 in 1901 to peak at over 180,000 in the summer of 1911.[36]

With its natural amenities remaining the major attraction there was never the same pressure to invest in entertainments on the scale of the larger resorts, but Ilfracombe, haunted by the fear of being left behind again as at mid-century, found it necessary to keep up with its south Devon rivals. From the early 1860s steps were taken to supplement the work of the Local Board which was prevented by law from promoting the resort directly, by establishing a voluntary Improvement Committee to publicise the town and oversee its musical entertainments. From the 1870s the need for a little 'mild dissipation' for visitors familiar with a wide range of entertainments at home was universally acknowledged. But the prevailing ethos that holidays were as much for the 'improvement' as the amusement of those taking them ensured the highest propriety at all times. Much of the overbearing primness of the health resort died hard as family holidays gained in importance. Major concessions like mixed bathing appeared only in the new century and the District Council, following the pattern set by the Local Board, 'resolutely declined to encourage the usual "sands" entertainments'.[37]

Private investment in amusements none the less increased alongside the widening appeal of the resort. With the arrival of the railway imminent an Oxford Music Hall was opened in 1873, which also provided serious drama in the absence of a theatre, and, after the failure of an entertainments complex near the front, was even periodically converted into a roller-skating rink to cater for the rising number of younger visitors. In the following decade the range of entertainments widened further. The town's serious lack of a wide beach frontage was to some extent overcome in 1880 by the Ilfracombe Hotel's covered sea-water swimming pool where numerous galas and aquatic entertainments became a major attraction. Such facilities were also part of the continuous campaign to extend the season. The Victoria Pavilion, built to commemorate the Golden Jubilee, for example, provided a winter garden in the form of a miniature Crystal Palace. With its potted palms, aquaria and sun-deck it epitomised late Victorian holidaymaking at Ilfracombe. But it soon proved quite inadequate to cope with the demand for summer season concerts and by the 1890s additional facilities were being provided at several large hotels like the Runnacleave. In 1901 a Kursaal was opened on the pier and the Council's Alexandra Theatre followed two years later. A wide range of nationally recognised performers appeared at the town, from virtuosos like Kreisler to vaudeville comedians George Robey and General Tom Thumb.[38]

The role of the local authority in all this, with statutory prohibitions on advertising the town and direct promotion of entertainments, remained ambiguous. Not until 1914, after years of haggling over concert rights, did it undertake to run its own musical entertainment, and by then the amusements provided by many resorts were again perceptibly changing, with Ilfracombe's first cinema opening in 1909, hot on the heels of Torquay. But, though publicly helpless, many councillors privately contributed greatly to such developments. Indeed whenever private enterprise faltered and the pressure for economy allowed, they proved ready to safeguard the resort by all available means, complementing their basic task of ensuring the well-being of a population that might quadruple for three or four months each year. The Council's record in this was one of steady endeavour but mixed success. Not until 1904, with the building of a new pipeline from Exmoor, was the town adequately provided with water; in several hot summers the supply dried up altogether. The disposal of largely untreated refuse into the sea remained a potential health hazard, as did much of the housing around the harbour, and attempts to municipalise the sometimes unreliable gas and electricity companies failed. In protecting much of the land around the town from building encroachments, however, the authorities were more successful: the purchase of beauty spots like Capstone Hill and Ropery Meadow in the 1870s and Cairn Top and Hillsborough Hill in the last years of the century, providing many scenic walks that enhanced the resort's romantic attractions. In 1905 the Council finally took over the harbour and pier from the manorial trustees who had already improved its facilities to cope with the crowds of summer trippers. With it the picturesque Lantern Hill close by and several tracts of land that became additional recreation grounds were saved from the building speculator.[39]

But notwithstanding such safeguards the physical expansion of the town reached unprecedented levels between the late 1870s and early 1890s. Rows of detached and terraced houses spread even higher up the hills above the town and began to spill over into adjoining valleys. Ilfracombe's rising popularity as a residential and retirement centre also stimulated several large-scale developments. All were within walking distance of the town and front and took on a suburban air. Principal among them was G. E. Russell's Wildercombe Park of detached and semi-detached villas to let or for sale between £600 and £1500, close to and modelled on the earlier Torrs Park. At its eastern limit Chambercombe Park slowly engulfed farmland, building operations extending in similar fashion from the late 1880s to the 1900s.[40] But most development was still on a small scale and Ilfracombe retained its compact appearance right through to 1914. Many properties in the best situations were let as lodgings or converted into boarding houses. Such accommodation was more usually purpose built, however, like the imposing Granville Hotel established high above the town by a former lodging-house keeper, or the substantial private hotels lining the new Wilder Road and charging from two guineas *en pension* weekly. Not all visitors could afford this standard of accommodation of course, and by the turn of the century a wide range of smaller boarding houses provided rooms from as little as 1s 6d per night.[41]

With such wide appeal as both a fashionable and a middle-class resort and excursion centre Ilfracombe thus reached its heyday in the twenty years before 1914. Despite cries in the national press that 'it is a much to be pitied place ... trying to hold its own against the cheap tripper and the speculative builder', it managed to maintain its high social tone, and holidaymaking at the resort retained much in common with that half a century earlier. But its physical appearance and economic structure had altered substantially as catering for an ever-expanding body of visitors became an increasingly important source of employment. Indeed by 1880, the *Ilfracombe Chronicle*, summarising contemporary impressions, proclaimed 'one would almost imagine one half of the population exist by letting out lodgings'.[42] Certainly thirty per cent of directory entries in 1878 and thirty-seven per cent in 1910 did provide accommodation in some way, including much higher numbers of men than earlier, evidence of the transformation of the industry from a secondary, largely female occupation to the major source of income for the families involved. More detailed investigation of Ilfracombe's economic transformation is precluded by the absence of adequate Census information, but the more partial evidence of the directories reveals the steadily rising importance of the town's holiday industry and its residential and retirement functions. Alongside these there grew up a substantial service sector of professionals, retailers and other workers in shops, building, transport and allied trades, though the extent to which these redressed the basic problem of seasonal unemployment remains unclear. With most of its labour force born locally, Ilfracombe never experienced annual influxes of casual workers on the scale of the larger resorts. But like all such places it depended heavily on an army of domestic servants that for most of the period constituted over a quarter of the female labour force. For many the holiday industry continued to provide at best a precarious livelihood, as soup kitchens and sales of furniture appeared after poor seasons, but most clung on to this opportunity for economic advancement.

Indeed the holiday industry provided the one means by which Victorian Ilfracombe might advance. As its traditional economy withered, the impetus to resort promotion gathered momentum, but internal and external influences on its development remained inextricably intertwined. A first flush of local enterprise produced many improvements, but not until its future as a health resort was jeopardised by disease and distress did the small community take up its new economic role wholeheartedly. Even then support for numerous ventures had to be sought outside the town which already depended to an uncomfortable degree on external agencies to provide, for example, the all-important transport links. Its location was always both its chief strength and weakness: a north-facing situation, inadequate beaches and limited open space for expansion, and, above all, its inaccessibility helped account for the relative slowness with which its scenic and other attractions came to be enjoyed. Much of the energy of those promoting the resort was spent attempting to overcome these obstacles. Yet Ilfracombe largely succeeded in coming to terms with its dual market situation, continuing to cultivate its fashionable clientèle and assimilate growing numbers of excursionists. For the most part the leisure patterns of the two sides of Ilfracombe's visitor population had sufficient in common not to threaten their generally peaceful coexistence, and by 1914 Ilfracombe was well-established as a holiday playground for young and old from a wide range of social and geographical backgrounds. With its economic transformation complete the town appeared to thrive on the variety of its experience as residential and retirement functions also increased in importance. But in the new conditions of post-war society the expectations raised in its Edwardian heyday proved illusory. In most essentials Ilfracombe remains the product of its nineteenth-century creators: an inheritance that provides much of its present-day charm.

NOTES

1 This article is based on parts of my thesis, 'The development of Ilfracombe as a resort in the nineteenth century', M.A., University of Wales, 1978.

2 F. J. Snell, *North Devon* (1906), p. 71.

3 See, for example, J. A. R. Pimlott, *The Englishman's Holiday: A Social History* (1947, repr. with new introduction 1976), pp. 50–4; E. R. Delderfield, *Exmouth Milestones* (Exmouth, 1948), pp. 35–6; W. G. Hoskins, *A New Survey of England: Devon* (1954).

4 *Exeter Flying Post*, 17 July 1788.

5 Shaw, *A Tour of the West of England in 1788* (1789), quoted in D. W. Bowring, *Ilfracombe Throughout the Ages* (Exeter, 1951), pp. 64–5; W. G. Maton, 'Observations on the western counties, 1794–6', in R. Pearse-Chope (ed.), *Early Tours in Devon and Cornwall* (Newton Abbot, 1967), p. 277.

6 Pimlott, *op. cit.*, pp. 96–7.

7 H. J. Perkin, 'The "social tone" of Victorian seaside resorts in the north-west', *Northern History* 11 (1976 for 1975), pp. 180–94.

8 Pimlott, *op. cit.*, pp. 61–3; *Exeter Flying Post*, 16 July 1789 *et seq.*; *North Devon Journal*, 20–27 July 1827.

9 G. Farr, *Ships and Harbours of Exmoor* (Dulverton, 1970), *passim*.

10 Public Record Office (P.R.O.), HO 107/1893 (Census Enumerator's Schedule); *North Devon Journal*, 27 July 1848.

11 Ilfracombe Tithe Survey Map and Apportionment, 1840 (copy in Ilfracombe Museum).

12 Sir Bourchier Palk Wrey, 1788–1879. The absence of relevant family papers is a serious gap in the sources for the town's growth. The Ilfracombe estate was subsequently administered in trust.

13 R. Warner, *A Walk through some of the Western Counties of England* (Bath, 1800), p. 119; *Ilfracombe Chronicle*, 12 November 1904; *Ilfracombe Observer*, 26 April 1890; *North Devon Herald*, 14 September 1893.

14 T. H. Cornish, *Sketch of the Rise and Progress of the Principal Towns of the North of Devon* (Bristol, 1828), pp. 29–30; *North Devon Journal*, 29 June 1827 *et seq.*; various deeds kindly lent by owners.

15 J. Banfield, *Guide to Ilfracombe* (1836 edn.), p. 12; *North Devon Journal*, 19 September 1936.

16 Eg. *ibid.*, 25 May 1848.

17 *Ibid.*, 27 April 1837; 10–17 November 1842; 12–26 January 1843.

18 T. W. Rammell, *Report to the General Board of Health on . . . the Sanitary Condition . . . of Ilfracombe* (1850); W. H. Rogers, 'The Barnstaple Turnpike Trust', *Transactions Devon Association* 74 (1942), pp. 144, 146–7, 149–52; *North Devon Journal*, 24 March 1836 *et seq.*

19 For conditions of employment at this time see e.g. W. G. Hoskins, *Old Devon* (1971), pp. 203–4; *North Devon Journal*, 7–21 September 1843; 19 April 1849; 25 April 1850.

20 P.R.O., MH 13/99 Correspondence of the General Board of Health with Ilfracombe 12 April 1848–15 October 1849 and later Ilfracombe Board of Health; T. W. Rammell, *op. cit.*; *North Devon Journal*, 22 February 1849; 21 June 1849; 29 November 1849; 19 September 1850 *et seq.*

21 Minutes, Ilfracombe Local Board of Health, Devon Record Office, R2458 A/C1 15 September 1851 *et seq.*; P.R.O., MH 13/99 3 December 1851 *et seq.*; *North Devon Journal*, 31 July 1851 *et seq.*

22 G. Farr, *Ships and Harbours . . .*, pp. 20, 22 and his *West Country Passenger Steamers* (Prescot, 1967), pp. 71–3, 78, 90–3.

23 *North Devon Journal*, 12 May 1836; 30 July 1841 *et seq.*; D. St John Thomas, *A Regional History of the Railways of Great Britain*, vol I, *The West Country* (1960), pp. 11, 42–50, 62 *et seq.*

24 R. A. Williams, *The London and South Western Railway*, vol. I (Newton Abbot, 1968), pp. 107–18.

25 J. Simmons, 'South Western *v.* Great Western: railway competition in Devon and Cornwall', *Journal of Transport History* 4, (1959), pp. 18–19; E. T. MacDermot (ed. C. R. Clinker), *History of the Great Western Railway*, vol. II (1964 edn.), pp. 77–81, 84–5.

26 R. A. Williams, *op. cit.*, vol. II (1973), pp. 229–36; F. E. Box, 'The Barnstaple and Ilfracombe Railway', *Railway Magazine* 45 (1919), pp. 408–14; 46 (1920), pp. 24–9.

27 P.R.O., RG 10/2187, Census Enumerator's Schedule.

28 *Bright's Intelligencer* (September 1860); *North Devon Journal*, 23 September 1860; 12 September 1861; 30 January 1862 *et seq.*

29 P.R.O., BT 31/30721 Shareholders' Lists, Ilfracombe Hotel Company, 1863 *et seq.*; *North Devon Journal*, 1 September 1870; 2 November 1871.

30 *Ilfracombe Gazette*, 9 August 1884; *North Devon Journal*, 3 November 1891.

31 *Ilfracombe Chronicle*, 7–12 August 1886.

32 Eg. *North Devon Journal*, 10 August 1827; 5 June 1828; 4 June 1829.

33 Perhaps its most famous literary association was with her uncle, Charles Kingsley, whose *Westward Ho!* was published in 1855. See S. Chitty, *Charles Kingsley's Landscape* (Newton Abbot, 1976), pp. 12, 18–30; *North Devon Journal*, 26 January 1865.

34 *Ibid.*, 7 September 1871.

35 Minutes of Evidence, S. C. H. C., Ilfracombe Harbour and Improvement Bill, Devon R.O., R 2458/H18, pp. 22, 26–7; Minutes Ilfracombe Urban

District Council, 7 November 1899; *Ilfracombe Chronicle*, 11 August 1896; *North Devon Journal*, 17 September 1896 *et seq.*

36 Devon R.O., R 2458/H18, p. 22; *Ilfracombe Chronicle*, 18 October 1913.

37 Eg. *North Devon Journal*, 25 June 1862; 24 July 1862; *Ilfracombe Chronicle*, 2 May 1874; 14 October 1903; W. Mate, *Ilfracombe Illustrated* (1905 edn.), p. 20.

38 W. White, *Directory of Devonshire* (1878 edn.), p. 493; *Ilfracombe Chronicle*, 7 August 1880; 4 September 1880; 20 November 1880; 29 December 1888; 31 December 1904; 30 December 1905; 21 September 1912.

39 See Minutes, Ilfracombe Local Board of Health, and later District Council, Devon R.O., R 2458A/C I–25; R 2458/H18; also P.R.O., MH 12/2161–5, 1893 *et seq.*

40 *Ilfracombe Gazette*, 8 November 1884 *et seq.*; *Ilfracombe Chronicle*, 3 September 1885; 8 September 1888 *et seq.*

41 See e.g. *Pearson's Gossipy Guide to Ilfracombe and the North Devon Coast* (*c.* 1901). For earlier statements of the range and costs of accommodation, *North Devon Journal*, 27 July 1849; 24 July 1856; *Bright's Intelligencer*, 2 May 1861 *inter alia*.

42 Cited *Ilfracombe Gazette and Observer*, 5 September 1896. See too *Ilfracombe Chronicle*, 3 July 1880.

H.ANELAY

orking-class home

I

On 31 May 1838 there took place England's final 'Last Labourers' Revolt', when a group of about thirty-five farm labourers led by 'Sir William Courtenay', a former wine-merchant turned radical politician and messiah, launched a furious attack on a detachment of troops drawn up before them on the edge of Bossenden Wood in north east Kent. The brief but bloody conflict caused more casualties than the whole of the Captain Swing rising, in which no lives were lost until the courts intervened, and the final death-toll on that day – Courtenay, eight labourers, two constables and an army lieutenant – exceeded even the Peterloo Massacre.[1]

This paper is less concerned with the battle itself, described by E. P. Thompson as 'perhaps the most desperate on English soil since 1745',[2] than with the implications of the contemporary response to the tragedy. Coming as it did at the end of almost a decade of rural violence,[3] and coinciding with the birth of Chartism, the rising gave the authorities every cause for concern. Their search for a remedy led to an extensive re-examination of the way of life of those who seemed so vulnerable to the appeal of prophets and demagogues. The answers they found in turn posed major new questions about the nature and significance of the domestic reading habits of the working class.

There were three possible explanations of the event. The first was economic. There had been poverty and unemployment in the area, and the recently imposed New Poor Law was bitterly resented. Courtenay had begun his career in Kent by standing in the 1832 General Election as a Spencean radical, committed to the abolition of tithes and primogeniture.[4] Although the religious element had become more pronounced as his campaign reached its climax, he had led his followers under the banner of a loaf of bread atop a pole, and had rallied his ragged band on the eve of battle by promising fifty acres to each man who fought with him.

The second explanation was legal. There had been a clear breakdown of law enforcement in the weeks leading up to the conflict, and both contemporaries and later historians have argued that the final bloodshed might have been greatly reduced by a more tactful handling of the troops who were belatedly summoned after Courtenay had shot a parish constable sent to arrest him.

Finally, there was a cultural explanation. A man who had spent most of the period since the 1832 Election in Kent County Lunatic Asylum had been able to make so complete a conquest of a substantial group of farm workers that carrying nothing but staves they had thrown themselves upon well-armed troops believing that Courtenay would be resurrected if he fell in battle. Something had gone badly wrong with the agencies responsible for instilling sound judgement in the minds of the labouring poor.

Of the three explanations, the first was decisively rejected, usually without much argument. Some credence was given to the second, and in the following year the Home Secretary, Lord John Russell, who had been severely criticised for allowing Courtenay out of the asylum in the autumn of 1837, piloted the County Police Act through the House of Commons. However the Kent magistracy, who had been found so wanting in the crisis, were to wait until 1857 before exercising their option to form a constabulary.

It was to be the cultural analysis which won the day. Within two years a church was being built in the newly-formed parish of Dunkirk in the middle of the trouble area, and a church school was soon to follow. The event featured largely in the debate which led to the increase of the grant to the Anglican and Nonconformist school societies in 1838.[5] This reaction was part of a wider response to the political unrest of the period. The decade between 1836 and 1845 saw a major expansion in the programme of ecclesiastical building, with the construction of 761 new Anglican churches,[6] and the church school societies entered a period of rapid growth in the 1840s.[7] What was of more interest, both for the light it cast on the changing attitude towards the relationship between working-class culture and politics, and for the detailed evidence it provided on the state of that culture, was the action taken by the recently-formed pressure group, the Central Society for Education. In the immediate aftermath of the rising, it dispatched a London barrister named Frederick Liardet to make a thorough survey of the physical and moral condition of the villages from which the rebels had been drawn. In his twenty-thousand-word report, which was published the following year,[8] he reached the conclusion that the problem was essentially one of re-creation. It was, he claimed, what the labouring poor read, and what they failed to read, in their homes after work, which lay at the root of the violence which had taken place.

II

As an observer, Liardet was not without his preconceptions. He was a member of the Central Society for Education's committee of management, and his principles reflected those of both his parent body and the other newly-formed statistical societies which were urgently conducting their own investigations into the working class. Their research was founded on a conviction that the causes of the apparently remorseless increase in crime and political discontent lay in the physical environment

and moral condition of the working-class family.[9] The societies largely
ignored the workplace and rates of pay, and concentrated instead on the
twin problems of public health and education. Although the direction of
the causal flow between the two forces was often unclear, most of the
investigations, and especially those of the Central Society for Education,
were designed to prove that a moral regeneration of labouring poor
would be an effective first step towards the creation of a stable, hierarchical society. In this sense, the findings of the reports which poured forth
from the late 1830s onwards tell us as much about the bodies which
commissioned them as about their supposed subject matter, yet it
remains the case that the statistical societies were genuinely trying to
apply new techniques to new questions. Partly because of the assump-
tions which underpinned their analysis, and partly in spite of them, the
surveys provide the historian with a unique and largely neglected insight
into the cultural life of the working-class home.

At the very least, the approach of the societies demanded some physical contact with those they would examine, so Liardet duly took up
residence amongst the Kent peasantry, and set about interviewing wit-
nesses, counting what could be counted, and organising his material into
a rudimentary comparative study of the three communities from which
Courtenay had recruited his followers. He reached two broad conclusions. Firstly, that whilst there had been and in some areas still were
distressingly high levels of pauperism, and whilst there was some over-
crowding and poor housekeeping, the physical circumstances of the
labouring poor were not so reduced as to make a rational and moral way
of life utterly impossible. The proportion of the population receiving
relief in the three communities varied from one in eight in Herne Hill to
over one in four in Dunkirk.[10] However only one of the eight fatalities
and four of the twenty-seven awaiting trial were or recently had been
paupers.[11] Equally, although there were some overcrowded and 'dirty
and uncomfortable' houses, 84 per cent of the labouring families had
three rooms or more and most of these lived in 'middling' or 'very
comfortable and clean' conditions.

His second conclusion was that the major problem in the sphere of
culture was not a lack of books, but rather the absence of the right sort
of literature and of the correct attitude towards it. Possession of books
ranged from 52 per cent of households in Dunkirk to 75 per cent in
Herne Hill,[12] figures which were much in line with the data collected
elsewhere by the Society and the other statistical societies. In other areas,
book ownership tended to be slightly higher: surveys of groups of
parishes in Essex, Herefordshire, Norfolk and an adjacent area of Kent
returned figures of 83, 78, 91 and 90 per cent respectively.[13] In the
towns, the societies usually found that at least 70 per cent of households

contained literature of some description. A massive survey of six thousand working-class families in Bristol in 1839 discovered books in 73.2 per cent of the homes;[14] Grays Inn, West Bromwich, Trevethin and Blaenavon in Monmouthshire, Kingston-upon-Hull and St George's, Hanover Square in London produced findings of 78, 85, 86, 75 and 89 per cent.[15] Of the twenty-three investigations of book ownership in a total of over twenty-five thousand working-class homes carried out in this period, only one, a Central Society for Education survey of an Irish slum in Marylebone, found more than half to be devoid of any literature.[16]

When the societies turned their attention from volume to quality, they discovered an overwhelming preponderance of religious works.[17] Liardet and the other investigators of rural homes could find few of the newspapers, cheap novels and improving penny magazines which were appearing in ever increasing numbers during the decade.[18] Even in the towns, where such literature was more common, it was still very unusual to find a working-class domestic library composed solely of secular items. Taken as a whole, the surveys bear striking witness to the comparative literariness of the traditional popular culture.[19] The efforts of the tract distributors, commercial publishers and multiform political and educational agencies were beginning to transform the availability of printed material, but the statistical societies had proved beyond question that the written word, most frequently in the form of the classic prose of the Bible and Prayer Book, was no stranger to the homes of the labouring poor.

It was clear, therefore, that the usual cultural explanation of popular unrest would no longer suffice. Not only were there already Bibles and Testaments in many working-class homes, and, in the countryside at least, correspondingly few seditious works, it was also evident that Courtenay's followers were amongst the most literate and respectable members of their communities.[20] Those who lost their lives in the onslaught on the troops included the sixty-one-year-old smallholder Edward Wraight, 'a man of reserved gloomy temper, who was reckoned a shrewd character by his neighbours',[21] and the farm servant George Griggs, who 'had been in his youth a constant attendant at the Sunday School, and is mentioned as having made great progress in religious knowledge'.[22] Even the one reputed sheep-stealer in their midst, William Burford, had in his cottage 'a Testament and one or two other books of a religious nature'.[23]

Liardet therefore put forward a new and more subtle analysis. His preoccupation with domestic reading arose from the disintegration of traditional means of instilling discipline in the labouring poor. Even in the countryside the transmission of values through a hierarchical community was ceasing to function.[24] In Dunkirk, the worst trouble spot, the villagers were 'left entirely to themselves having neither gentry, clergymen, surgeon nor anybody above their own condition to connect them with the civilisation of the higher classes'.[25] Such a collapse of personal authority had already become evident in the towns,[26] and the consequence was to direct the attention of those anxious to prevent the overthrow of property towards literature as a more generalised channel of indoctrination,[27] and towards the working-class family as the last remaining social structure capable of nurturing and sustaining habits of discipline and rational behaviour.

There were, however, grave defects in the inherited pattern of domestic reading, and this was Liardet's most urgent message both to his own organisation, whose president, the Lord Chief Justice, Lord Denman, was to try the rioters, and to the propertied classes as a whole. It was necessary, first of all, to examine the use which was made of the tiny libraries which had been passed down from generation to generation. 'The returns state,' he wrote of Boughton under the Blean, 'that in two cottages only did the parents employ their evenings in reading; in thirty-eight cases the time after labour was described as being spent "about home", but not in reading; and in seven instances the husband went out to seek for company at the beer-house, or in the cottages of his neighbours'.[28] Although he suspected that his respondents may have understated their drinking habits, all his findings pointed towards a sharp distinction between owning and reading books. Indeed, given the prevailing levels of literacy, especially in the countryside, it is probable that more families owned books than could read them, at least with any fluency.

Yet the very survival of the libraries indicated that the families still attached considerable importance to religious literature, and their support of a number of day and Sunday schools suggested some commitment to the skills of literacy. This apparent paradox lay at the heart of Liardet's argument. The spiritual texts which were to be found in the homes of the labouring poor played both too small and too large a role in their mental universe. They were infrequently read, yet they dominated the meagre resources of the working-class literary culture. As a result, the Bible was not only an inadequate safeguard against the breakdown of order, it actually played a significant part in undermining the judgement of the labourers and their families: 'it may be doubted', observed Liardet, 'if a course of exclusive religious reading, has not a tendency to narrow the mind, and instill fallacious ideas'.[29] Courtenay's ascendancy owed much to his capacity to use the Bible, which he was adept at quoting,[30] to seduce the intellects of those who had too much respect for and too little understanding of its contents. Thus also 'It appeared to him' explained a witness at the trial of the rioters, 'that Courtenay and his clergy had read the same religious books'; thus also was explained the influence of Courtenay's chief lieutenant in the area, Mrs Foreman, who not only had the reputation of 'being able to dispute with any person on the Bible',[31] but, with splendid irony, had been the teacher at the flourishing day school run by the vicar of Herne Hill: 'Among these simple people the capacity to read, and to converse with any degree of fluency upon the subjects treated of, is an infallible proof of superior talents; and as Mrs —— possessed these talents, she became the oracle of the community.'[32]

Two lessons could be drawn from this analysis. The first was that the reading matter of the working class had to be secularised. The diet of religious literature should be broadened to include works on political and legal duties, the rationale of the poor laws and the *laissez-faire* economy, biographies of famous men, 'especially such as have risen by their own efforts from obscurity',[33] and descriptions of nature and of other lands. Liardet particularly welcomed the activity of the Society for the Diffusion of Useful Knowledge, which in conjunction with the Mechanics' Institutes was making strenuous efforts to redefine the working-class conception of the value of the written word.[34]

The second lesson was that in this cultural revolution, the role to be played by the working-class home was decidely ambiguous. On the one hand Liardet and all those engaged in spreading middle-class civilisation to those beneath them were able to conjure up the immensely seductive image of the labourer and his family sitting around the fire after the day's work was done, reading improving tracts and penny magazines. They derived encouragement from the high levels of book ownership which had been established, and from the undoubted working-class respect for literature and the literate.

On the other hand, the working-class home was, in the last resort, a private institution, despite the occasional incursions of would-be social scientists and other philanthropists. However successful the efforts to enlarge the libraries of the poor, their behaviour in their own homes could not be policed as it might be in the workplace or in more organised forms of recreation. Even if the head of the household could be dissuaded from going out to the pub, there was, when it came to it, little that could be done to prevent him spending the evening not reading but merely 'About home, doing sometimes one thing sometimes another; but, most times, going to bed for want of something to do.'[35] To contemporary observers it seemed that this collapse into mental torpor could be quite as damaging to the reasoning power of the labourer as more active forms of dissipation.

Here, as elsewhere, the middle class could not trust their inferiors with an institution like the home which they increasingly saw as a cornerstone of their own way of life.[36] Working-class parents appeared to lack both the physical and moral resources to sustain the sort of domestic existence which could regenerate their culture. Thus Liardet found himself anticipating subsequent promoters of rational recreation by advocating 'amusements, and other sources of innocent and healthful excitement' which could take place out of doors or in public institutions under the watchful eye of the educated classes.[37] In respect of working-class reading, where the church schools and bodies such as the SDUK and the Mechanics' Institutes vigorously sought to direct the consumption of literature,[38] and in respect of the working-class home, where most of this literature was to be read if it was to be read at all, the middle-class educators constantly found themselves torn between a faith in the reasoning power of the working man and a fear that in practice it would not be used, or would be used for the wrong purpose.

III

It is, of course, possible to doubt whether the Battle of Bossenden Wood could have been prevented by the distribution of 'a small book, explaining, in a familiar manner, the legal rights and duties of persons as members of society', or whether the improvements in education or domestic recreation demanded by the new pressure groups would have prevented the emergence of Chartism.[39] Yet the significance of the surveys carried out by the Central Society for Education and the other statistical organisations extends beyond the insights they yield into the prevailing conceptions and misconceptions of the springs of working-class discontent. The autobiographies of working men who lived through this period suggest that the findings of the investigations into the domestic culture of the labouring poor were largely correct, and furthermore, that there were some important affinities between the approach of the educated and of the self-educated members of society to the question of reading in the working-class home.

At the outset, those within the working-class community who had embarked upon the pursuit of knowledge showed a similar concern to enlarge the framework within which they had taken their first steps towards literacy. In their autobiographies, which were themselves a product of a secularisation of their view of themselves and their past,[40] they describe a journey away from a background dominated by religious literature to a new working-class culture in which spiritual works battled for attention with every form of fiction and non-fiction. If they had received some formal schooling, they would have been taught to read by means of the Bible, irrespective of whether the church was directly involved in the institution. Even the most sophisticated elementary school, such as the junior section of Manchester Free Grammar School, organised the teaching of reading around the single text. Here, the young Samuel Bamford gradually progressed through the 'spelling', 'testament', 'lower bible', and 'middle bible' classes, until he became 'the first scholar in the first bible class, and consequently was the first English speller and reader in the school'.[41] At home, the children practised their skills on libraries very similar to those described by the Central Society. Taken from school at the age of ten, J. G. Farn found further mental development hampered by the limitations of his parents' bookshelf: 'the only books to which I had access being Watts' "World to Come," Bunyan's "Pilgrim's Progress," the Bible, a Hymn-book, Hervey's "Meditations," and a controversial work on an important theological point'.[42] Looking back from a period which had seen the working-class home invaded by the 'flimsy and flaming sensations' of the penny and halfpenny novel, many of the autobiographers could share Charles Shaw's nostalgia for the time when 'they drank, however rarely, at the "well of English undefiled"'.[43] The Bible, Bunyan, Watts, and, if they were particularly lucky, Milton, had provided them with immense intellectual and imaginative stimulation. Yet always there came a time, when, as the tailor Thomas Carter wrote, 'there were many things which I wished to know, upon which both the Bible and my other instructors were silent'.[44]

Such knowledge could be distinguished from both the serious literature they found in their homes and their schools, and the occasional chap-books purchased from travelling booksellers, by its quality of utility. 'My prevailing desire was to acquire some useful knowledge,'[45] recalled Carter. The brief introduction to the Bible provided at school was no substitute. 'Now, that school,' wrote the Spitalfields cobbler John James Bezer of his Dissenting Sunday school, 'did not even learn me to read; six hours a week, certainly not *one* hour of useful knowledge; plenty of cant, and what my teachers used to call *explaining* difficult texts in the Bible, but little, very little else'.[46] The value of the information sought by the readers had little to do with their occupational lives. 'Skill' and 'Book Knowledge' rarely overlapped, except in so far as a basic literacy was a usual requirement for entry into a skilled trade.[47] Rather it served the wider purpose of demystifying the world in which the working men found themselves.

In part this was a question of doing battle with the accumulated growth of folk wisdom and folk ignorance which separated the uneducated from their natural environment. The anomymous Suffolk Farm Labourer was one of many autobiographers who wrote at length on the prevalence of superstition in the traditional popular culture.[48] He had

seen a man 'swam for a wizard' as late as 1826, and had no doubt where
the responsibility for such credulity lay: 'The belief in Witchcraft was a
legacy of the previous century, and a relic of the ignorance of the people
which Church parsons with their undisputed sway had done nothing to
remove.'[49] Here the Central Society was on the same side as the autobiographers, and indeed was speaking the same language. Liardet saw
the 'credulous ignorance' and 'the belief in witchcraft which still exists
to a considerable extent' as being a further indication of the irrational
state of the church-educated farm labourers.[50] Again, the root cause was
the narrowness of their domestic reading: 'It is particularly to be remarked that not in a single cottage was there found any one book (not of
a religious nature) capable of giving any useful knowledge of men and
things.'[51]

But in part, useful knowledge was seen by self-educated working men
as a means of arming themselves to do battle with the established order
which the Central Society was striving to protect.[52] For Joseph Arch,
who organised the first successful agricultural labourers' trade union, the
travesty of an education handed out to a fortunate few in the early church
schools had reinforced rather than undermined the ingrained deference
of the farm worker: 'The literacy acquired by a minority of agricultural
labourers had hitherto served only the ends of their masters: of course he
might learn his catechism; that and things similar to it, was the right,
proper, and suitable knowledge for such as he; he would be the more
likely to stay contentedly in his place to the end of his working days.'[53]
The common language concealed a decisive difference of interpretation.
Knowledge became useful when it caused the reader to challenge the
world view of those who had traditionally ruled his life.

The written word was coming to play a central role in all forms of
working-class protest, and newspapers, broadsides, tracts and posters
were to be found wherever discontent spilled over into active protest.
Yet there was an inescapable element of privacy and domesticity in the
long and painful pursuit of knowledge. Just as the autodidacts were
initially at one with bodies such as the CSE and the SDUK in advocating
the broadening and secularisation of the content of working-class reading, so they shared the view that the consumption of this literature would
demand a major change in the pattern of domestic recreation.

In the first instance, the readers were increasingly forced to accept
that a complete divorce was to be made between work and recreation,
and that reading essentially belonged to the latter category. There is
evidence to suggest that once it had been occasionally possible to combine
self-education and manual labour. Those who worked on the land,
particularly in occupations such as tending livestock, might sometimes
read or even write a little. The poet Robert Story remembered how, on

being given his first book of verse, Watts's *Divine Songs for Children*, he, 'carried it with me to the hills whither I was sent as a herd-boy, and pored over it in the loneliest places – my heart burning with secret rapture'.[54] James Hogg had to exercise considerable ingenuity to overcome the obstacles with which he was faced:

> Having very little spare time from my flock, which was unruly enough, I folded and stitched a few sheets of paper, which I carried in my pocket. I had no ink-horn; but, in place of it, I borrowed a small vial, which I fixed in a hole in the breast of my waistcoat; and having a cork fastened by a piece of twine, it answered the purpose fully as well. Thus equipped, whenever a leisure minute or two offered, and I had nothing else to do, I sat down and wrote out my thoughts as I found them.[55]

Those who worked in the towns in artisan workshops occasionally enjoyed similar opportunities. Some trades were obviously particularly suited to the acquisition of knowledge. The journeyman bookbinder Benjamin Stott found some compensation in his occupation for the polluted atmosphere of his native Manchester: 'He has, however, to counteract this disadvantage, had an opportunity, for the business that he follows, of cultivating his ardent love of literature.'[56] Many workshops were either too noisy, or filled with journeymen interested only in enforcing the complex rituals of alcoholic consumption,[57] but there was just a chance that the would-be reader would come across the ideal environment. Another working-class poet, J. A. Leatherland, described his transition from a ribbon factory to a small workshop of velvet weavers: 'Here I worked in a room with seven others – young men of quite different habits to my former shopmates. Gilbert's Map of the World hung at one end of the room, and entomological specimens adorned the window sills. Here, instead of teasing and tormenting one another, all were affable and courteous, and each ardently bent on acquiring knowledge.'[58] But domestic artisans usually made the reverse transition, and Leatherland himself was later forced to return to the factory where further self-cultivation was out of the question. As the factory system and its accompanying noise and discipline took hold, so the very slender possibilities of combining work and reading dwindled into nothing.

Secondly, the pursuit of books inevitably engendered a retreat from many traditional forms of communal recreation. Various factors combined to cause the reader to distance himself from the pastimes of his friends and neighbours. There were the practical problems facing the self-educator. If any surplus money and time were to be found, expenditure of either commodity in other forms of recreation had to be kept to a minimum. 'It was at this period,' wrote Farn of his intellectual awakening in his late teens, 'that real inquiries began. For the first time in my life I had occasionally a few pence at my disposal, and, contrary to the custom of most boys of my age, I denied myself every trifling enjoyment, in order to expend the money in the purchase of books.'[59] Reading was, of necessity, a solitary activity. 'I never had much relish for the pastimes of youth,' recalled John Clare, 'instead of going out on the green at the town end on winter Sundays to play football I stuck to my corner stool poring over a book ...'[60]

The readers' conception of the identity and purpose of their activity played a part in this withdrawal. There was the image of the abstracted intellectual, or better still, of the romantic poet, to which some of the autobiographers subscribed. The Cornish tin-miner John Harris thought it necessary to renounce 'the noisy multitude for silence and the shades' if he wished to be a poet: 'This love of solitude made me a little singular, though I was cautious not to give offence. I shunned the crowd then, and I shun the crowd now.'[61] There was the ideological hostility to the culture of drink, which the drinkers frequently reciprocated. The command over himself which the reader sought was directly opposed to the drunkard's abdication of his moral and rational being. 'Then it was known', wrote the sometime shipwright, actor and house painter Christopher Thomson of the time before working men pursued useful knowledge, 'that the drunkard was never likely to trouble the law-makers with clamours for commercial freedom, universal suffrage, and a fair share of the proceeds of labour; and, with the class raised above the sot, to see a man "glorious" only excited their mirth, seldom their pity.'[62] Finally there was the role of literature in temporarily abstracting the reader from the grim reality of his surroundings. There was an instant, and not altogether illusory freedom to be gained from the printed word. 'When alone', wrote George Healey, then working in a silk mill, 'I would say, "My mind to me a kingdom is"; then I sought the abode of study in search of learning. This I found to be "a certain cure for every woe" and "an inexhaustible spring of pure delight".'[63]

The consequence was that the reader was forced to seek peace and quiet, in the countryside when it was accessible, and when the seasons, the weather and the hours of work permitted; otherwise in the home. Domestic recreation, from both a practical and an ideological standpoint, had to take on a new significance in the culture of the working class. At this point the hopes of the middle-class educators and the needs of the working-class readers appeared to intersect. In Liardet's ideal working-class home there would be found, 'when the out-door work was over, the cottage family, sitting by a cheerful fire, and engaged in some light and profitable handicraft ... [being] entertained by a member of it reading some interesting particulars respecting the labours in which they are ordinarily engaged, or the natural objects with which they are conversant'.[64] However, for the readers this picture of domestic bliss was far removed from the reality of their endeavours to pursue knowledge amidst their families.

The only instances recorded by the autobiographers which bore any resemblance to the ideal are to be found in the accounts of their childhood. It would appear that at least some working-class parents were prepared to use such literature as they possessed, or even to purchase new items, to amuse or inform their children.[65] But as the child grew into manhood it became increasingly difficult to integrate his intellectual activity with the domestic routine of the household. The contented fireside group was under any circumstances an unlikely prospect. The cabinet-maker Henry Price was particularly scornful about the tableau. 'The Merry Homes of England Around their fires by night. Some one has sung about them. But they could not have known much about them. The vast majority of them in the Towns and Cities Have no room to be merry in. The Bread Winner has to be up and off early, and home late and too tired to be merry'.[66] In the countryside matters were no better, not even silence could be guaranteed: James Bowd, who had followed in his father's footsteps as a farm labourer and was now raising his own family, found himself living in 'a house with Only two Rooms and no Yard nor Garden and the Blacksmith's hammer and tongs on one side of us at four O'Clock in the Morning, and the Cobbler's Hammer and Lapstone on the other side of us till nine or ten at Night not much solid Joy and Lasting peace either'.[67]

In the context of these meagre recreational resources the pursuit of knowledge merely added further strain to an already difficult situation. The reader needed seclusion amidst the bustle of his family. It was very rare indeed for his home to be large enough to give him a spare room. John Harris had to wait until he was fifty-three years old before an award of £50 from the Royal Literary Fund enabled him to 'build a little study for myself over our kitchen', and realise 'what I had been anxiously desiring for a lifetime'.[68] The reader needed time free from the demands of his family if he was to achieve any self-education in the short evenings after work. 'I am afraid', wrote the 'Dundee Factory Boy', 'if I were to encourage the reader on the path of self-improvement by telling him the difficulties I had, even as a shoemaker, to encounter, and the number of books I read frequently when I should have been in my bed, that he would scarcely believe me.'[69] For this reason the reader also needed light, an expensive commodity in the ill-lit working-class homes.[70] As a young man, Ben Brierley had to have recourse to the firelight by which to read his books, which proved a perilous business: 'In the study of my favourite authors, I was not allowed a candle during winter nights, until my hair underwent a constant singeing process'.[71] Finally the reader needed money, which might otherwise be spent on the other material and recreational needs of the family. Not only could he rarely afford to buy proper books,[72] the small library he painfully acquired would be constantly vulnerable to the inevitable financial disasters of the family economy. The apprentice pawnbroker William Brown noted that books were amongst the most common items to be pledged when a family was in trouble,[73] and the miners' leader Edward Rymer, who reckoned that his home was broken up fourteen times in twenty-six years as a result of his union activity, wearily recounted how he had to 'Pawn books and clothing to procure bread, rent and fire'.[74]

The pursuit of knowledge could make the working-class home even less of a nest, a spiritual refuge from the outside world than it might have been. Rather than providing a focal point of a new pattern of domestic recreation, the reader's activity served to intensify his awareness of the inadequacy of the available facilities. It was not only a question of material deprivation. A single-minded programme of self-education could only exacerbate the emotional strains within the family. As the mechanic Thomas Wood observed, 'A home with seven or eight children on one floor is a fine opportunity for the display of patience on the part of a "student" or an earnest reader'.[75] Where an interest in books might bind together parents and children, the evidence of the autobiographies suggests very little joint enterprise between husbands and wives. If the male reader required, as he often did, help and encouragement, he looked not to his family but to other working men in the community. In turn wives were usually excluded from the mutual improvement societies which did so much to sustain their husbands' self-education.[76] This exclusion may very well be the reason why there are so disproportionately few autobiographies by working-class women.[77] In the home, serious reading was a matter of competition rather than co-operation over the allocation of scarce recreational resources.

Here again, the function of the working-class home seemed ambiguous. The commitment to books drove the self-improving working man to make unprecedented demands on his domestic recreation, yet the difficulties he encountered amidst his family constantly forced him out to seek the company of other working men who had embarked upon the pursuit of knowledge. Almost all the autobiographers who tried to educate themselves made contact with what might be termed a 'learned neighbour', a friend (always male) or workmate who could provide the essential intellectual stimulus, moral support and practical assistance. 'Hours and hours we have wandered together by the side of the Eden', wrote the Carlisle handloom weaver William Farish of himself and a fellow reader, 'discussing in our own way politics and philosophy, and anon reading the poets, or working out problems in Nesbit.'[78] Where the community was large enough, this individual co-operation could be translated into institutional endeavour in the form of artisans' libraries and mutual improvement societies.[79] Farish was a founder member of an organisation which had split off from the Carlisle Mechanics' Institute, 'through the reluctance of the weaver in his clogs and fustian jacket to meet in the same room with the better clad, and possibly better mannered, shop assistants and clerks of the city'. The weavers fitted up a six-loom weaving shop with desks and seats and here 'Those who could read taught those who could not, and those who could cypher did the same for the less advanced'.[80]

IV

When Sir William Courtenay, Knight of Malta, Earl of Devon and King of Jerusalem, fell in battle, his line died with him. No more prophets came forth from the West to lead agricultural labourers in risings against the propertied classes. Yet the issues raised in the response to the violence of May 1838 and the mounting unrest elsewhere in the country were to live on for decades to come. Driven by a combination of faith in the influence of rational inquiry and deep anxiety about the state of class relations, the statistical societies had identified a problem which was to remain, for different reasons, a major presence in the outlook of educated and self-educated alike.

For those on whose behalf the Central Society for Education and its sister organisations had carried out their surveys, the question of reading in the working-class home was to grow more urgent and complicated as the years passed. In the late 1830s, the investigations seemed to indicate that the libraries of the labouring poor were too limited and too neglected. But as the volume of cheap literature increased and leisure time was gradually extended, new dangers arose. Either the working-class readers bought the penny novels and Sunday newspapers and had their judgements further corrupted by sensation and fantasy, or the more serious among them moved on from their Bibles to works which questioned every aspect of the established order. In time, commentators would look back with nostalgia to the situation which Liardet and his fellow statisticians had revealed. 'Years ago', wrote a contributor to the *Nineteenth Century* in 1886, 'had one walked into almost any poor but respectable man's room in the kingdom, one would probably have found two books at least – the Bible and Pilgrim's Progress. Both were held in extreme veneration. Now it is to be feared that very few working men and women read the Pilgrim's Progress, and the Bible is far from being what it was – the book of the home.'[81] The domestic reading of the labouring poor epitomised the dilemma in which the more advanced section of the middle class found themselves. Their conviction that the secret of har-

monious class relations lay in the field of leisure rather than work raised
the intractable difficulty of the independent judgement of the working
man. By definition, recreation was spontaneous, nobody could be forced
to play. Nowhere was this more evident than in the sphere of domestic
reading, which combined two key elements of the culture the middle
class was trying to spread downwards, rational amusement and the
enclosed family. Immense efforts were made to shape the literary taste
of the working class through elementary and adult education, but in the
end, the choice of books, and their use in the home, could not be
controlled.

The minority of serious working-class readers could also find no easy
solution to the challenge posed by the crisis in their culture. In their way,
they were as anxious as their betters to overthrow the conception of
reality held by those who were vulnerable to the gospel of a new messiah.
The world of superstitious belief, of irrational explanations of their
environment, had to be defeated if ever they were to exercise any control
over the forces which shaped their existence. This meant reading, and it
meant moving onwards and outwards from the religious texts with which
Courtenay's followers had been so familiar. That there existed a tradition
of keeping and sometimes consulting the classic spiritual texts meant
that there was a genuine continuity between the self-taught Bible scholars who tended to take the lead in millenarian movements and the more
widely-read autodidacts who played so large a part in organising Chartism. In their struggle against older modes of interpreting their surroundings, they were extending rather than betraying existing forms of behaviour. Yet their activities created immense tensions in the pattern of
working-class leisure. Their commitment to books demanded an enhanced status for domestic recreation, but even for the most sober and
prosperous artisan, the home was less a refuge from the world than a
cockpit wherein its privations were most directly experienced.[82] It was
perhaps for this reason that the 'Family Magazines' aimed at the
working-class reader failed to prosper,[83] whereas those designed for the
rising middle class in their new villas were one of the great publishing
success stories of the 1840s and 1850s.

Self-improvement was both a private and a corporate pursuit. There
was a constant movement in the lives of the working-class readers
between a withdrawal into the home from older drink-centred pastimes
and an advance into new forms of social, and by extension, political
organisation. The readers could not close their front doors on the injus-
tice and inequality of their working lives. But neither could they hope to
come to terms with the new industrial society unless they laboured
amidst their family to break the shackles which for so long had impri-
soned their minds. Few of the working men who came to the fore in the

prolonged political struggle of the decade which followed the Battle of Bossenden Wood had not, at some time in their lives, tried to read as their children played around them, or sat up late at night with a book and a guttering candle. However difficult and inadequate an experience, reading in the home came to be an essential element in the emergence of an independent working-class culture.

NOTES

1 See the eye witness accounts in *The Globe*, 1 and 2 June 1838. The most detailed study of the event is to be found in P. G. Rogers, *Battle in Bossenden Wood* (1961). Courtenay's real name was John Nichols Tom. See also J. F. C. Harrison, *The Second Coming* (1979), pp. 213-5.

2 E. P. Thompson, *The Making of the English Working Class* (Harmondsworth, 1968), p. 881.

3 J. P. D. Dunbabin, *Rural Discontent in Nineteenth Century Britain* (1974), pp. 18-26; E. J. Hobsbawm and G. Rudé, *Captain Swing* (Harmondsworth, 1973), pp. 241-8; J. Stevenson, *Popular Disturbances in England 1700-1870* (1979), pp. 236-44.

4 See the election addresses and articles collected in *The Eccentric and Singular Productions of Sir W. Courtenay, K. M.* (Canterbury, [1883]).

5 See especially the speech of Charles Wyse in the House of Commons on 19 June 1839, in which he quoted extensively from Liardet's report, drawing particular attention to the quality and content of working-class reading (*Hansard*, 19 June 1839, cols. 538-9). Similar use was made by Lord Lansdowne in the House of Lords (*Hansard*, 5 July 1839, cols. 1261-2).

6 A. D. Gilbert, *Religion and Society in Industrial England* (1976), p. 130.

7 M. Sturt, *The Education of the People* (1967), pp. 160-1.

8 F. Liardet, 'State of the peasantry in the County of Kent', in Central Society of Education, *Third Publication* (1839), pp. 87-139.

9 See M. J. Cullen, *The Statistical movement in Early Victorian Britain* (Hassocks, 1975), pp. 136-49 and *passim*.

10 F. Liardet, *op. cit.*, pp. 98, 116, 120.

11 *Ibid.*, p. 96.

12 *Ibid.*, pp. 108, 118, 122.

13 Central Society of Education, *Second Publication* (1838), pp. 259, 260-3. *Third Publication*, pp. 368-72; *First Publication* (1837), pp. 342-4. See also a survey of the parish of Evesholt, Bedfordshire, by J. E. Martin which found 94% ownership: *Journal of the Statistical Society of London* (hereafter *JSSL*) 6 (1843), pp. 255-6.

14 *JSSL* 2 (1839), pp. 368-75.

15 *JSSL* 1 (1839), pp. 541-2; *JSSL* 2 (1839), pp. 375-8; 3 (1840-1), pp. 366-75; *JSSL*, 5 (1842), pp. 212-21.

16 CSE, *Second Publication*, pp. 250-72. Three in eight of the families 'possessed some kind of books, chiefly those connected with the formularies of the Catholic faith.'

17 The domination by the Bible of the serious literature of the poor is discussed by Louis James in *Print and the People* (Harmondsworth, 1978), p. 29.

18 See Louis James, *Fiction for the Working Man* (Harmondsworth, 1974), pp. 32–50; Victor Neuberg, *Popular Literature* (Harmondsworth, 1977), pp. 123–223; R. J. Altick, *The English Common Reader* (Chicago, Ill., 1963), pp. 267–86; 332–47. Older forms of popular literature such as chapbooks and broadsides, were also not recorded, and it is possible that the investigators often disregarded what they regarded as wholly ephemeral literature.

19 For the problems raised by the concept of the oral tradition, see David Vincent, 'The decline of the oral tradition in popular culture', in R. Storch (ed.), *Popular Culture and Custom in Nineteenth Century England* (1982), pp. 20–47.

20 This was commonly the case with millenarian movements. See Harrison, *op. cit.*, pp. 221–2, 229.

21 Liardet, *op. cit.*, p. 92.

22 *Ibid.*, p. 96.

23 *Ibid.*, p. 96.

24 Hobsbawm and Rudé, *op. cit.*, pp. 239–40.

25 Liardet, *op. cit.*, p. 133.

26 See R. D. Storch, 'The problem of working-class leisure: some roots of middle-class moral reform in the industrial North: 1825–50', in A. P. Donajgrodzki (ed.), *Social Control in Nineteenth-Century Britain* (1978), pp. 138–62.

27 R. K. Webb, *The British Working Class Reader 1790–1848* (1955), pp. 36–59 and *passim*.

28 Liardet, *op. cit.*, p. 118.

29 *Ibid.*, p. 128.

30 He was particularly fond of declaiming from the fifth chapter of the General Epistle of St James: 'Go to now, ye rich men, weep and howl for your miseries that shall come upon you ... Behold, the hire of the labourers who have reaped down your fields, which is of you kept back by fraud, crieth: and the cries of them which have reaped are entered into the ears of the Lord of sabbath.'

31 *The Globe*, 10 August 1838; Liardet, *op. cit.*, p. 92.

32 *Ibid.*, p. 93.

33 *Ibid.*, p. 130.

34 For the SDUK, see Webb, *op. cit.*, pp. 66–73, 114–22; T. Kelly, *A History of Adult Education in Great Britain* (Liverpool, 1970), chapters 8 and 11; David Vincent, *Bread, Knowledge and Freedom*, (1981), pp. 133–65.

35 Liardet, *op. cit.*, p. 35.

36 For the increasing role of reading in the home in the middle-class pattern of recreation see E. Burton, *The Early Victorians at Home* (1974), pp. 238–42; R. Irwin, 'The English domestic library in the nineteenth century', *Library Association Record* (October 1954), pp. 382–9; J. Walvin, *Leisure and Society, 1830–1950* (1978), p. 56.

37 *Ibid.*, p. 36. For the problem of the working-class home and 'rational recreation', see P. Bailey, *Leisure and Class in Victorian England* (1978), p. 97.

38 The most elaborate contemporary definition of the ideal programme of reading for the working man is to be found in the twenty-seven-page reading list in B. F. Duppa's *A Manual for Mechanics' Institutions* (SDUK, 1839). Only seventeen of the five hundred entries were fiction.

39 Liardet, *op. cit.*, pp. 131–2.

40 See D. Vincent, *op. cit.*, pp. 14–19.

41 S. Bamford, *Early Days* (1849), pp. 82, 89.

42 J. C. Farn, 'The autobiography of a living publicist', *The Reasoner* (16 September–23 December 1857), p. 197. Also, T. Wood, *The Autobiography of Thomas Wood, 1822–1880* (1956), p. 9; W. Howitt, *The Rural Life of England* (3rd edn., 1844), vol. 1, p. 256.

43 [C. Shaw], *When I was a Child, by An Old Potter* (1903), p. 207.

44 T. Carter, *Memoirs of a Working Man* (1845), p. 38.

45 T. Carter, *op. cit.*, p. 28.

46 J. J. Bezer, 'The Autobiography of one of the Chartist rebels of 1848', in D. Vincent (ed.), *Testaments of Radicalism* (1977), p. 157.

47 For the training of the new industrial workforce, see S. Pollard, *The Genesis of Modern Management* (1965), pp. 171–8.

48 For a more extended discussion of the attitude of the self-educated to superstition see D. Vincent, *art. cit.*,

49 'Autobiography of a Suffolk Farm Labourer With Recollections of Incidents and Events that have occurred in Suffolk during the Sixty Years from 1816 to 1876', ed. 'Rambler', *Suffolk Times and Mercury* (2 November 1894– 16 August 1895), pt. 2 ch. 3. See also W. Lovett, *Life and Struggles of William Lovett* (1876), p. 9. For the relationship between belief in religion and in the supernatural in the countryside in this period see J. Obelkevich, *Religion and Rural Society: South Lindsey 1825–1875* (Oxford, 1976), chapter VI; K. Thomas, *Religion and the Decline of Magic* (Harmondsworth, 1973), pp. 797–8.

50 Liardet, *op. cit.*, p. 137.

51 *Ibid.*, p. 128.

52 For a clear exposition of the relationship between the middle-class conception of 'useful knowledge' and more direct forms of policing the working class, see J. W. Hudson, *The History of Adult Education* (1851), p. v.

53 J. Arch, *Joseph Arch, The Story of his Life. Told by Himself.* (1898), p. 25. See also J. Hawker, *A Victorian Poacher, James Hawker's Journal*, ed. Garth Christian (Oxford, 1978), p. 91.

54 R. Story, 'Preface', in *The Poetical Works of Robert Story* (1857), pp. v–vi.

55 J. Hogg, *Memoir of the Author's Life* (Edinburgh, 1972 edn.), pp. 10–11.

56 B. Scott, *Songs for the Millions and other Poems* (1843), p. x.

57 See B. Harrison, *Drink and the Victorians* (1971), pp. 39–40; J. D. Burn, *The Autobiography of a Beggar Boy*, ed. D. Vincent (1978), pp. 156–7; Lovett, *Life and Struggles*, p. 31.

58 J. A. Leatherland, *Essays and Poems with a brief Autobiographical Memoir* (London, 1862), p. 9. See also R. Spurr, 'Autobiography', published as R. J. Owen, ed., 'The Autobiography of Robert Spurr', *Baptist Quarterly* 26 (April 1976), p. 284.

59 Farn, *op. cit.*, p. 197.

60 J. Clare, 'The Autobiography 1793–1824', in J. W. and A. Tibble (eds.), *The Prose of John Clare* (1951), p. 15. See also W. E. Adams, *Memoirs of a Social Atom* (1903), vol. 1, pp. 107–8.

61 J. Harris, *My Autobiography* (1882), p. 27. The syndrome of 'Mooning with the Muses' was well described by B. Brierley in *Home Memories and Recollections of a Life* (Manchester, 1886), p. 33.

62 C. Thomson, *The Autobiography of an Artisan* (1847), p. 313. See also Hawker, *op. cit.*, pp. 24-5.

63 G. Healey, *Life and Remarkable Career of George Healey* (Birmingham, *c.* 1890), p. 17. See also W. Heaton, *The Old Soldier; The Wandering Lover; and other poems; together with a Sketch of the Author's Life* (1857), p. xxiii; C. Shaw, *op. cit.*, p. 92.

64 Liardet, *op. cit.*, p. 130.

65 J. Bowd, 'The life of a farm worker', *The Countryman* LI. ii (1955), pp. 293-4; D. Vincent, *op. cit.*, p. 102.

66 H. E. Price, 'Diary' [MS Autobiography] (*c.* 1904), p. 67. See also *Report from the Select Committee on Public Libraries*, P.P. 1849, vol. XVII, 2751, 2753.

67 Bowd, *op. cit.*, p. 297.

68 Harris, *op. cit.*, p. 62. See also Shaw, *op. cit.*, p. 224.

69 *Chapters in the Life of a Dundee Factory Boy*, ed. J. Myles (Dundee, 1850), p. 64.

70 W. T. O'Dea, *The Social History of Lighting* (1958), pp. 40-54.

71 Brierley, *op. cit.*, pp. 31-2.

72 For the difficulties of acquiring books in this period, see Vincent, *op. cit.* pp. 113-20.

73 W. Brown, *A Narrative of the Life and Adventures of William Brown* (York, 1829), p. 18.

74 E. A. Rymer, *The Martyrdom of the Mine* ... (Middlesbrough, 1898), p. 30.

75 Wood, *op. cit.*, p. 9.

76 On the hostility of working-class men to participation by their wives in self-improvement see J. Hole, *An Essay on the Management of Literary, Scientific and Mechanics' Institutions* (1853), p. 35; D. Thompson, 'Women and nineteenth-century radical politics: a lost dimension', in J. Mitchell and A. Oakley (eds.), *The Rights and Wrongs of Women* (Harmondsworth, 1976), pp. 112-38. Also Thomson, *op. cit.*, pp. 379-82.

77 Of the 142 working-class autobiographies covering the first half of the nineteenth century which have so far come to light, only six are by women.

78 W. Farish, *The Autobiography of William Farish* (1889), p. 47. 'Nesbit' was probably A. Nesbit, *A Treatise on Practical Arithmetic* (1826).

79 These were sometimes to be found in public houses. See Hudson, *op. cit.*, pp. 148, 211.

80 Farish, *op. cit.*, p. 46.

81 E. G. Salmon, 'What the working classes read', *Nineteenth century* XX (1886), p. 115.

82 For an interesting plea that middle-class educators should take more account of the "class characteristics' of the working man's material life before prescribing courses of reading, see 'The byways of literature. Reading for the million', *Blackwood's Magazine* (August 1858), LXXXIV, pp. 200-16.

83 See, James, *Fiction for the Working Man* ..., pp. 44, 144-34. Despite its apparent concern for day-to-day realism, the 'domestic story' which came to dominate penny issue novels in the 1840s was designed to afford the reader an escape from the actual conditions of the working class home.

12 JAMES WALVIN
Children's pleasures

One striking feature of the population of Victorian England and Wales was the number of children. From 1801 to 1914 the Census returns show that those aged fourteen and under always formed at least one third of the overall population. In 1841 there were some $5\frac{3}{4}$ million children, by 1901 ten million. Not surprisingly contemporaries thought that children were ubiquitous and unavoidable. Their physical presence, noise and social activities were inescapable features of contemporary (especially urban) life and this fact did not change substantially until effective compulsory schooling began to remove the great majority of them from public view during much of the working day. Soon afterwards the fall in family size began to reduce the relative numbers of children.

Many aspects of the experience of children have been explored by historians, notably the problems of their health, work and education, yet one of the most striking and, in contemporary terms, most important features of their collective and individual lives – their play and recreation – has in general been left to the antiquarian and folklorist. But even a casual glance at the history of children at play reveals a story which is not only fascinating in itself but also sheds light on wider and more significant phenomena.

By the late nineteenth century the British prided themselves on their sporting prowess. In the course of the century a number of games had evolved from pre-industrial forms, often transformed within the English public schools into recognisably modern sports, watched and played by millions at both amateur and professional levels. A parallel sporting ethos derived from within the public schools and proponents of that ethos were determined to see the benefits of a sporting life enjoyed by all. And what better place to begin than among the young? Inside the public schools themselves the commitment to sporting activity had, by late in the century, become little short of fanaticism. Among its disciples, the coming of compulsory education provided the opportunity to encourage similar sporting endeavour at all social levels.

The Victorian and Edwardian sporting ethos was primarily masculine. Boys' games were encouraged for their own sake, for the alleged physical good of the boys and, ultimately, for the future well-being of the nation.

> Brave boys make brave men. Good soldiers, dauntless hunters, adventurous explorers, and good volunteers, all owe a great deal to the pastimes they enjoyed between school hours and in vacations. Indeed much of the greatness of our nation is to be attributed to the training which takes place in the playground. For summer we have a capital game in cricket; for winter, when it is impossible to play cricket, we have football . . .[1]

By the end of the century it was widely accepted that certain games played a crucial role in a child's education – and were also vital to the nation's future. This belief was itself integral to the public school sporting tradition and was confirmed by the comments of the Clarendon Commission in 1864.

> The cricket and football fields ... are not merely places of amusement; they help to form some of the valuable social qualities and manly virtues, and they hold, like the classrooms and boarding houses, a distinct and important place in public school education.[2]

The view that physical recreation was good for the body (of boys at least) became an unchallenged assumption. 'Every boy should learn to run, and to leap, to sit, to kneel, to crawl; in fact to make a proper use of his bodily powers; a man who cannot do this is only half a man.'[3] Contemporary revelations about 'the Condition of England Question' gave added strength to such convictions, and reinforced the determination to propagate the benefits of sporting activity among those most in need, i.e. the lower orders. This conviction helped to establish within the new Board Schools a series of games, preferably those which combined the virtues of cheapness with easily-organised mass participation. Gymnastics, initially based on a military model, was an early incorporation and was widely used both for boys and girls; the exercises later being modified to provide more 'suitable' recreation for girls. It was, however, football which rapidly established itself as *the* major school game for boys – a fact which undoubtedly helped to cement the national commitment to that game in adult life.[4] Time and again teachers and educationalists testified to the importance and popularity of football among school boys – in public and Board schools alike. Given this emphasis on games it was natural that ordinary school playgrounds came to be accorded the importance of the public school playing fields. There was no doubt, one man argued, that:

> Good playgrounds attached to schools have a perceptible influence on the inclination of children to go to school, especially in the case of boys. Those whose physical restlessness leads to absent themselves from schools, whenever they can do so, find their wants met by the games which take place in the playground in the intervals between lessons ...[5]

It is not surprising, in the light of the public school influence on the development of the Victorian sporting ethos, that the debate about school games and recreations was concerned primarily with boys' activities. Indeed it was assumed that organised games *ought* to be a male preserve. Even in gymnastics, it was argued, girls ought to have less energetic exercises because 'of their greater delicacy and less strength'.[6] Although more and more girls turned to outdoor and physical recreation in the last decade of the century (a trend accentuated in the early years of the twentieth century by the proliferation of girls' boarding schools with their own distinctive athletic ethos), Victorians tried to nurture the belief that girls ought to seek their recreational satisfaction in more sedate pursuits. It is symptomatic that one girls' book, *The Girl's Own Toy-maker and Book of Recreation* devoted only three of its pages to outdoor games.[7] While educational opinion – often purveyed through the medium of books and magazines – paid inordinate and growing attention to the importance of encouraging physical activity among boys, there was relatively little corresponding attention given to girls' physical recreation. Indeed there was a marked degree of hostility to girls' outdoor games, not merely because they were considered by many to be unladylike and unseemly but also, and perhaps most important, because they distracted girls from the home. Time and again Victorian girls were encouraged to follow recreational pursuits which were domestic and which would have practical importance for their future lives – as wives, mothers or domestics. Toy making and dressmaking, for instance, were thought to offer ideal training for adult life.[8] 'Home duties then, should have the first place with girls, because home is the nursery in which they learn the lessons which will make their price beyond rubies, and their names blessed among their daughters.'[9] Dolls, dressmaking, reading, music: these and other domestic recreations were the staple recreational diet of generations of middle- and upper-class girls. Moreover, compulsory schooling enabled these qualities to be passed on to girls whose domestic circumstances denied them access to such home-based female recreations. There were even educationalists who believed that while boys were enjoying games in the school playground the girls ought to be indoors cleaning and tidying the school; preparing themselves for the domestic chores of adult life.[10]

Despite a widespread antipathy to girls' recreations, changes began to make themselves felt late in the century. As games became ever more popular, through schools, commercial involvement, professionalism and *via* press coverage, it was natural that many girls would find themselves attracted to outdoor recreations. More and more girls and young women began to enjoy tennis, croquet, golf and cycling. In the words of the *Girl's Companion* of 1895: 'Our girls have welcomed new outdoor sports, and taken to many new indoor pastimes both physical and mental.'[11] Indeed it is indicative of the growing female presence in outdoor sports that commercial concerns began to cater for that interest.

Such recreations made little impression on girls of the lower classes, unless they encountered them at school. Tennis and croquet were generally played in the grounds of private homes or clubs. Cycling was costly – except at the seaside or amusement parks where cycles could be hired by the hour. Thus while girls and women had staked a claim to the right to enjoy many of the newer sporting fads these recreations, like contemporary female political activity, tended to be the preserve of middle- and upper-class women. In terms of organised games and mass participatory sports, girls and women had made precious little headway.

To discuss children's games and recreations largely in terms of organised, commercial or educational activities would be to miss the major point, for the most obvious of all children's games were those which grew out of the independent and spontaneous social world of childhood. Although often encouraged by parents and teachers, the importance of informal children's games was the simple fact that they belonged to an independent cultural world and owed allegiance only incidentally to adults. Unlike more formal games, few children were denied access to them because of sex or class. It was the informal, *ad hoc*, games of the street and field which provided the overwhelming majority of children with the recreational enjoyments of childhood and which (though none realised it) linked them to the forgotten pleasures of generations past and of others yet unborn.

Despite certain similarities, children's games tended to differ between town and country. Country games, for instance, were, in general, determined by the rhythms of rural life just as those in the towns were shaped by the restrictions of an urban environment. And, as in the world of adult recreations (though obviously not to the same extent) work usually shaped the nature of local children's games. Children of rural labourers were often tied to the work of their families. At the busier times of harvest, lambing, planting – or hectic periods dictated by the vagaries of the weather – those children found little opportunity for play and recreation. Older children, particularly the girls, were normally expected to care for the gaggles of smaller children. Rural children, no less than the better-remembered offspring of the early factory workers, found their enjoyments limited by the restrictions and demands of local work and family life.

Many of their games were seasonal. If a sharp winter made domestic life a little harsher it was partly offset by the delights of impromptu winter games, skating, sledging and snowballing. Custom-made skates could be bought from shoemakers, though poor children did not need such refinements to enjoy winter games. It is significant that Victorian books which described and listed children's games invariably included such winter pastimes. Boys' magazines praised the qualities of outdoor life in winter.

> In spite of wind and weather, the hardy English boy will have his outdoor pastime. He dearly loves an exhilarating game, is not afraid of snowballing, an awkward fall from that difficult 'outside edge' of his skate, or a kick from the toe of an opposing football player. This is as it should be.[12]

Football was the ubiquitous winter game and whatever happened in the more crowded urban environments, rural games of football survived in their essentially pre-industrial form. With the passage of time, of course, these games were increasingly influenced by the codification and changes effected from within the public schools. By late century it was argued that football was ideally suited for cold weather – and indeed ought not to be played when it was warm. 'Only in cold, or at least in cool weather, can this game be played, as it requires such incessant movement and such strenuous exertion on the part of every player, that no one would be able to endure a spirited game in the summer time.'[13] Footballers did not, of course, need formal equipment (though it was increasingly available for those able to afford it). Even the football was easily made from animal bladders, as it had been since time out of mind.

> In November came pig killing time, and soon our ears would be tormented with the screams of the expiring pig . . . then the pig was washed and cleaned. As children we hung round waiting for the bladder, which when drained we blew up with a clay pipe stem, and then used it for a football.[14]

In summer cricket held sway. It was, said one mid-century book on children's games, 'the king of games. Every boy in England should learn it.'[15] Village boys made their own bats and wickets and played in local lanes and fields. Apprentices to carpenters often made excellent cricket equipment and the strength of the local game was frequently enhanced by the encouragement of the local village school.[16] It was, above all, a game with powerful and traditional local, often parochial, roots. Furthermore the rural game grew in popularity with the development of county and Test cricket though its strength remained in the localities.

It was, however, the recreational opportunities afforded by the woods and fields which gave children their greatest chance for fun and games in the country, though obviously this differed greatly between regions. Children everywhere seemed to find endless enjoyment in climbing, fishing, hunting, collecting food, fruit and eggs – sometimes illicitly. John Clare, that perceptive though tormented poet of rural England, offers a wealth of information about the recreations and enjoyments of rural children.

> I used to be very fond of fishing and of a sunday morning I have been out before the sun delving for worms in some weed blanketed dunghill . . . I used also to be very fond of poking about the hedges in spring to hunt pooties [snails] and I was no less fond of robbing the poor birds nests or searching among the prickly firze on the heath poking a stick into the rabbit holes and carefully observing when I took it out if there was down at the end of it which was the sign of a nest with young then in went the arm up to the shoulder and then fear came upon us that a snake might be concealed in the hole and then our blood ran cold within us and started us off to other sports.[17]

Even when at school rural children found plenty of opportunity, at break and when school was over, to enjoy the natural habitat. Clare, again, wrote:

> Harken that happy shout – the school house door
> Is open thrown and out the younkers [youths] teem
> Some run and leap frog on the rushy moor
> And others dabble in the shallow stream
> Catching young fish and turning pepple oer
> For muscle claims.[18]

Half a century later, the Reverend Francis Kilvert described the informal rural games among children in Herefordshire: 'I was delighted to hear Teddy Evans proposing to some other children to play the old game of "Fox a Dandley." Then they chose "dens" and began running about catching each other ... I had no idea the old game was still played by the present generation of children.'[19] Five years later Kilvert came across two 'urchins' playing in an empty field. ' "Please, Sir, we'm gwine to play blindman's buff." The two children were quite alone. The strip of dusky meadow was like a marsh and every footstep trod water out of the soaked land, but the two little images went solemnly on with their game as if they were in a magnificent playground with a hundred children to play with.'[20] The hunting and catching games of rural children were a constant source of concern because they so often involved needless suffering to birds and animals. Time and again children's books returned to the need to prevent children's cruelty to animals. 'Children and young persons accustomed to country life ... will often wantonly inflict protracted and horrible pain on other animals, especially if they are popularly called *vermin* ...'[21] It is impossible to say whether children were crueller in country than in towns but the proximity of animals seems to have given children in the country ample scope for indulging whatever cruelties they fancied. They seemed to prey on animals and birds as a regular part of their youthful pleasures. Recalling his Victorian childhood in Yorkshire, John Mortimer wrote: 'I was equally cruel and destructive to young animals, such as rabbits and birds. With boys possessed of a similar barbarous inclination, I have obtained many a pocket full of young rabbits, and many a hatful of jackdaw's eggs ...'[22]

The routines of rural life were occasionally brightened by colourful and eye-catching attractions. At the religious festivals, village and agricultural fairs, organised school shows and outings, children were able to enjoy themselves in a distinctive and memorable way. Each region and even each village had its own specific children's customs for such occasions. At a more general level Guy Fawkes' day was in effect a national children's day; a national holiday which existed long before the concept of national holidays (though until mid-century it was also an adult festival characterised by turbulence and rowdiness). Christmas occupied a similar role and was important in rural life long before the Victorian transformation of that festival into its modern form. But in addition to these national celebrations there was an amazing variety of parochial children's customs, generally held on days of religious significance, notably Shrove Tuesday, which offered children a multitude of delights.

One highlight eagerly awaited by rural children was the visit of a travelling show with its food stalls, machines, exotic animals, music and noise; a major annual event which lasted throughout a long day and remained among the most durable of childhood memories. There were even travelling circuses and menageries criss-crossing the country and bringing the most exotic of sights into the most unlikely of places.[23]

Colourful and memorable as they were, such treats were exceptional. For the most part, rural children made their own pleasures in much less spectacular ways. Many of their commonplace games required equipment or specialised toys; hoops, kites, tops, marbles and countless other items, but all of these could easily be improvised or substitutes found, and it is one of the recurring features of children's history that the young made their own toys from whatever materials came to hand. Of the apparently infinite variety of games played by children throughout the nineteenth century, few were inaccessible solely because of the cost of the equipment.[24]

Urban children may have been less blessed than their rural peers in having more limited and less attractive natural facilities for games and recreations. The scope for open play and adventure in the countryside was clearly greater than in many of the more crowded urban areas. Yet it would be mistaken to think of Britain as being sharply divided between town and country. In many industrial areas the countryside was very close indeed. The Yorkshire textile area is a good example, for the region was dominated not by endless urban sprawl but by a collection of small towns and villages which, though crowded and often filthy, were hemmed in by a rugged and beautiful countryside. In many Yorkshire and Lancashire textile towns, and in the mining communities of South Wales and the North-East, the countryside began, quite literally, at the end of the street. For many Victorian town dwellers, for most of the nineteenth century the country was closer to hand than we might imagine.

None the less there were armies of Victorian children whose lives were utterly determined by unpleasant urban environments. Despite everything, however, children's games survived and adapted themselves to the harshest of urban conditions. In the early nineteenth century the bigger industrial cities came to share the urban vices once monopolised by London. For many children the problems were not simply environmental, for in those industries employing child labour there was often little surplus time or energy for pleasure and games.[25]

It was in the bigger cities that children seemed ubiquitous; they seemed to swarm over the pavements, alleys and courtyards, their noise resounding above all else. Octavia Hill, campaigning for 'Open Spaces' for the poor in the mid-century, commented that, on entering a court: 'the children are crawling or sitting on the hard hot stones till every corner of the place looks alive, and it seems as if I must step on them if I am to walk up the Court'.[26] Parents in crowded homes would at the first opportunity drive their offspring from the home and into the streets. The result was a little less noise in the home – but the unavoidable presence of children on the streets – a presence only remedied (for part of the year) by the coming of compulsory schooling.

> As you pass through one of those low, densely-crowded districts of London you will be struck by swarms of children everywhere collected ... Their parents live huddled in dirty single rooms ... and whenever the rain is not actually pouring down in torrents, they turn their children out to find amusement and subsistence, in the streets.[27]

It was on the streets that generations of poorer children found their pleasures and this fact is one of the reasons why local authorities legislated against children's play on their local streets. Looking at such groups of children, the observer might see a galaxy of games and amusements.

> Amongst the revellers there is a boy, who for the last five minutes has been hanging by his legs to a bit of temporary railing, with his hair sweeping the ground. On quitting it, he goes to a retired corner of a plot gravely putting his head and hands upon the ground, at a short distance from the wall, turns his heels up in the air, until he touches the house with his feet. This accomplished, he whistles a melody, claps his shoeless soles together, goes through certain telegraphic evolutions with his legs ...[28]

Even the most wretched of circumstances did not prevent children from playing. Henry Mayhew, probing the lives of London's poor, found an abundance of children's games and recreations: 'There are few who are in the habit of noting what they may observe of poor children in the streets and quieter localities, who have not seen little boys playing at marbles, or gambling with halfpennies, farthings or buttons, with older lads ...'[29] In one poor courtyard near Drury Lane, Mayhew discovered, 'In one corner was a group of four or five little boys gambling and squabbling for nuts ...'. Among older boys, Mayhew thought that 'the Penny Gaff [penny theatre] and Two Penny Hop [dance] were very popular'. Similarly he noted: The Jew-Boys of the streets play at draughts or dominoes in coffee shops where they frequent.'[30] Indeed dominoes was a commodity generally sold by poor, rootless children: 'most of the boys who vend this article play at the game themselves, and with some skill'. Even more surprising were the distances such children travelled, partly to work but also for enjoyment. Mayhew encountered cases of children from London travelling to Wolverhampton for the races.[31]

The street gangs of urban children were a constant source of adult complaint, as indeed they had been since time immemorial. According to *Punch* in 1853 London's streets were sometimes impassable because of children playing 'shuttlecock' and 'tipcat'. 'The mania for playing at cat is no less absurd than dangerous, for it is a game at which nobody seems to win and which, apparently, has no other aim than the windows of the houses and heads of the passengers.'[32]

Games of marbles were equally inescapable on the streets, and the game was transformed in the nineteenth century by the flood of cheap marbles on to the British market. In the words of *Every Boy's Magazine* in 1867, 'Foreign marbles have been introduced prodigiously cheaper, it is true, than our old British marbles, and infinitely worse . . .'.[33] What is striking about this is the fact that even such an apparently insignificant toy as this had become part of a fiercely competitive international industry. We have to remember that toys of all kinds formed a new and growing industry which sought to satisfy the diverse interests of children of both sexes and of all social classes. Naturally, toymakers tended to concentrate their efforts on the upper end of the market, but so universal was the desire for toys that cheaper versions (in addition to home-made versions) could be found right down the social scale. Indeed by 1850 there was a whole industry – ironically using child labour – which specialised in making toys for the poor. The indefatigable Mayhew discovered one manufacturer of these so-called 'Bristol' toys.

> The first Bristol toys are the common toys made for the children of the poor, and generally retailed at a penny. They were first made in Bristol, but they have been manufactured in London for the last 50 years . . . Bristol toys are carts, horses, omnibuses, chaises, steamers and such like – nearly all wheel-toys.

This was a trade particularly susceptible to economic fluctuations. One toymaker told Mayhew, 'As all my goods go to the poor, and are a sort of luxury to the children, I can tell what's up with working and poor people by the state of my trade'.[34]

Despite this growing industry there remained thousands of children who had to rely upon the traditional street games and upon their own inventiveness. Dolls made of straw, balls of crumpled paper, old ropes used for skipping, and hoops from barrels – all could readily be found. See-saws were made from old planks and swings made by hitching a rope to a tree, lamp-post or pole. Dolls could be made from rags.

Robert Roberts's description of life in Edwardian Salford told of the lure of the streets where there flourished a rich and varied culture of children's games and songs.[35] Much the same was true of any urban area, each of which had its own cycle and informal calendar of games and songs. In Newcastle, for instance, 'These various games used to come out every year, no-one used to say anything to my knowledge, we would find ourselves playing marbles, then marbles would vanish, we would be playing with various shaped tops and whips, or tops and string.'[36]

The poorer and more crowded a home, the more likely it was that its children would pursue their games on the streets and alleyways. Often, however, the weather or the time of the year forced them to stay indoors but even the poorer children managed to create games and fun from the most cramped and unyielding of circumstance. Furniture and other household items were converted to the temporary needs of imaginative children's play. Girls 'dressed up', played at being wives and mothers, cooking or washing – make-believe clothes in imitation of the real world around them – and waiting for them in the near future. When they did not own their own dolls' house, an old orange box was equally useful.[37] For children whose parents could not afford a day at the seaside, it was always possible to recreate the seaside in the home.

> The table was a good, strong, unpolished table, and stood up to the rough treatment. We turned it upside down and fastened an old sheet, from our dressing-up box, from one leg to the opposite corner. Our spades and pales came into this game of course; the spades being used as oars, in case the sails were not a success; and the pails were very useful to bail out the imaginary water we had shipped.[38]

Such reconstructions were, literally, without limit.

> I spent hours, sat on a board rested on the arms of the arm chair, with another in front of me, my mother used to tie a piece of cord on the back of the chair in front of me and that was the reins so that I could drive in my childish dreams, the butter and eggs to Morpeth as my grandparents or Uncle Bob used to do. The whole arrangement represented to me a horse and trap.[39]

In Robert Roberts's Salford home, a corner shop:

> We built hamlets of thatched cottages, roofing gas mantle boxes with wisps of straw, sticky with albumen from the egg crate. We borrowed lumps of washing soda from a sack under the counter to make cliffs, gorges or the Rocky Mountains, using flour, sugar and salt sweepings from the shelves to scatter creation with snow and ice, and peopled it with figures carved from pop bottle corks.

Roberts's two sisters 'once erected for me a splendid Greek temple from half-pound blocks of Sunlight soap ... and carton board, with rows of candles for columns ...'.[40]

For many children the problem of which games to play was complicated by an embarrassment of riches. Children of the more prosperous middle and upper classes formed an expanding and lucrative market for that growing commercial world of toy and book manufacturers. The products of the toy industry were remarkable for their range, diversity and qualities. Toys had been commercially manufactured since classical antiquity, but the origins of the modern toy industry lay in the emergence of German toymaking in the late Middle Ages. German traders sold their imaginative wares throughout Europe establishing for the Germans an early reputation as superb toymakers. Throughout much of the nineteenth century they remained the world's pre-eminent toy manufacturers – one business alone had a catalogue of 1200 items – but patents records show the growth of the indigenous British toy industry. Though there was an upsurge in the manufacture of specialised children's books and toys in the course of the eighteenth century (itself perhaps an indication of changing attitudes towards the child)[41] it was the advent of mass production of toys, notably tin soldiers which, in common with other industrial processes, both stimulated further interest and created a wider market for toys.

Prosperous children were faced with an amazing and ever-expanding range of toys. Dolls' houses (which might be made by the estate carpenter) had complex miniature contents and inhabitants. Sometimes toys were used for specific educational ends. Jigsaws, geographic and historical games of reconstruction were designed both to entertain and to instruct. Here, as in so many other areas of Victorian life, the example of royalty was important. The Queen's well-publicised commitment to her children and grandchildren was accompanied by an unusual collection of contemporary children's toys (many of which are enshrined in the royal collections now on display to the public).

The expansion of toymaking in Victorian England was remarkable. It was a reflection of the growing consumer market and an indication of the harnessing of new sciences and techniques to industrial processes. Victorian toys were increasingly influenced by the technical achievements of society at large. There were clockwork toys, optical toys, magic lanterns, walking toys, fireworks and engines; china and pottery toys. Again, in the words of Henry Mayhew:

> Optics gives its burning glass, its microscopes, its magic lanterns, its sterescope, its thaumatrope, its phantasmascope ... electricity its Leyden jars, galvanic batteries, electrotypes, etc; chemistry its balloons, fireworks, and crackers; mechanics its clock-work mice – its steam and other carriages,

pneumatics contributes its kites and windmills; acoustics its Jew-harps, musical glasses, accordions and all the long train of musical instruments; astronomy lends it orreries; in fine, there is scarcely a branch of knowledge which is not made to pay tribute to the amusement of the young.[42]

Many of these children's consumer durables were hawked on the streets – often by children – but the more expensive toys were sold in specialist shops. The number and range of toys increased substantially towards the end of the century, with German metal toys still dominant; the English tended to specialise in wood.[43] Technical improvements, notably in printing and colour production, led to an upsurge in attractive and colourful children's books, including the 'indestructible' linen books for infants. Many books were, of course, more than mere reading matter. There were elaborate coloured illustrations, books with mechanisms which sprang to life when opened; books designed as houses; books which turned into miniature theatres and books to be cut up as scrap or collage.[44]

The toy industry was highly technical and highly skilled; it was international and always open to new ideas and eye-catching concepts. Its products were often practical and educational. Saturated as the market might sometimes have seemed, there was always scope for innovative ideas. Plasticine (1897), hollow rather than solid soldiers and animals, clockwork trains, steam engines, gollywogs (1895), the 'teddy bear' (an American idea deriving from President Theodore Roosevelt's refusal to shoot a bear on a hunting expedition) – these and countless other objects found their way into the severely competitive market of children's toys before 1914. For the prosperous and discerning parent there was an abundance of playthings to set before their children.[45]

Wealthier parents tried to insulate their offspring from the harmful influence of their inferiors by consigning them to the ever-watchful nanny in the nursery. The nursery thus became the focal point for those children's routines until they were old enough to be sent to a tutor, academy or boarding school. Indeed it is indicative that there evolved an architecture and interior design for the nursery. Rooms set aside for children were commonplace as early as the seventeenth century. But as society became more prosperous and the homes of the well-to-do grew in size, individual nurseries became more commonplace. Sometimes they served both as a schoolroom and a playroom and with the development of the large Victorian house, the nursery came to be located at the extremities of the building, close to the servants, where the noise of the children would not disturb their parents. The daily routines of these children were thus quite distinctive. They tended to visit rather than live with their parents, being ushered in to see them at recognised times; for meals, family gatherings and prayers. From this separation of parents and child there emerged the British nanny (who was in effect a foster parent).[46] Of course, these lavish and costly arrangements characterised only the upper reaches of society. But the pattern was often followed by those much lower down the social scale, with a result that nurseries found their way even into modest middle-class homes.

There was, quite clearly, no single 'typical' child's environment for play. It varied greatly from place to place, across time and, perhaps more strikingly, between the different social classes. Yet, despite the efforts of parents to insulate their children from their inferiors, there was unavoidable contact. Furthermore there were remarkable similarities between the recreational culture of children of different social classes. All inherited and bequeathed ancient rhymes, songs and games of childhood; they created games at home and on the streets, in the landed-home or in the fields. And many of them were provided with a growing abundance of custom-made toys and games. Poorer children, on the other hand, simply created make-shift copies of commercial versions. It would, however, be naive to expect that games and recreations were enjoyed equally by every single child throughout the century; there were doubtless countless children whose misery and physical conditions prohibited anything but mere survival. 'Never no time to play,' was one wretched child's response to a question from one of Charles Booth's researchers.[47] Notwithstanding the extent and depth of such misery, the modern reader is struck by the remarkable vitality of children's games and play, often *despite* prevailing circumstances. That after all is perhaps one of the most often recurring themes in the history of childhood.

NOTES

1 *The Boys' Journal*, II (1865), p. 1.
2 Quoted in J. Walvin, *The People's Game, a Social History of British Football* (1975), p. 38.
3 *Peter Parley's Annual* (1840), p. 129.
4 I have dealt with this argument in my book *The People's Game*.
5 *Parl. Papers*, Final Report of the Commissioners on the Working of the Elementary Education Acts, 1888, Part III, Ln. 2, p. 64.
6 J. T. Burgess, *Elementary Gymnastics for the Young and Sedentary* (1866), p. 9.
7 E. Landells, *The Girls' Own Toy-maker and Book of Recreations* (1860), pp. 152–4.
8 *Ibid.*, p. vi.
9 Mrs Valentine (ed.), *The Girls' Home Companion* (1895) p. 751.
10 *Parl. Papers*, Education, General, 4; Report of the Assistant Commissioners on the State of Popular Education in England, 1861. Evidence of Rev. James Fraser, p. 99.
11 Mrs Valentine, *op. cit.*, Preface.

12 *The Boys' Journal* II (1865), p. 51; *The Girls' Home Companion*, p. 35.

13. E. Routledge, ed. *Routledge's Every Day Journal* (1863), p. 37.

14 I. Stickland, *The Voices of Children, 1700–1914* (Oxford, 1973), p. 194.

15 W. Martin, *The Book of Sports for Boys and Girls* (1853), p. 52.

16 P. Horn, *The Victorian Country Child* (1974), p. 151.

17 'Prose on the pleasures of childhood', in (eds.), E. Robinson and J. Summerfield *Selected Poems and Prose of John Clare* (Oxford, 1967), p. 18.

18 *Ibid.*, p. 154; Horn, *op. cit.*, p. 33.

19 W. Plomer (ed.), *Kilvert's Diary* (1977 edn.), p. 45.

20 *Ibid.*, p. 297.

21 T. Jackson, *Our Dumb Neighbours* (*c.* 1870), pp. vii–viii.

22 J.D. Hicks (ed.), *A Victorian Childhood on the Wolds.* East Yorkshire Local History Society (Beverley, 1978), p. 10.

23 Horn, *op. cit.*, chapter 9.

24 *The Book of Games* (1805); *The Boys' Book of Sports* (1860).

25 See chapter 4 in J. Walvin, *A Child's World: a social history of English Childhood, 1800–1914* (1982).

26 E.M. Bell, *Octavia Hill* (1942), pp. 146–7.

27 Stickland, *op. cit.*, p. 154.

28 *Ibid.*

29 H. Mayhew, *London Labour and the London Poor*, 4 vols. (New York, 1968 edn.), vol. I, p. 469.

30 *Ibid.*, p. 476.

31 *Ibid.*, p. 478.

32 Quoted in I. and P. Opie, *Children's Games* (Oxford, 1969), p. 11, n. 1.

33 N. Temple (ed.), *Seen and Not Heard* (1970), p. 168.

34. H. Mayhew, 21 February 1850, in E.P. Thompson and Eileen Yeo (eds.), *The Unknown Mayhew* (Harmondsworth, 1973), p. 339.

35 R. Roberts, *The Classic Slum* (Harmondsworth, 1971 edn.), pp. 153–4.

36 Stickland, *op. cit.*, pp. 205–6.

37. *Ibid.*, p. 194.

38. *Ibid.*, p. 200.

39. *Ibid.*, p. 203.

40 R. Roberts, *A Ragged Schooling* (Manchester, 1978), pp. 26–7.

41 P. Flick, *Discovering Toys and Toy Museums* (Aylesbury, 1977 edn.), pp. 7–8.

42 Mayhew, 21 February 1850, *The Unknown Mayhew*, p. 337.

43 Flick, *op. cit.*, pp. 16–17.

44 *Ibid.*, pp. 19–20.

45 This is dealt with in chapter 5 of *A Child's World*.

46 J. Gathorne-Hardy, *The Rise and Fall of the British Nanny* (1972), pp. 57–8.

47 Quoted in J. Walvin, *Leisure and Society 1830–1950* (1978), p. 118.